THE
AFRICAN JIHAD

THE AFRICAN JIHAD

Bin Laden's Quest for the Horn of Africa

Gregory Alonso Pirio

The Red Sea Press, Inc.
Publishers & Distributors of Third World Books

P.O. Box 1892　　　　　　P.O. Box 48
Trenton, NJ 08607　　　　Asmara, ERITREA

The Red Sea Press, Inc.
Publishers & Distributors of Third World Books

P.O. Box 1892	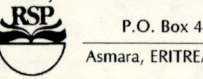	P.O. Box 48
Trenton, NJ 08607		Asmara, ERITREA

Copyright © 2007 Gregory Alonso Pirio

All rights reserved. No part of this publication may be reproduced, stored in a retrieval system or transmitted in any form or by any means, electronic, mechanical, photocopying, recording or otherwise without the prior written permission of the publisher.

Book design: Aliya Books
Cover design: Ashraful Haque
Front cover photo: Joao Silva/*The New York Times*/Redux

Library of Congress Cataloging-in-Publication Data

Pirio, Gregory Alonso.
 African jihad : Bin Laden's quest for the Horn of Africa / Gregory Alonso Pirio.
 p. cm.
 ISBN 1-56902-277-1 (cloth) -- ISBN 1-56902-278-X (pbk.)
1. Qaida (Organization) 2. Islamic fundamentalism--Horn of Africa. 3. Jihad. I. Title.
 HV6433.4.A3553P57 2007
 363.325096--dc22
  2007015696

CONTENTS

Author's Note vii
Map of Somalia ix
List of Abbreviations xi

Introduction 1

Chapter One
Sudan and Al Qaeda: The Jihadist Onslaught 13

Chapter Two
Jihadist Somalia: Al Itihaad Al Islamiya 43

Chapter Three
Jihadism in Somalia's Islamic Courts 77

Chapter Four
Eritrean Islamic Jihad/Eritrean Islamic Salvation Front .. 105

Chapter Five
Kenya: Jihadism in an Open Society 121

Chapter Six
Radical Islamic Expression in Tanzania:
Domain of a Growing Minority 157

Concluding Remarks
The Changing Dynamics of Jihadism in the Greater Horn
of Africa (November 2006) 187

Postscript— February 24, 2007
The Battle for the Horn of Africa and Its Aftermath 201

Index 219

AUTHOR'S NOTE

As the manuscript for this book was being copyedited for publication in December 2006, a military struggle to define the future of the Horn of Africa region intensified when the forces of the Somali Union of Islamic Courts launched an offensive against the rival Transitional Federal Government based in the inland Somali city of Baidoa. The large-scale Ethiopian military intervention in support of the Transitional Federal Government and its forces led to a routing of the militias of the Union of Islamic Courts. In response to these dramatic and rapidly unfolding events, which in many respects were foreshadowed in the original book manuscript, I have added a Post-Script to the original manuscript. It was completed on February 24, 2007 and was entitled "The Battle for the Horn of Africa and its Aftermath." This update allows the reader the opportunity to more fully appreciate the extent to which international jihadism, promoted in the region by Osama bin Laden's Al Qaeda movement, continues to play out in the politicomilitary equation of the region.

By way of acknowledgement, I want to recognize the many people upon whom I have depended to write this manuscript. The names of the many researchers and journalists to which I am indebted are found in the chapter endnotes. I particularly want to thank the journalists, many of them African, who regularly put their safety at risk in assignments with the goal of bringing to light stories from dangerous places. I have had to glean through thousands of their stories to patch together the tale of jihadism in the Greater Horn of Africa that is the subject of this book. In my own career in journalism and broadcasting, I have long been inspired by the dedication to the pursuit of truth and their courage of such journalists.

I also want to express my appreciation to Dr. Hrach Gregorian, then of IAQ, Inc., as well as to Dr. Jacob Kipp and Karl Prinslow of the Foreign Military Studies Office for their encouragement and support for my initial research into radical Islamic expression in Africa. The opportunity to edit a number of studies of radical Islamic movements in Africa enabled me to better value the internationalist character of this phenomenon and reinforced in me the importance of not limiting the discussion of this issue to any particular nation state.

MAP OF SOMALIA

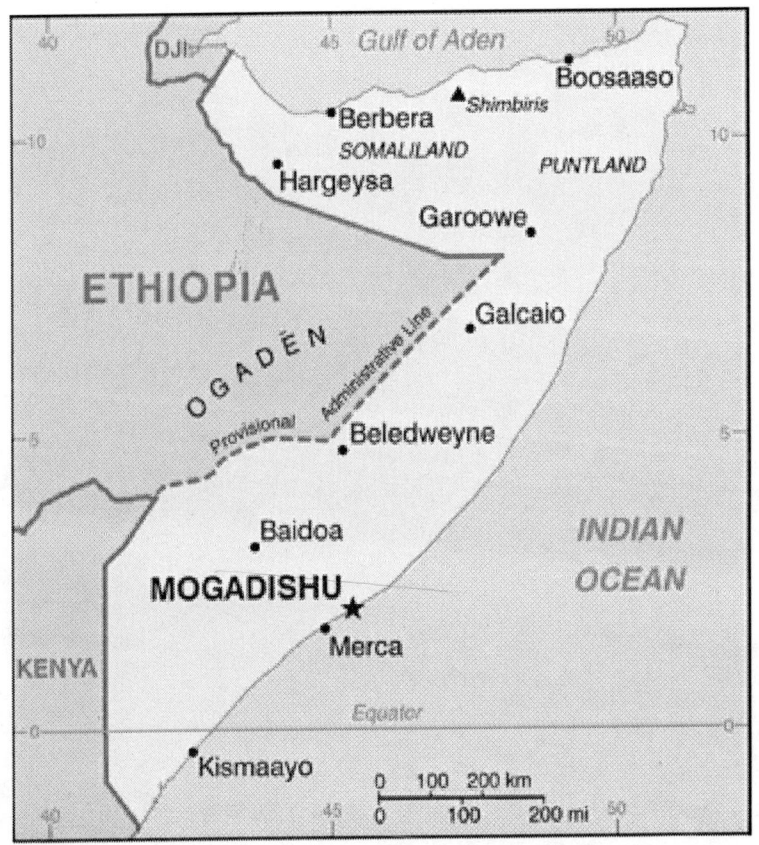

LIST OF ABBREVIATIONS

ADF	Allied Democratic Forces
BAKWATA	*Muslims Baraza Kuu la Waislam wa Tanzania* (Tanzana Muslim Council)
BALUKTA	*Baraza la Uendelazaji Koran Tanzania* (Tanzania Koranic Council)
CCM	*Chama Cha Mapinduzi* (Party of the Revolution)
CIA	Central Intelligence Agency
CUF	Civic United Front
EAMWS	East African Muslim Welfare Society
EDF	Equatoria Defense Force
EIJ	Eritrean Islamic Jihad
EIJ/EISF	Eritrean Islamic Jihad/ Eritrean Islamic Salvation Front
EISF	Eritrean Islamic Salvation Front
ELF	Eritrean Liberation Front
ENA	Eritrean National Alliance
EPLF	Eritrean People's Liberation Front
EPRDF	Ethiopian People's Revolutionary Democratic Front
FBI	Federal Bureau of Investigation
IFLO	Islamic Front for the Liberation of Oromia
IGAD	Intergovernmental Authority on Development
IPK	Islamic Party of Kenya
KANU	Kenya African National Union
LRA	Lord's Resistance Army
MIRA	Mercy International Relief Agency

NDA	National Democratic Alliance
NIF	National Islamic Front
OLF	Oromo Liberation Front
ONLF	Ogaden National Liberation Front
PAIC	Popular Arab and Islamic Conference
PDSJ	People's Front for Democracy and Justice
SLA	Sudanese Liberation Army
SPLM/A	Sudanese People's Liberation Movement/Army
SRRC	Somali Reconciliation and Restoration Council
TFG	Transitional Federal Government
TNG	Transitional National Government
Uamsho	*Jumuia ya Uamsho na Mihadhara* (Revival and Propagation Organization)
UIC	Union of Islamic Courts
UMA	United Muslims of Africa
UNOSOM II	United Nations Operation Somalia II
USC	United Somali Congress
UWAMDI	*Umoja wa Wahubiri wa Mlingano wa Dini* (Union of Preachers for Propagation of Religion)
Warsha	*Washa ya Waandishi wa Kiislam* (Muslim Writers Workshop)

INTRODUCTION

In 1992, Essam al-Ridi, an Egyptian *émigré* living in Dallas, Texas, purchased from a Southern California broker a surplus U.S. Air Force T-39A jet for the Saudi-born, multimillionaire Osama bin Laden. The jet was a military version of the twin-engine Sabreliner built by North American Rockwell that since the late 1950s had been used to transport U.S. generals and VIPs. Al-Ridi deceived the broker by pretending that the jet was destined for the personal use of a wealthy Egyptian family. He had it overhauled at Van Nuys Airport in Southern California (not far from where I now sit writing this book) and had it made to look like a civilian craft. At a small airport in Lancaster, California, a local pilot coached al-Ridi in flying the aircraft; and then in January 1993, al-Ridi piloted it from Dallas, not to Cairo but to Khartoum, Sudan, where bin Laden had established his Al Qaeda (The Base) headquarters in 1991 and from whence he planned, with Sudanese support, to turn the Greater Horn of Africa into a region under the rule of an Islamist state.

Al-Ridi had first met bin Laden in the early 1980s in Peshawar, Pakistan. After moving to Texas, al-Ridi had proven useful to bin Laden by arranging for shipments of night-vision goggles and .50 caliber rifles for *mujahidin* troops (Islamic fighters). These soldiers, consisting of both Afghans and recruits from many other, mostly Muslim countries, fought on behalf of loosely-aligned opposition groups that opposed the Soviet occupation of Afghanistan during the 1980s.

Then in 1992, Wadith el Hage, a naturalized-U.S. citizen from Lebanon, who was later found guilty for the 1998 bombing of the U.S. embassies in Tanzania and Kenya, approached al-Ridi, telling him that he could be of further service to bin Laden. El Hage said that bin Laden was in need of a jet plane to transport some FM-912 Stinger missiles from Peshawar to Khartoum — the highly-accurate, manned portable infrared homing surface-to-air missiles developed in the United States and supplied by its military. Al-Ridi obliged bin Laden's request and received $230,000 from Al Qaeda to pay for the jet.

However, the T-39A aircraft was never used to transport the Stinger missiles. In the aircraft's only known operational flight, al-Ridi ferried from Khartoum to Nairobi, Kenya, five top Al Qaeda commanders, including bin Laden's senior commander, Mohamed Atef, in late 1993. The commanders were *en route* to Somalia as part of Al Qaeda's support for a Somali jihadist organization, *Al Itihaad Al Islamiya* (the Islamic Union), which had recently declared *jihad* (a military struggle against non-Muslim combatants) against the United States. Bin Laden was determined to rid the Horn of Africa region of U.S. influence, and Al Itihaad was a useful ally in achieving this aim. With Al Qaeda and Sudanese backing, Al Itihaad targeted U.S. troops, who were part of a U.S.-led United Nations humanitarian intervention in Somalia, dubbed Operation Restore Hope by the U.S. military. (There is great irony in Al Qaeda's use of a surplus U.S. military aircraft to support a secret operation against U.S. forces in Somalia.) One of Al Itihaad's commanders who collaborated with Al Qaeda was the Somali Hassan Dahir Aweys.[1]

Fast forward to the summer of 2006: The picture of Hassan Dahir Aweys, with a broad, winning smile and dressed in a blue button-downed collared shirt, could be found on many news and Horn-of-Africa-oriented web sites. Sheikh Aweys had plenty of reasons to smile. He had risen in status from an army colonel, once decorated for heroism in Somali's 1977 war with Ethiopia,[2] to become leader of the militarily ascendant Union of Islamic Courts (UIC). Sheikh Aweys had just been chosen as leader of the *Majlis al-Shura* (Consultative Council), a policy-making body overseeing the UIC,[3] just as the UIC was consolidating its control of the country's one-time capital Mogadishu and much of southern Somalia. Normally inattentive to events in Somalia, the international media had begun in-depth coverage of the story of the UIC's growing power, and much of the media spotlight had been placed on Sheikh Aweys, who was frequently described as a hardliner.

Sheikh Aweys's accomplishment was all the more remarkable since he had reportedly gone underground in early 2002 after the United States and the United Nations designated him and his Al Itihaad organization as allies of Al Qaeda. It was only in 2004 that he reemerged as a prominent leader of the council governing the Islamic Courts in Mogadishu.[4]

From the perspective of the UIC, its militias were defeating the forces of local secular clan-based factional leaders — often referred to as "warlords" in the international media. Since the collapse of the country's central government in January 1991, clan-based militia factions had divided Mogadishu and the rest of southern Somalia into fiefdoms, and many of these militias had been accused of widespread human rights abuses. The UIC saw its forces as liberating the Somali population from what it considered the tyranny of the factional militias. The UIC contended that it was spreading peace and order to chaotic and dangerous Somalia through the establishment of branch Islamic Courts administering Islamic law. Prominent UIC leaders labeled Muslims who resisted its effort to establish its Islamist order as nonbelievers. As it expanded its control, the UIC began collecting taxes, taking over former police stations, imposing adherence to strict cultural codes, and restricted media freedoms — leaving the impression that it was establishing the infrastructure for an Islamic state.

With Sheikh Aweys at the helm of the Islamic Courts, it was as if the worse-case counterterrorism scenario was unfolding. For years, counterterrorism analysts had been warning that stateless Somalia had the potential of becoming a haven for Al Qaeda and other international jihadist groups just as what had occurred in Afghanistan under the rule of the Taliban — the Sunni puritanical Islamist movement that ruled most of Afghanistan from 1996 until 2001. Then, as the Islamic Courts movement was consolidating its grip on southern Somalia, hardliners within the Islamic Courts — under the leadership of Sheikh Aweys, who had historic ties to Al Qaeda — were reportedly pushing aside more moderate leaders.[5] Many media reports expressed growing alarm that a Taliban-style movement with links to international terrorism was now poised to establish a militant Islamist state in Somalia, which had been bereft of a central government since 1991.

All of this concern was not without merit, and the journey of power and force that Sheikh Aweys had begun since joining Al Itihaad in 1991 is central to understanding why the growing dominance of the Islamic Courts could be viewed as a threat to regional stability and a setback to international counterterrorism efforts. The ascendancy of Sheikh Aweys within Somalia was also part and parcel of the larger drama that has unfolded in the Horn of Africa since the international jihadist movement determinedly set out in the early 1990s to establish Islamist hegemony there.

Hassan Dahir Aweys's career has indeed been one of intimate involvement with the wider international jihadist movement. After the Somali dictator Mohamed Siad Barre had been forced from power by triumphant rebel movements, the one-time Colonel Aweys reportedly served with the forces of the rebel United Somali Congress, but switched his allegiance to Al Itihaad. Aweys quickly rose to play a prominent role in Al Itihaad as a military commander, and he achieved the position of vice-chairman at a time when Al Itihaad had become allied with the nascent Al Qaeda movement of Osama bin Laden, with other international jihadist organizations, and with Sudan under the rule of the National Islamic Front. Al Itihaad worked hand in glove with its foreign sponsors to carry out their jihadist agenda for the Horn of Africa region. From these sponsors, Al Itihaad received arms, money, military personnel and training, as well as social welfare assistance for populations under its control.

In 1991, bin Laden had moved his jihadist fighters from Afghanistan to Sudan at the invitation of Hassan al-Turabi, the Islamist architect of Sudan's National Islamic Front movement. Al-Turabi articulated a grand vision for the Arabization of Africa, and Al Qaeda plotted to establish an Islamic state in the Horn of Africa as a launching pad to take control of Yemen and acquire its ultimate prize, Saudi Arabia. The interests of Sudan and Al Qaeda conjoined, and together they made

Introduction

a jihadist grab to gain control of the Horn of Africa and East Africa that brought terrorism, numerous proxy wars, and immense suffering to the people there. This book tells the tale both of their alliances with multiple organizations in the region and of their multifaceted actions undertaken with the aim of achieving destabilization of neighboring states and ultimately military and political dominance. The Al Itihaad faction within the Islamic Courts can be viewed in part as a legacy of Al Qaeda and Sudan's efforts to achieve regional hegemony through the promotion of an international jihadist agenda.

In Somalia, Al Itihaad became an ally of Sudan and Al Qaeda in opposing U.S. influence in the region and in destabilizing Ethiopia; and in the 1990s, Al Itihaad declared *jihad* successively against the United States and Ethiopia. In 1991, just as Sudan began hosting Al Qaeda forces, the United States began to lead a UN humanitarian relief operation in Somalia whose original goal of providing famine relief to needy Somalis drifted into a nationbuilding exercise undertaken by the United Nations in a Somalia bereft of a central government. In alliance with the forces of Somali factional leader, Mohamed Farah Aidid, and with training from Al Qaeda operatives, Aweys is thought by some to have led the operation widely known as *Black Hawk Down* — the downing of a U.S. army helicopter in Mogadishu and the subsequent loss of life of eighteen American soldiers and hundreds of Somalis. *Black Hawk Down* was later memorialized in a bestselling nonfiction book[6] and an Academy Award winning movie of the same title. UN investigators believed that Al Itihaad forces also supported Al Qaeda in its preparation for the 1998 Al Qaeda bombing of the U.S. embassies in Nairobi, Kenya, and in Dar es Salaam, Tanzania. The Nairobi embassy bombing resulted in 213 deaths and over 5,000 injuries, the overwhelming majority of which were Kenyan. In Dar es Salaam, eleven Tanzanians were killed and eight-four wounded.

Al Itihaad's vision of uniting ethnic Somalis in Djibouti, Ethiopia, Kenya and Somalia into a single pan-Somali Islamic state, variously referred to as a caliphate or emirate, fit into Sudan's and Al Qaeda's plans for the region, and so with Al Qaeda and Sudanese support, Al Itihaad carried out military operations inside Ethiopia and undertook a terrorist campaign against soft targets. Al Itihaad eventually suffered military reversals at the hands of Ethiopia, and Sheikh Aweys experimented with different strategies to keep the militarily weakened Al Itihaad as a viable revolutionary force. Sheikh Aweys ultimately founded as part of this effort an Islamic Court in southern Mogadishu, whose compound reportedly came to look much more like a military base than a court. As early as 1999, Sheikh Aweys's Islamic Court militia had begun challenging the hegemony of the so-called warlords in southern Somalia. On June 26, 2006, in Mogadishu, Sheikh Hassan Dahir Aweys achieved unquestioned new prominence as chairman of the UIC's Consultative Council.[7] Any doubts about the ability and resiliency of Sheikh Aweys to keep his jihadist agenda on track seemed to be put to rest.

THE LOOMING CONFRONTATION

In the city of Baidoa in the Bay region northwest of Mogadishu, a so-called Transitional Federal Government (TFG) took seat in 2005 under the presidency of Abdullahi Yusuf Ahmed. He, like Sheikh Aweys, had been an army colonel. Abdullahi Yusuf had substantial credentials as an opponent of the Siad Barre regime. He defied the 1969 *coup d'état* that brought Siad Barre to power, spent time in prison for his opposition, and fought in various ways to overthrow the Siad Barre regime including as leader of the rebel Somali Salvation Democratic Front.

The TFG had been created in Kenya in 2004 after lengthy reconciliation talks hosted by the Inter-Governmental Authority on Development (IGAD), which comprised Djibouti, Eritrea, Ethiopia, Kenya, Somalia, Sudan and Uganda. The lengthy reconciliation process helped clan-based factions overcome differences to establish an interim government as a way of restoring a central government to Somalia. The African Union and the United Nations supported this process, and the United States encouraged the formation of a functional transitional government.

Confrontation between the TFG and the jihadist factions within the Islamic Courts seemed inevitable though. Mogadishu's Islamic Courts did not enjoy representation within the TFG, and TFG president, Abdulahi Yusuf Ahmed, had been a fierce opponent and vocal critic of Al Itihaad and other Islamist and jihadist groupings based in Mogadishu. Some UIC leaders in Mogadishu have regarded the TFG as a creature of

Introduction

what they deride as "Christian" Ethiopia, and they considered Yusuf to be a close ally of Ethiopia. Yusuf had been administrator of Puntland, a region in northeastern Somalia centered around Garowe (Nugaal region), whose leaders in 1998 declared it to be an autonomous administrative region that aspired to one day join a reconstituted and federated Somali republic. Reportedly, with Ethiopian support, Puntland's forces under Yusuf successfully fought efforts backed by Al Itihaad and other jihadist groupings to remove Yusuf as president of Puntland. Yusuf had also been a vocal critic of the Wahabist (also often refered to as Salafist) brand of Islam that Al Itihaad has promoted in Somalia. Wahabist theology advocates a puritanical and legalistic stance in matters of faith and religious practice and rejects the mystical tradition of Islam known as Sufism. As Puntland president, Yusuf defended Somalia's more traditional moderate Sufi-based Islam against what he felt was the encroachment of theologically rigid Wahabism.

Somali jihadists and Islamists based in Mogadishu seemed to have ample reason to resist the seating of the TFG in the nation's capital. In what seemed to be a clear message to the TFG about its intentions to take up office in Mogadishu, in May 2005 TFG prime minister, Ali Mohamed Gedi, escaped unharmed from a bombing — a signature jihadist attack — at a rally with supporters at Mogadishu's stadium that left at least ten people dead and sixty injured.[8] The blast occurred on the fourth day of Gedi's maiden tour of the capital, aimed at building support for his government and at ending a bitter dispute over when and where the TFG should establish itself in Somalia as it relocated from Kenya.[9] Then, when in November 2005, Gedi made another trip to Mogadishu to try to negotiate again the arrival of the TFG government to Mogadishu, unknown assailants killed two people and wounded twelve in an attack on his convoy.[10] In September 2006, two suicide bombs exploded in Baidoa in what was a failed attempt on the life of Abdullahi Yusuf. The suicide bombings brought with them the chilling prospect that terrorist techniques used in the Middle East had been introduced to Somalia for the first time. A Somali group close to Sheikh Aweys is believed to have carried out a number of assassinations, but the identities of those carrying out these attacks have not been revealed. In the case of the suicide bombings, a BBC reporter in Baidoa said that those arrested for the bombings came from a group close to the UIC — a likely reference to a jihadist youth movement that had been promoted by Sheikh Aweys.[11]

Taking a Stand in Mogadishu

The prospect of a stable, secular TFG authority in Mogadishu that would not tolerate the presence of Al Qaeda and other jihadist groupings and that would have the backing of Al Itihaad's nemesis, Ethiopia, was bound to be a serious threat to the investment in organizations and individuals that the international jihadist movement, particularly Al Qaeda, had made in Somalia since 1991. Mogadishu then became the place where the jihadists would make a stand in a region that was once central to its strategy to take over the Arabic peninsula and to restore the Muslim world to the rule of a powerful Caliphate.

The National Islamic Front government of Sudan and Al Qaeda, which was based in Sudan from 1991 to 1996, had fueled Islamist ambitions in the region and helped set into motion most, if not all, of the jihadist groups operating in the Greater Horn of Africa. This book examines the rise and present state of jihadist and other Islamist groups in the Greater Horn of Africa. The book seeks to explain the international linkages of these militant Islamist groups and sources of support, especially foreign support. This book also aims to provide readers with an explanation of the social, economic, and political context in which these groups arose.

The region's jihadist groups had experienced a shrinkage in their sphere of operation, leaving southern Somalia, especially Mogadishu, the last enclave in the Greater Horn of Africa region in which the international jihadists could act with relative impunity. Sudan's growing moderation in international affairs since 1996, including its increasing cooperation with international counterterrorism efforts, deprived the militant Islamists of a steady partner and base of operations. And the increasingly effective counterterrorism vigilance of Kenya and Tanzania after the 1998 embassies bombing also left stateless Somalia as the only viable terrain in which the international jihadists could use as a base of operations that they needed to carry out their agenda.

Introduction 9

For his part, Sheikh Aweys dismissed the allegations that Mogadishu's Islamic Courts were a breeding ground for a new generation of militants linked to Al Qaeda. He said that the claims made by other Somali politicians in this regard were made to satisfy "the West and its allied Christians in the region," using the Islamists' preferred description for neighboring Ethiopia.[12] Yet, reports of "Arab" and other foreign jihadists supporting the UIC forces in its battle against the factional militias cast doubts on Sheikh Aweys' denials.

The juxtaposition between the TFG and the Islamic Courts also carried the threat of an internationalization of the Somali strife. The United States had entered the equation by covertly sponsoring a counterterrorism alliance of secular factional leaders who attempted unsuccessfully to neutralize Mogadishu's jihadists. Ethiopia, which had intervened militarily in Somalia in the past to prevent Al Itihaad from destabilizing Ethiopia in an alliance with armed Ethiopian opposition groups, deployed troops in July 2006 to defend the TFG seated in Baidoa from the encroaching UIC militias.

On the other side, Eritrea, which had fought a bloody 1998-2000 border war with Ethiopia, had been beefing up the military arsenal of the Al Itihaad faction within the UIC, and the United Nations reported that 2,000 uniformed and fully equipped Eritrean forces were on the ground in Somalia in the fall of 2006. Eritrea denied the UN claims. Eritrea also reportedly supplied Ethiopia's armed opposition based in Somalia, and these Ethiopian rebel forces reportedly had fought alongside the Islamic Court militias in their bid to consolidate their control over Mogadishu.[13]

THE HORN OF AFRICA'S WIDER JIHADIST DREAM

For the purposes of this book, the Greater Horn of Africa includes Djibouti, Ethiopia, Eritrea, Kenya, Somalia, Sudan, Tanzania, and Uganda. Against Ethiopia, Al Qaeda and Sudan supported the Islamic Front for the Liberation of Oromia and Al Itihaad; in Uganda, they backed the Allied Democratic Forces. In Eritrea, the Eritrean Islamic Jihad (EIJ) has been the main focus of Islamic extremism. Until fall 2004, the EIJ advocated the establishment of an Islamic State in Eritrea and engaged in an intermittent armed struggle to achieve it. During the course of its history, the EIJ had received support from the National Islamic Front government in Sudan and from Al Qaeda.

In Kenya, Al Qaeda had been able to exploit Kenya's relatively open political and economic systems to establish a regional operational center there. However, the increasing vigilance of the Kenyan government appears to have limited the capacity of international terrorists to operate within its territory. Al Itihaad has also been active in Kenya's North Eastern Province in generating support for its vision of a pan-Somali Islamic caliphate, and during the 1990s, Sudan provided support to the Islamic Party of Kenya.

In Tanzania, Al Qaeda operated a cell, organized businesses, and plotted terrorist bombings through an Islamic charity. The semiautonomous island province of Zanzibar has emerged as a hotbed of radical Islamic activism as Islamic nationalists seek the restoration of an Islamic state to Zanzibar.

SOME CLARIFICATIONS

The term *Islamist* is used to describe those groups that seek the establishment of an Islamic state, and that theologically promote a *wahabist* or *salafist* version of Islam. *Islamism* is a set of political ideologies that hold that Islam is not only a religion, but also a political system that governs the legal, economic and social imperatives of the state according to its interpretation of Islamic Law. Islamists advocate that the *sharia* — a legal system based on the Koran, other revered texts and Islamic tradition of jurisprudence — be the basis for regulating public and some private aspects of life.

The term *jihadist* is used to describe those Islamists who espouse violent action, whether military action or terrorism, to achieve their aims. Jihadists see themselves as waging war against *kafirun*, or unbelievers. They see their struggle as a just war legitimated by a religious, political and military interpretation of the Islamic concept of *jihad*. Jihadists often see their actions as part of a local and global struggle to decenter the West in world affairs in order to establish *Hakimiyyat Allah* or "God's rule" on a global scale.

In this book, the term, *international jihadist*, is used to describe those who clearly see themselves as part of a global movement, maintain operational relationships with groupings in other countries, and are willing to act both locally and globally in support of a jihadist agenda. Al Qaeda has been the premier international jihadist organization, and it has acted as if there are no distinctions between local and global jihadist struggles.

Jihadists use the term *jihadi* to describe themselves. In so doing, they have appropriated the term *jihad* which refers to peaceful inner spiritual striving that is a widely respected Islamic ideal; and they have used it to sanction violent struggle against nonbelievers and Muslims who disagree with their version of Islam. This leaves us with the uncomfortable position of using a spiritual term dear to millions of Muslims throughout the world to describe those espousing an ideology based on hateful violence — quite an antithesis to ideals of the spiritual struggle that is the more traditional meaning of jihad.

NOTES

1. Stephen Braun and Judy Pasternak, "Long before Sept. 11, Bin Laden Aircraft Flew under the Radar," *Los Angeles Times*, November 18, 2001; Deborah Feyerick and Phillip Hirschkom, "Embassy Bombing Defendant Linked to bin Laden," *CNN*, February 14, 2001, http://archives.cnn.com/2001/LAW/02/14/embassy.bombing.02/index.html posted at: 10:46 p.m. EST (0346 GMT); United States v. Usama (sic) bin Laden et al., S (7) 98 Cr. 1023 (LBS), (United States District Court Southern District of New York), 34.
2. International Crisis Group, *Somali's Islamists*, Africa Report no. 100, December 12, 2005, 5; Joseph Winter, "Profile: Somalia's Islamist Leader," *BBC*, June 30, 2006, http://news.bbc.co.uk/1/hi/world/africa/5120242.stm.
3. Rod Norland, "Heroes, Terrorists and Osama," *Newsweek*, July 22, 2006, http://ethiomedia.com/carepress/aweys_interview.html.
4. "Islamist Denounces Somali Government," *The East African Standard*, August 30, 2005.
5. Craig Timberg, "Radicals Gain Edge in Somali Capital: Moderates Lose Key Positions in Islamic Militias," *Washington Post*, July 4, 2006.
6. Mark Bowden, *Black Hawk Down* (London: Bandam Press, 1999). Bowden's account of this incident does not shed light on Al Qaeda's nor Al Itihaad's involvement.
7. "Islamic Courts Set Up Consultative Council," *IRIN*, June 26, 2006.
8. Mohamed Olad Hassan, "Somali Prime Minister Unhurt by Blast at Rally," *Associated Press*, May 3, 2005. Some have disputed that this was an assassination attempt but rather report this to have been an acciden-

tal firing of a grenade. Other have linked it to jihadists. See "Security Alert," *The East African Standard*, Nairobi, June 15, 2005, allafrica.com/stories/ 200506060753. html; Johnson Muthumbi, "Somalia Minister linked to al-Qa'idah," *The People*, July 6, 2005; International Crisis Group, *Counter-Terrorism in Somalia: Losing Hearts and Minds*, Africa Report no. 95, July 11, 2005, 14.

9. Ali Musa Abdi, "Bomb Blast Kills Eight at Mogadishu Stadium," *Agence France-Presse (AFP)* in Middle East on Line, May 3, 2005, http://www.middle-east-online.com/english/?id=13392. Earlier in 2005, BBC correspondent and producer, Kate Peyton, was shot dead in Mogadishu after speaking to TFG officials who had gone to Mogadishu to see if it was safe for them to relocate from Kenya. A Sudanese national was later arrested in Kenya for the assassination, leaving the impression that the killing was the handiwork of an international jihadist operative. Reporters sans Frontieres alleged a link with a Mogadishu-based Islamic Court. Prime Minister Gedi contended that the killing of Ms. Peyton was designed to demonstrate Mogadishu as unsafe and to discourage international support for peace and reconciliation in Somalia. *Reporters sans Frontieres, Somalia: One Year After BBC Reporter Kate Peyton's Murder Investigation Has Gone Nowhere*, February 8, 2006; Cathy Majtenyi, "Terrorism Suspects in Kenya Said to Have Links to Journalist's Murder in Somalia," *VOANews*, February 22, 2005, http://www.voanews.com/english/archive/2005-02/2005-02-22-voa15.cfm.

10. "Somalia's Prime Minister Escapes Attack on his Convoy as Gunmen Throw Grenades, Mine Explodes," *Associated Press*, November 6, 2005.

11. "Somalia Suicide Bombing Arrests," *BBC*, September 28, 2006, http://news.bbc.co.uk/go/pr/fr/-/2/hi/africa/5389636.stm.

12. "Islamist Denounces Somali Government," *The East African Standard,* August 30, 2005.

13. "Eritrea Denies its Troops in Somalia," *Associated Press*, October 29, 2006.

Chapter One

SUDAN AND AL QAEDA
The Jihadist Onslaught

In May 1996, Osama bin Laden chartered an aircraft for a flight out of Sudan—just days after Khartoum had asked him to vacate the country. President Omar Hasan Ahmad al-Bashir was seeking to improve Sudan's relations with the United States and reportedly ceded to an American diplomatic request to expel bin Laden. Struggling for political dominance over Hassan al-Turabi, who was mastermind of the country's jihadist policies, Sudan's President al-Bashir had recently made another gesture of moderation to the West when he delivered the terrorist known as "Carlos the Jackal" to France.

By one account, bin Laden had the chartered aircraft taxi down the runway at the Khartoum airport. The plane accelerated as if to take off, but then it came to an abrupt stop. In a bid to escape being intercepted or shot down, bin Laden and his entourage deplaned and on the runway boarded a second plane, which had not reported its flight plan. Bin Laden then headed to his ultimate destination, Jalalabad, Afghanistan.

Bin Laden's care in avoiding harm's way was well justified. He had his enemies, and some U.S. officials had raised the possibility of shooting down his chartered aircraft. According to the *Washington Post*, however, "the idea was never seriously pursued because the United States had not yet linked bin Laden to killing Americans, and it was inconceivable that then U.S. President William Clinton would sign the 'lethal finding' necessary under these circumstances."[1]

Bin Laden's dramatic departure ended a period of intimate cooperation between the National Islamic Front (NIF) government of Sudan and Al Qaeda. The NIF government had set out to achieve Islamist political hegemony in the Greater Horn of Africa region by promoting armed opposition against neighboring countries and by harboring and abetting Islamic terrorists who backed Sudan's strategy of Islamist expansionism. From 1991 to 1996, the linchpin terrorist organization operating from within Sudan was bin Laden's nascent Al Qaeda organization, which worked hand in glove with the Sudanese government in supporting terrorists and armed insurgents in an effort to undermine the governments of neighboring states. By the time bin Laden left Sudan, he left behind an operational network of Al Qaeda cells and allied organizations active in the countries of Eritrea, Ethiopia, Kenya, Somalia, Tanzania, and Uganda.

Sudan and Al Qaeda launched a plan of widespread aggression against Ethiopia, Eritrea, Kenya, and Uganda, and their combined efforts sought both to drive the United States out of Somalia and to bring about an Islamist state in Somalia. During the 1990s both the Khartoum government and Al Qaeda fueled Islamist ambitions in the region and helped set into motion most, if not all, of the armed radical Islamic movements operating in the Greater Horn of Africa.

Sudan's aggression toward its neighbors stemmed in part from its bid to cut off support for the rebel Sudanese People's Liberation Movement/Army (SPLM/A) and other Sudanese armed rebel factions. In 1983, civil war broke out in Sudan, following the attempt by the northern Islamic political elite in the country to control the oil wealth located in the south. Sudan's government, based in the largely Muslim northern region, then became pitted against rebel forces, based in the southern part of the country inhabited predominately by people practicing Christian and traditional African religions. Of the estimated Sudanese population of more than 35 million, Sunni

Muslims comprise 70 per cent; pratitioners of traditional African religions 25 percent; and Christians 5 percent.

The NIF government in Khartoum sought to legitimize its war against rebel forces by articulating a vision of itself as the protector of Islam in Sudan. Political opponents were denounced as anti-Islamic, and the war against southern political and military organizations was considered a jihad. Jihad was also waged in the northern Kordofan state against the "African" Nuba population, which was both Christian and Muslim because of support given by elements of the Nuba population to the SPLM/A. For the dominant southern movement, the SPLM/A, the war was viewed as a means to free southerners from political domination and religious persecution.[2]

Muslim groups based in the North launched two other sets of rebellions. In 1997, the National Democratic Alliance (NDA)—a coalition of northern Sudanese parties in a loose alliance with the SPLM/A—carried out intermittent military offensives in eastern Sudan from bases inside Eritrea. In 2003, the Sudanese Liberation Movement and the Justice and Equality Movement created a third rebel front in the Muslim Darfur region of western Sudan.

The Sudanese state organized several wars by proxy in its strategic quest to gain regional dominance and to undermine regional support for the Sudanese opposition based in southern Sudan and later in Eritrea. Khartoum preferred supporting armed Islamist groups in Eritrea, Ethiopia, Somalia, and Uganda, when possible, but also backed non-Muslim insurgencies, when necessary, as it did in Ethiopia and Uganda. Sudan also sought to initiate jihad in Kenya and Tanzania but with little effect. Additionally, Sudan sponsored terrorist activities and armed rebel forces in Algeria, Chad, Egypt, Libya, Tunisia and Yemen. These latter countries lie outside the scope of the present discussion.

An ideology of expansionist Islamic fundamentalism, which sought to "Arabize" all of Sudan and the Horn of Africa region and to impose strict adherence to sharia, underpinned Sudan's regional aggression.[3] The Sudanese state became Islamist when a 1989 military *coup d'état* brought Colonel (later Lieutenant General) Omar Hasan Ahmad al-Bashir to power. The ideological driving force behind the regime's effort to propel political Islam as the dominant regional force was Hassan al-Turabi and his NIF.

A number of factors eventually contributed to a gradual moderation of the regime's policies of aggression, including its support for both international terrorism and regional jihadist groups. These factors helped to hasten the ouster of al-Turabi from power. They included:

- Sudan's increasing international isolation, including UN sanctions;
- Concerted diplomatic engagement by the U.S. government; and
- The patent failures of Sudan's Islamist policies to provide the hoped-for security in both the international and domestic spheres.

As a result, the Khartoum government and the insurgent SPLM/A reached in January 2005 the Comprehensive Peace Agreement that formally ended Africa's longest civil conflict. The southern movement joined with Sudan's ruling party, the National Congress Party, in a coalition government. The agreement also called for free elections in 2009 and an independence referendum for the South. Also in 2005, the NDA joined Sudan's new unity government after reaching a reconciliation agreement brokered by Egypt.[4]

HASSAN AL-TURABI

Hassan al-Turabi was the architect of Khartoum's Islamist ideology that buttressed the military regime's hold on power and quest for regional dominance. With a law degree from Khartoum University and advanced degrees from the University of London and the Sorbonne, al-Turabi's intellectual prowess and personal charm often masked his political cunning and ruthlessness.

As a young man, al-Turabi came to Khartoum in 1951 to study law. While other students promoted secular solutions to the problems in Sudan, al-Turabi joined the Sudanese branch of *Al-Ikhwan Al-Moslemoon* (Muslim Brotherhood), just as the parent organization in Egypt was entering a phase of fomenting political revolution.

A twenty-two-year-old elementary school teacher, Hasan al-Banna, founded the Muslim Brotherhood in 1928 as an Islamic revivalist movement following the collapse of the Ottoman Empire and the subsequent end of the caliphate system of government that had united Muslims in the region for hundreds of years. Al Banna contended that Islam was more than a religious observance; it was, rather, a comprehensive way of life. He propagated the tenets of puritanical *Wahabism*, and he insisted that the Brotherhood's male students receive *jihadia* training rather than what had been traditional Islamic education. Soon after its founding, the Muslim Brothers set up branches in neighboring countries, including Sudan, and worked actively to spread the principal Islamist idea: That Islam is "creed and state, book and sword, and a way of life." These principles conflicted with what was then the mainstream view of Muslim scholars, namely that Islam should be restricted within the walls of the mosque. The Muslim Brothers also adopted an anticolonialist and antiimperialist stance in their rhetoric about the West.[5]

The Muslim Brotherhood sought to institutionalize Islamic law throughout Sudan, and the legal scholar, al-Turabi, became secretary general of Sudan's Muslim Brotherhood in 1964.[6] When General Jafa'ar Nimeiri took power in a coup in 1969, he dissolved Sudan's Brotherhood and arrested its leadership, including al-Turabi. Dr. al-Turabi returned to political life in 1977, upon reconciliation with Nimeiri. General Nimeiri then designated al-Turabi his attorney general. A former dean of the law school at the University of Khartoum, al-Turabi, played a leading role in the introduction of sharia. The enforcement of sharia-dictated amputations and hangings provoked a public outcry that contributed to the popular and nonviolent overthrow of Nimeiri in 1985 and a brief reinstatement of parliamentary democracy.[7]

After the overthrow of Nimeiri, al-Turabi proved instrumental in setting up the NIF, a Brotherhood-dominated organization that included several other small Islamic parties. Following al-Bashir's 1989 coup, the military government arrested al-Turabi, as well as the leaders of other political parties, and held him in solitary confinement for several months. Nevertheless, this action failed to dispel the pervasive belief in Sudan that al-Turabi and the NIF actively collaborated with Colonel Bashir in the coup. Not long after al-Bashir's rise to power, the NIF influence within the government became evident in its policies and in the presence of several NIF members in the cabinet.[8] Al-Turabi's incarceration was likely a ploy designed to dupe the Egyptian government into extending recognition to the military government before the new regime revealed its Islamist orientation, which surely would not have received Cairo's approval. From that time until 1999, al-Turabi was the power behind the throne. He maneuvered the NIF police state and associated militias to consolidate Islamist power and to prevent popular uprisings as had occurred in response to the sharia implementation of the Nimeiri period.[9]

Throughout his long political career, al-Turabi maintained links with the wider Islamist international movement. Indeed, he reportedly had close contact with Dr. Ayman al-Zawahiri. Al-Zawahiri founded the Egyptian Islamic Jihad, which merged with Osama bin-Laden's Al Qaeda group to create the "World Islamic Front for Jihad Against Jews and Crusaders."[10] Al-Zawahiri became bin Laden's personal physician and close confidant and eventually his second in command.[11]

THE NATIONAL ISLAMIC FRONT IN SUDANESE NATIONAL POLITICS

Al-Bashir forged an alliance with the NIF in an attempt to create legitimacy for his military regime. The Mulsim Brotherhood and later the NIF drew its support almost exclusively from university-educated, middle class males. The NIF never succeeded in growing much beyond this traditional base of support, which remained a small minority within Sudan. Al-Bashir's and the NIF's political success rested largely in repressing the democratic opposition. The NIF moved to undermine the trade union movement, which historically opposed the authoritarian military state, and purged democratic sympathizers within the military and government bureaucracy.[12] The regime also employed divide-and-rule tactics when dealing with various ethnic groups within the country.

The failure of the NIF to broaden its base of support may be explained, at least in part, by Sudan's Islamic history. Al-Turabi's austere legalistic view of Islam remained at odds with mainstream Islam in Sudan, which is heavily influenced by the Sufi orders or brotherhoods. Sufism is an Islamic mystical tradition in which Muslims seek to find the truth of divine love and knowledge through direct personal experience of God.

Sufi practice often consists of a variety of mystical paths that are designed to ascertain the nature of man and God and to facilitate the experience of the presence of divine love and wisdom in the world. The Sufi orders or brotherhoods are responsible for preserving and passing on the tradition's esoteric knowledge.

Sudan remains one of the strongholds of Sufism in the Muslim world, and although not directly involved in politics, Sudan's traditional Sufi orders have historically been pillars of support to the moderate UMMA party of former Prime Minister Sadiq al-Mahdi.[13] Sufism in Sudan does have its own reformist traditions of purifying Islamic practice, but the Sufi mandate of tolerance with "family, neighbors and all others in the world" was often at odds with the al-Turabi's NIF view of Islam that preached the Arabization of Africa and the Islamization of the United States.[14] According to Dr. Hasan Al Fatih Qaribullah, a leading sheikh of the Sufi movement in Khartoum, "If there is a family in Sudan that does not have at least one Sufi member, it is not Sudanese."[15] Sufi notions of moderation had hobbled al-Turabi's efforts to make his more intellectualized version of Islam the dominant tendency in Sudan.

PAIC: Al-Turabi's Internationalism

Under al-Turabi's guidance, the Sudanese government created an open-door policy for jihadists, which led the U.S. State Department to designate Sudan as a state sponsor of terrorism in August 1993.[16] In 1990-1991, al-Turabi established an international Islamist umbrella organization—the Popular Arab Islamic Conference (PAIC), over which he presided as Secretary General. He formed the PAIC with the immediate aim of opposing U.S. involvement in the First Gulf War, which had received support from moderate Arab states. Al-Turabi envisioned the PAIC, which was headquartered in Khartoum, as a counterweight to the more conservative Saudi-dominated Organization of Islamic Conference representing the governments of fifty-six predominately Muslim countries.

Al-Turabi's sense of Arab nationalism limited, however, the appeal of the organization and circumscribed its effectiveness in "black" Africa. The word Arab in the name, Popular Arab and Islamic Conference, posed a problem for many non-

Arab Muslims interested in the organization. Non-Arab African, Asians, European and North American delegates to the 1995 PAIC conference demanded that "Arab" be deleted from PAIC, contending they did not fit into an organization that was labeled Arab. The majority non-Arab delegates voted for a change of name, whereupon the Arab delegates walked out in protest. Al-Turabi intervened by postponing the issue with the promise of taking it up at the following year's meeting,[17] but the name change never took place.

THE BIN LADEN CONNECTION

During the "open door" period, jihadist organizations converged on Khartoum, including the Palestinian *Tanzim al Jihad* (Islamic Jihad Squad), the *Harakat al-Jihad al-Islami al-Filastini* (Palestinian Islamic Jihad), the Egyptian *al Jama'a al Islamiya* (The Islamic Group), the Palestinian *Fatah al-Majles al-Thawry* (better known as the Abu Nidal Organization), Lebanon's *Hezbollah* (Party of God) and the Palestinian *Hamas* (*Harakat al-Muqawama al-Islamiyya* or Islamic Resistance Movement).[18] One little known international jihadist organization at that time, Al Qaeda, also established itself in Sudan and soon surrounded itself with a number of other smaller jihadist and terrorist organizations.

In 1991, bin Laden took advantage of Sudan's jihadist "open door" by relocating himself from Saudi Arabia where the government had been putting him under increasing pressure and by transporting his terrorist "shock troops" from Afghanistan to Sudan. There he established a powerful military and political presence, using a variety of business ventures to finance his activities. His move to Sudan came at the invitation of al-Turabi. He reportedly had known Bin Laden since 1984 when the Saudi-born bin Laden first visited Sudan and became acquainted with the leadership of the Sudanese Islamist movement.

Bin Laden's relocation to Sudan paid big financial dividends for the cash-strapped NIF government and produced substantial economic benefits for the country. Bin Laden joined the Turabi-led NIF with an initial fee of $5 million. Bin Laden also reportedly brought at least $350 million into the country, and provided valuable services to the Sudanese government, such as floating critical foreign exchange transactions when the government was short of foreign currency.[19] Bin Laden operated through a number of business enterprises. *Wadi al-Aqiq* served as a holding company in Sudan and has, accordingly, been described as the "mother" of the other companies. As Al Qaeda solidified its position in Sudan, other business ventures followed, including the Ladin International Company, an import-export concern; Taba Investment, an investment firm; *Hijra* Construction, which built bridges and roads; *Qudarat* Transport Company; Khartoum Tannery; and the *al-Themar al-Mubaraka* Company, which grew sesame, peanuts and white corn for Al Qaeda fighters on a farm near Ed Damazin. At this farm, Al Qaeda provided its members with refresher courses in light weapons and explosives. Among his biggest business achievements, one of Bin Laden's firms built the 700 kilometer road linking Khartoum, Shindi and Atbarah.[20]

A defecting Sudanese military officer closely involved with bin Laden's operations in Sudan described bin Laden's supporters as a highly organized network of armed jihadist groups that traced their roots to the war in Afghanistan in the 1980s. In an interview with Human Rights Watch, the defector said the groups were linked through an "advisory committee" which bin Laden controlled. According to the military defector, the advisory council included representatives from such far-flung armed groups as the Egyptian Islamic Group, the Islamic Front for the Liberation of Oromia in Ethiopia, the Eritrean Islamic Jihad, the Islamic forces of Sheikh Abdullah in Uganda (which later joined Uganda's rebel Allied Democratic Forces), Algeria's Islamic Salvation Front, and the Moro Liberation Front from Mindanao, Philippines.

Among the more than 500 veterans of the Afghan war then based in Sudan, there were Tunisians, Algerians, Sudanese, Saudis, Syrians, Iraqis, Moroccans, Somalis, Ethiopians, Eritreans, Chechnyans, Bosnians and six African-Americans. These fighters were organized into groups and dispersed to camps throughout Sudan--near Khartoum, Port Sudan, the Damazin area of eastern Sudan and at a base in the southern Equatoria province situated near Uganda. One base, near Hamesh Koreb along the Eritrea border, was overrun in March 1997 by forces of the Sudanese opposition, who claim they captured large stores of Iranian military equipment there.

The main military camp of the Afghan Arabs was near Soba, ten kilometers south of Khartoum, along the Blue Nile. The Soba camp covered twenty acres and was a highly restricted area. Iranians previously based in Lebanon's Beka'a Valley were among those involved in training the mujahidin guerrillas at this camp. One account indicates that bin Ladin financed the building and supervision of twenty-three camps for Afghanistan's so-called Arab mujahidin. In 1993, 500 mujahidin fighters from Afghanistan, who were part of the Pakistani Islamist terrorist organization, Harkat-ul-Mujahideen, were forced out of Pakistan and made their way to Sudan, from whence many went to Somalia to join forces with the Somali jihadist militia, Al Itihaad.[21]

At the camps, guerrillas were schooled in the use of explosives, forgery, coding, and related skills. Officers who carried out successful operations in the region were rewarded with money and arms. Weapons for the guerrillas were imported mainly from Iran and China through Port Sudan, and then trucked to Khartoum where the Ministry of Defense turned them over to bin Laden's representatives. Some arms were also routinely relocated to a warehouse in Yemen for forwarding to other operational areas including Somalia. Bin Laden purchased a jet plane and used chartered planes to ferry his jihadist troops and materiel in the region. He also owned a ship, and he used that and other vessels to transport materiel to Somalia and Kenya.[22]

THE WARS BY PROXY

1993 was a decisive year in Sudan's efforts to launch a regional offensive. The al-Bashir government came to wage war through proxies with Eritrea, Ethiopia and Uganda and militarily backed the largest Islamist faction in Somalia. Sudan's attempt to set up a jihadist militia in Tanzania was thwarted by the Tanzanian government. Al Qaeda launched numerous operations in these neighboring states at times in apparent coordination with Sudan, and also set up active and large operations in Kenya, Somalia, Tanzania and Uganda.

In the case of Uganda, Khartoum was seeking to prevent the use of its neighbor's territory as a base and arms conduit for the rebel SPLM/A. As for Eritrea and Ethiopia, the Sudanese government was seeking to export Islamist revolution. When the governments in Addis Ababa and Asmara came to power in the early 1990s, they maintained cordial relations with Khartoum. Indeed, Khartoum had provided support for and harbored bases of the Ethiopian and Eritrean movements that overthrew the Ethiopian dictatorship of Mengistu Haile Mariam. However, by 1993 it was apparent that Khartoum was assuming a hostile stance with the result that both Ethiopia and Eritrea began to support Sudanese rebel groups including the SPLM/A and, later, the northern-based NDA.

Khartoum also became alarmed that the U.S.-led UN intervention in Somalia in 1991 might shift the regional balance of power against Sudan, bring a large Muslim nation under Western influence and lead to U.S. occupation of southern Sudan. The United Nations entered Somalia to supply humanitarian relief to millions of Somalis facing the specter of starvation after the collapse of the central government. However, the mandate of the UN mission expanded to include nation building until continued opposition by Somali politicomilitary factions forced the UN to withdraw in 1995. Sudan and Al Qaeda were determined to undermine U.S. influence in the region, and Al Qaeda took center stage in the targeting of Kenya for hosting considerable U.S. diplomatic and intelligence assets that provided support to the SPLM/A.

THE UGANDAN FRONT

In 1993, the Khartoum government began supporting a small and relatively inactive residual guerrilla force on the Ugandan border in an area inhabited by Acholi-speaking people. This was the Lord's Resistance Army (LRA), a Christian-inspired millenarian movement founded by the prophetess Alice Lakwena, who rebelled against the Ugandan government in 1987 and took refuge in Kenya after her defeat. Joseph Kony, then took the reins of the LRA; he is a visionary who has claimed to be guided by spirits and has been known to daub his fighters with a magic substance to protect them against bullets. Kony apparently wished to establish a state based on his unique interpretation of biblical millenarianism. The LRA has been accused of widespread human rights violations, including mutilation, torture, rape, the abduction of civilians, the use of child soldiers and a number of massacres. The Sudanese government not only supported the LRA against the

Ugandan government; the Sudanese military also reportedly deployed LRA forces to fight against Sudanese rebel militias in southern Sudan.

In 1996, the Sudanese made contact with another anti-government Ugandan organization, the Nile West Bank Liberation Front under the command of Juma Oris. It operated from bases within the then Zaire (later renamed the Democratic Republic of Congo) and Sudan, and the Front carried out its actions largely in the far northwestern Kaya region of Uganda. It was predominantly made up of Muslims from the local Nubi, Kakwa and Aringa ethnic communities. Its officers were mainly ex-members of the army of former Ugandan president, Idi Amin. The Front was both less violent and less militarily active than the LRA. By 1998, as a result of actions by the government's Uganda People's Defense Force, the Front as a group was no longer capable of significant activity.[23]

Another Ugandan group that received support from Sudan and also from Al Qaeda was the Allied Democratic Forces (ADF). The ADF, which adopted an Islamist ideology, emerged out of a core group of puritanical Moslems from *Tabligh Jamaat* (Proselytizing Group)—a normally apolitical missionary movement with roots in South Asia, but which in Zanzibar and other parts of East Africa has given rise to militant Islamist preaching and in the case of Uganda an armed insurrection. Determined to put an end to what they considered to be the marginalization of Muslims in Uganda, a faction of Uganda's *Tablighis* resorted to armed struggle in the hopes of establishing an Islamic state that would respect their interests.

Together with the obscure and largely defunct National Army for the Liberation of Uganda, the Tablighis moved to western Uganda to start the rebellion under the ADF umbrella. Among ADF's recruits, there were Rwandan Hutu supporters of the former government responsible for the 1994 genocide in Rwanda, fighters from the local Bakonja ethnic community in then Zaire, and unemployed youth from various Baganda, Banyoro and Batoro ethnic communities in Uganda.[24] The ADF set up rear bases in neighboring Zaire where it could receive military support from Sudan and from whence it began recruiting and training fighters with the promise of money and education. Al Qaeda helped to set up camps for training ADF fighters, and when bin Laden's organization relocated its headquarters to Afghanistan in 1996, ADF members traveled there to undergo training as explosives experts. The Ugandan government attributed numerous terrorist bombings that rocked the capital, Kampala, between 1997 and 1999 to the ADF.

Even after bin Laden's departure, Sudan continued to support the Ugandan jihadists. As late as June 2004, Uganda and the Democratic Republic of Congo were engaged in negotiations on how to dispose of about 2.5 tons of arms that the Sudanese government had supplied to ADF rebels based in the Congo.[25]

THE ERITREAN FRONT

Khartoum backed the Eritrean Islamic Jihad (EIJ), which launched an armed struggle against what it termed the "Christian regime" governing Eritrea with the goal of establishing an Islamic state. Al Qaeda also gave training and financial support, and reportedly considered the taking of Eritrea as a strategic prize that could be used as a staging area for operations against Ethiopia and against Yemen, where Al Qaeda-allied groups were already ensconced. The first serious incidents of EIJ military actions occurred at the end of 1992. EIJ members laid mines on desert tracks near the Sudanese border and infiltrated small groups of fighters inside Eritrea. In September 1993, new clashes took place, and the government captured several EIJ members who confessed they had been trained in camps inside Sudan. The government also said it killed several jihadist fighters from Afghanistan, Morocco and Yemen who were most likely part of bin Laden's Al Qaeda network then operating from Sudan.[26] The EIJ has carried on an intermittent, low intensity war with the Eritrean government since then, and seemed ready for action when called on by Khartoum.

THE ETHIOPIAN FRONT

The Sudanese government tried to recruit the Oromo Liberation Front (OLF) to wage its proxy war against Ethiopia. The Oromo are the largest ethnic community in Ethiopia — comprising 32.1 percent of the population according to the 1994 census and numbering around twenty-five million in 2005. The OLF, which advocates an independent Oromia state, has engaged in an armed struggle with the Ethiopia government since it pulled out of the provisional Ethiopian government in 1992 over allegation of political harassment and a demobilization dispute; but the OLF's predominantly Christian leadership was not comfortable working with Islamist Khartoum. In search of an alternative to the OLF, the Sudanese government promoted a purely Islamic Oromo organizations, the Islamic Front for the Liberation of Oromia (IFLO).[27] Originally called the *Jihad Oromo Ibrahim Bilisa*, IFLO was reportedly formed in 1978 after a split with the OLF. In mid 1990s, IFLO operated out of bases inside Somalia and with Sudanese support worked in alliance with Al Itihaad to carry out actions inside of Ethiopia. IFLO military actions were intermittent and relatively ineffective. It reportedly drew support from Oromo clans such as the Jara in the eastern Oromo area of Haraghe, and IFLO members have consisted of urban Muslim inhabitants of Harar and Dire Dawa, and the rural populations living around these towns and in the area to their west.[28]

THE SOMALI FRONT

The intensity of Sudanese involvement with Al Itihaad, which began in 1993, led many Somalis to regard the Somali organization as a foreign puppet. Al Itihaad emerged as a dominant military force in Somalia after the collapse of the central government in 1991 and launched a campaign to secure territory in the north and south of the country. It received support from Sudan, Al Qaeda, Iran and Saudi sources. By the end of 1993, Al Itihaad began small-scale actions in the Ogaden region of Ethiopia in a bid to establish a greater Islamic Somali state that would include Somali-speaking peoples within Ethiopia, Kenya and Djibouti. In December 1994, Al Itihaad began operations in parts of Ethiopia's Somali region, forcing the Ethiopian government to send troops to contain the situation,[29] and in 1996, the Sudanese *charge d'affaires* in Mogadishu called publicly for jihad against Ethiopia during a meeting with supporters of Al Itihaad.[30]

THE KENYAN FRONT AND AL QAEDA'S EAST AFRICA CELL

Sudan's support for the Islamic Party of Kenya (IPK) was consistent with Khartoum's policy of promoting an Islamists agenda in the region and as a means of undermining Kenyan support for the rebel SPLA.[31] The Sudanese government, however, specifically denied allegations in the press that it was training armed IPK insurgents in Sudan, and the author has not seen any credible evidence of a Sudanese-backed armed opposition to the Kenyan government.[32] During the period when the firebrand preacher, Sheikh Khalid Balala became *de facto* head of the IPK, Sudanese and Iranian support reportedly helped the IPK to effectively mobilize a mass following in Coast Province. Sheikh Balala had cemented his relationship with the Sudanese government during his several trips to Khartoum.[33]

In East Africa, including Kenya, Tanzania and possibly Uganda, Al Qaeda set up an active operation. Kenya operated as a "gateway" for its operations in Somalia. Al Qaeda members blended into Kenyan and Tanzanian society. Al Qaeda opened legitimate businesses that sold fish and dealt in various other commodities, and it operated two Islamic charities from Kenya. In 1993, Al Qaeda began assessing sites in Nairobi to hit American targets in retaliation for the U.S. intervention in Somalia.[34] The East Africa cell remained active after Al Qaeda's departure from Sudan and was responsible for bombing the American embassies in Dar es Salaam and Nairobi in 1998. Uganda claimed that it broke up Al Qaeda plots to bomb the U.S. embassy in Kampala and the Ugandan parliament. The Ugandan government also claimed that Al Qaeda members had plotted to assassinate President Yoweri Museveni in Kampala in 1999.

THE TANZANIAN FRONT

In 1993, Sudan reportedly supported *Baraza la Uendelazaji Koran Tanzania* (BALUKTA or the Tanzanian Koranic Council), that reportedly began training a militia to carry out jihad. Al Qaeda also established various business ventures in Tanzania and was behind the 1998 bombing of the U.S. embassy in Dar es Salaam. Officials of the Al Qaeda-linked, Saudi-based charity, Al Haramain, may have encouraged a spate of jihadist violence that hit Zanzibar in 2004.

INTERNATIONAL RESISTANCE TO SUDAN'S AGGRESSION

After 1989, when the al-Bashir-led coup deposed the elected government and imposed a military-Islamist junta on Sudan, the Sudanese government became internationally ostracized for its gross human rights abuses. Over the next several years, the international community often led by the United States imposed a series of restriction on Khartoum in response to Sudan's aggression and that of Al Qaeda. These actions ultimately obliged the Sudanese government to begin moderating its policies.

The first U.S. actions against the al-Bashir government were legislatively mandated votes in international bodies that were designed to block the Sudanese government from receiving aid from international lending institutions. When the U.S. State Department designated Sudan in 1993 as a state sponsor of terrorism, additional sanctions were imposed.[35] It was Sudan's complicity in the assassination attempt on Egyptian President Hosni Mubarak in Addis Ababa in 1995, however, that galvanized international opposition to Sudan, and this pressure ultimately prompted Khartoum to inform Osama bin Laden that he was no longer welcomed in Sudan.

The U.S. implicated bin Laden, Al Qaeda, and elements within the Sudanese government in the 1995 Mubarak assassination attempt. Three suspected members of the Egyptian terrorist organization, *Jama'at al-Islamiyaa*, survived the foiled operation. The suspects fled to Sudan, where they found a safe haven. An Islamic charity operating in Sudan, *Muwafaq*, or Blessed Relief, which was reportedly a front for bin Laden activities, acted as a conduit for funds that helped finance the failed assassination attempt. The son of Khalid bin Mahfouz, a controversial, Yemeni-born Saudi tycoon worth an estimated $2.5 billion, was on the board of the charity. Bin Mahfouz founded and ran the world's largest private bank until 1999, when the Saudi royal family quietly arranged for a government investment fund to buy out his 50 per cent stake in the National Commerical Bank, and then forced his dismissal. Mahouz was then confined to a military hospital in Taef, Saudi Arabia. One of his sisters is married to bin Laden.[36]

The United Nations imposed diplomatic sanctions on Sudan for Khartoum's failure to turn over to Ethiopia the assassination suspects and for Sudan's overall support for international terrorism.[37] Sudan never honored the extradition order. Minor diplomatic and air travel sanctions also went into effect; and these were not lifted until September 2001. For the same reasons, in late 1997, the U.S. implemented additional diplomatic and economic sanctions on Sudan prohibiting U.S. entities from doing business with the Sudanese government. The United States and Saudi Arabia pressured Sudan's government to expel Bin Laden and his terrorist network. Bin

Sudan and Al Qaeda: The Jihadist Onslaught

Laden then left Sudan in 1996 and headquartered Al Qaeda's operations in Afghanistan in an alliance with the Taliban.

In response to Sudan's regional aggression, including its sponsorship of terrorism, Ethiopia, Eritrea, and Uganda entered into what amounted to an U.S.-led "Frontline States" alliance against Sudan, and shortly after the imposition of UN sanctions, the U.S. government announced that Uganda, Ethiopia, and Eritrea were to be given non-offensive military equipment worth $20 million. It was widely perceived that this gesture was a rebuke of Sudan. It may have also allowed these three countries to funnel more materiel to Sudanese rebel groups.[38]

The Frontline States' strategy unraveled, however, when war broke out between Ethiopia and Eritrea in 1998, and when Uganda, the most pro-SPLM/A country in the region, became deeply embroiled in the Zaire conflict with the result that it had fewer resources to share with the Sudanese rebels. To offset the shortfall in regional support to the SPLM/A, the United States significantly increased its commitment of humanitarian aid to southern Sudan, allowing the SPLA to spend more of its meager funds on military equipment.[39]

In the middle of a bloody border war, both Ethiopia and Eritrea sought to normalize relations with Sudan—each in an effort to isolate the other. On December 8, 1999, Uganda and Sudan signed a peace agreement in Nairobi, Kenya. In the agreement the two signatories renounced sponsoring or harboring any rebel group fighting to destabilize the other's country.[40] Nonetheless, support continued to flow to armed opposition groups in both countries, if at an abated level.

In June 1998, Al Qaeda's cell in East Africa simultaneously attacked with suicide bombers the U.S. embassies in Nairobi, Kenya, and Dar es Salaam, Tanzania, killing hundreds, mostly Kenyans and Tanzanians. Al Qaeda in part was motivated by what it perceived to be U.S. support on behalf of the rebels in Southern Sudan. According to the Ugandan government, it foiled a plot to blow up the U.S. embassy in Kampala. In what was widely regarded as symbolic retaliation for the embassy bombings, on August 20, 1998, the United States struck Khartoum with two cruise missiles, destroying the Al Shifa pharmaceutical plant, which the United States suspected of being owned by bin Laden and of being involved in the embassy bombings and in chemical weapons manufacturing. One person was killed and eleven workers injured in the nighttime attack. A UN report later disputed the U.S. claim that the plant had been used for the production of chemical weapons. The United States also deployed cruise missiles in an attack against six Al Qaeda sites in Afghanistan. Although the U.S. attack in Khartoum was not aimed at the Sudanese government, jihadists in the region, including those in Sudan, interpreted it as a sign of U.S. intention to redouble its counterterrorism measures; and Sudan responded by accelerating its move away from its support for jihadist groups.

AL TURABI'S OUSTER: THE END OF ISLAMIST INTERNATIONALISM

In 1999, Sudanese President al-Bashir and his erstwhile ally al-Turabi became locked in a power struggle, as al-Turabi maneuvered to acquire some of al-Bashir's presidential powers. The struggle between al-Bashir and al-Turabi played out in the context of the Sudanese government's desire to end its designation as a state sponsor of terrorism. This desire certainly grew after the U.S. bombing of the Al Shifa pharmaceutical plant. The military strongman dealt decisively with al-Turabi, who was placed in and out of prison and under house arrest at various times after the falling out. Al-Turabi's ouster marked a turning point for a government that had become increasingly isolated in the international arena. It also saw a further moderation in the Islamist aggressiveness that had characterized the government since the early 1990s.

Al Turabi's ouster also highlighted an emergent division in the government regarding the continuation of an Islamist agenda. Just as control of oil resources lay at the heart of the outbreak of the civil war with the "South" in 1983, so too did the future dispensation of the country's petroleum wealth reportedly give context to how factions within the government regarded their Islamist options.

The "doves," led by the then minister for peace, Ghazi Salah al-Din Attabani (presidential advisor and spokesman), and backed by the foreign minister, Mustafa Osman Ismail, promoted peace with the Sudanese armed opposition based on an economic rationale. For Ghazi and his supporters, the Sudan's government would end up better off sharing the country's oil wealth with the South, since normalization of the situation offered the prospect of attracting Western investment with more advanced technological resources to exploit deposits. Another faction within the government, led by Vice-President Ali Osman Mohamed Taha, was opposed to this, seeing it as a trap that would weaken the government's Islamists credentials, at least in part. This faction argued that Chinese, Russian, Indian, and Algerian companies already on the ground would suffice as an alternative to Western investment.[41] The position of the doves would eventually win out as Khartoum reached its breakthrough peace agreements with the country's rebel movements in 2005.

Soon after al-Turabi's fall from al-Bashir's grace in December 1999, the Sudanese government closed down the office of Al Turabi's "Islamist International," the PAIC in February 2000. According to the PAIC Assistant Secretary, Ibrahim al-Sanusi, the government's closure of the PAIC in Khartoum amounted to an attempt to further erode the influence of al-Turabi. The PAIC contended that al-Bashir had succumbed to pressure from the United States and other countries to rein in hard line elements within his ruling elite.[42]

Counterterrorism cooperation with the United States then began in mid-2000; this significantly increased after the September 11, 2001 terrorist attacks, when Sudan began rounding up "Muslim extremists," including some with links to Al Qaeda. It was reported in 2005 that Sudan's intelligence agency, *Mukhabarat*, had cooperated with the U.S. global war on terror on various fronts. The Mukhabarat detained Al Qaeda suspects for interrogation by U.S. agents; it seized and turned over to the U.S. Federal Bureau of Investigation (FBI) evidence recovered in raids on suspected terrorists' homes, including fake passports; and Sudan expelled non-Sudanese extremists, putting them into the hands of other Arab intelligence agencies working closely with the U.S. Central Intelligence Agency (CIA). U.S. intelligence and diplomatic officials also credited Khartoum with foiling attacks against unnamed American targets by, among other things, detaining foreign militants moving through Sudan on their way to join insurgents opposing the U.S. military intervention in Iraq which had begun in 2003.[43]

In other areas of cooperation, the Sudanese government also took steps in 2003 to strengthen its legislative and administrative instruments for fighting terrorism. It ratified the International Convention for the Suppression of the Financing of Terrorism and the African Union's Convention on the Prevention and Combating of Terrorism, as well as the Convention of the Organization of the Islamic Conference on Combating Terrorism. The signing of the OIC convention represented a significant reversal for Khartoum, given that al-Turabi had once challenged OIC influence by establishing the PAIC as a rival international Islamic organization. The Sudanese minister of justice, Ali Mohamed Osman Yassin, also issued a decree establishing an office for combating terrorism. Sudan signed a counterterrorism cooperation agreement with the Algerian government, which had during the 1990s accused Sudan of harboring wanted Algerian terrorists. Sudan also signed a counterterrorism agreement with Yemen and Ethiopia.[44]

In 2004, new Al Qaeda training camps were identified on Sudanese soil, which left the unsettling impression that the Sudanese government, or at least elements of it, maintained relations with international terrorist organizations, even as Khartoum officially was cooperating with Washington in its war on terror. The Sudanese government continued to include many officials with a history of support both for international terrorist organizations and for a policy of aggression towards the country's neighbors.[45] In the United States, members of Congress raised a concern about the presence of such individuals in the Sudanese government, but the U.S. State Department expressed satisfaction that there was "no indication that al-Qaida elements have had a presence in Sudan with the knowledge and consent of the Sudanese Government for at least the past five years."[46]

The Sudanese government acted to remove the Al Qaeda presence in Sudan that was discovered in 2004. Authorities raided what was described as a probable terrorist training camp in Kordofan State, arresting more than a dozen operatives and seizing illegal weapons.

Western diplomats in Saudi Arabia said that in 2003 Al Qaeda had established camps in the Jebel Kurush Mountains, which run parallel to the Red Sea, and that these camps had become a vital staging ground for Al Qaeda. This Al Qaeda group in eastern Sudan reportedly took orders from Saudi Arabia's most wanted man, Saleh Awfi—the top Al Qaeda operative in Saudi Arabia who was killed in a Saudi operation in Medina in August 2005. As reported in one publication:

> There is significant traffic from these camps to the peninsula across the Red Sea. There is no real Sudanese government or army control over the mountains. The terrorists slip through the cracks, up into the hills where they can train, rest and build up the spirit of jihad. With things getting hot over here [in Saudi Arabia], they can get organized over there.[47]

Khartoum reportedly allowed U.S. Special Forces teams inside the country to hunt down these Saudi Arabian operatives. The presence of U.S. forces on Sudan soil may be viewed as an indication of just how far Sudan and the United States had come to cooperate in counterterrorism.[48]

Despite the growing satisfaction of Washington with Sudan's cooperation in counterterrorism, the State Department kept Sudan on its list of state sponsors of terrorism. State Department spokesmean, Richard Boucher, said in 2004 that it had done so, in part, because of the presence of Hamas and the Palestinian Islamic Jihad in Sudan.[49] Keeping Sudan on this list of state sponsors of terrorism with its mandatory restrictions of U.S. arms sales and foreign assistance also gave Washington some leverage with Khartoum, especially in regard to its widespread human rights violation in the Darfur conflict in western Sudan. Sudanese government forces and government-backed militias have been reportedly responsible for crimes against humanity, war crimes and "ethnic cleansing" involving aerial and ground attacks on civilians of the same ethnicity as members of two rebel groups in Darfur. Critics of the policy of the administration of President George W. Bush on the Darfur issue argued that the administration had not taken adequate measures against Khartoum given the enormity of the crimes in Darfur because of an unwillingness to directly confront Sudan on Darfur when Khartoum has been cooperating with Washington in the counterterrorism effort.[50]

THE DARFUR CONFLICT

Ironically, as the National Congress Party (formerly the NIF) was poised to reach historic agreements with the NDA and the SPLM/A and in so doing abandon its policy of the Arabization and Islamization of multiethnic, multilingual and multireligious Sudan as well as its policy of support for regional jihad, the hopes for restoring peace to Sudan were dashed. Al-Bashir's move against al-Turabi and away from the NIF's Islamist policies helped set the stage for the emergence of the conflict in Darfur. Leaders in the "black African" communities in western Sudan had earlier joined the Islamist movement under al-Turabi with the result that for about a decade Darfurian grievances about the social, economic, and political injustices on the part of the central government had been put on the back burner. Once al-Turabi was out of power, though, the Darfurian silence ended. According to Sudan expert Alex de Waal,

> In May 2000, Darfurian Islamists produced the "Black Book" in which they detailed the region's systematic underrespresentation in national governments throughout Sudan's independent history. It caused a stir throughout Sudan. In essence, it condemned the Islamist promise to Darfur as a sham. The Black Book was a key step in the polarization of the country along politically constructed "racial' rather than religious lines, and it laid the basis for a coalition between Darfur's radicals, who form the SLA (Sudanese Liberation Army), and its Islamists, who formed the other rebel organization, the Justice and Equality Movement.[51]

Out of jail, but out of power, al-Turabi came to the defense of the Darfurians—making an impassioned but enfeebled critique of the government's policies of widespread militia violence in Darfur that targeted civilian populations and calling for redress of the social injustices experienced by the people living in that region. Al-Turabi's sympathies clearly lay with the Islamist Justice and Equality Movement, but al-Turabi, who was detained for supporting the Islamist rebel movement, repeatedly denied involvement in the armed struggle.[52]

Another irony coming out of the Darfur conflict lay in the fact that just as the increasing moderation of the Sudanese government in regional affairs seemed to place Sudan on the brink of its much-desired international legitimacy, the wanton government-sponsored violence against Darfur's civilian population served to underscore the ruthlessness of the al-Bashir government, whether it was now jihadist or not, and its reputation as a rogue state was reinforced.

THE LEGACY OF SUDAN'S REGIONAL JIHADISM

The jihadist onslaught in the Greater Horn of Africa spearheaded by Sudan and Al Qaeda in the 1990s bequeathed a legacy of armed violence and terrorism. As recenly as 2004, Khartoum appeared to be continuing its direct support for the Eritrean Islamic Jihad (EIJ), and, according to the Ugandan military, elements of the Sudanese military reportedly continued to back the Ugandan rebel Lord's Resistance Army. However, with the SPLA and the NDA having entered the unity government in Khartoum, Sudan's strategic interest in supporting armed movements against its neighbors further waned.

Evidence suggested that in 2003 and 2004 Sudan renewed its backing for EIJ offensive actions in Eritrea and was behind the reinvigoration of the fighting force of the opposition Eritrean National Alliance (ENA), of which the EIJ is a member. Sudan's renewed interest in the Eritrean opposition was consistent with the government's long-standing search for internal security and for a counterweight to Asmara's renewed support of Sudan's NDA. Thus, after years of giving a cold shoulder to Eritrea's dissident groups, the al-Bashir government found new interest in supporting their activities. Sudan's ruling party, the National Congress Party, which replaced al-Turabi's NIF, used two Eritrean occasions—the Independence Commemoration of September 1, 2003, and the convention of the Eritrean Liberation Front-National Congress (ELF-NC)—to provide material and moral support to the exiled Eritrean opposition parties.[53]

Still, after the agreement between Khartoum and the opposition NDA in 2005, this author has not found any credible reports of military actions by the ENA or its constituents, leaving the impression that the Sudanese government support for the EIJ and other Eritrean opposition groups had once again become a casualty of improved relations between Asmara and Khartoum.

As for Uganda, Sudan's movement toward regional détente meant a lessening of support for both the ADF and LRA and helped set the context for the Ugandan government to put into motion military and peaceful solutions to the rebellion on its northern and eastern borders. As noted above, the ADF harbored a jihadist agenda, and the LRA is a millenarian militia with ideological roots in Christianity and traditional African religious beliefs.

Uganda sent troops to the Congo in 1998 to destroy camps of the Allied Democratic Front (ADF) and to cut off its supply lines from Sudan. Sudan's support to the ADF appears to have ceased after Khartoum and Kampala signed a peace agreement in 1999 brokered by former U.S. President Jimmy Carter. As a result, the ADF became fairly inactive, although there have been occasional reports, one in July 2004, of ADF actions in western Uganda. The Ugandan government said that these reports were false, but, nonetheless, it cautioned its citizens to be vigilant.[54] Kampala implemented what appears to have been a successful reconciliation program with exiled elements of the Tabliq sect, whose disaffected members formed the core of the ADF.[55]

Cut off from Sudanese backing, the ADF made an apparently failed effort in 2001 to court Iraq as a new patron. In a letter to the head of the Iraqi intelligence agency, a senior ADF operative outlined his group's efforts to set up an "international mujahidin team." Its mission, he said, "will be to smuggle arms on a global scale to holy warriors fighting against US, British and Israeli influences in Africa, the Middle East, Asia and the Far East." The letter, dated April 2001, was signed: "Your Brother, Bekkah Abdul Nassir, Chief of Diplomacy, ADF Forces." Nassir offered to "vet, recruit and send youth to train for the jihad at a center in Baghdad, which he described as "...headquarters for international Holy Warrior network....We should not allow the enemy to focus on Afghanistan and Iraq, but we should attack their international criminal forces inside every base," the letter said.[56]

The non-Muslim LRA continued to wreck havoc in northern Uganda, with 12,000 people reportedly killed throughout the length of the insurgency; its intensity diminished with waning Sudanese support and because of the Ugandan government's aggressive amnesty program and antiinsurgency operations, some of which have been criticized for their human rights violations. With the U.S. designation of the two Sudanese-backed armed insurgent groups in Uganda, the ADF and the LRA as terrorist organizations on December 5, 2001, Kampala's hand in negotiations with Khartoum was strengthened, and the two governments reached an agreement that allowed Ugandan troops to operate in Sudan against the LRA.[57]

Despite growing Sudanese cooperation, the Ugandan government claimed that elements within the Sudanese military continued to support the LRA, and evidence from diverse sources suggest that the LRA continued to be used by the Sudanese government against southern Sudanese rebel forces. The LRA reportedly worked hand in glove in 2004 with the local Sudanese military in Sudan's Equatoria region against the SPLA-allied militia, the Equatoria Defence Forces (EDF). According to a statement issued by the EDF, the LRA raided villages at Gangala near the Government garrison position of Jebel Mille. The raids took place from June 25 to 27, 2004. The EDF charged that the LRA, reportedly supported by the Sudanese government army, also attacked Jebel Guttni and Kor Englizi, overrunning and burning villages and looting property.[58]

While, on the one hand, Sudan was utilizing the Uganda rebel LRA in its war against a southern militia, on the other hand it was giving the green light to Uganda to launch an offensive inside Sudan against the LRA. In July 2004, Ugandan President Yoweri Museveni appointed his military assistant, Brigadier Kale Kayihura, as Uganda's special military liaison officer to the town of Juba in southern Sudan to coordinate with the Sudanese military an offensive against the LRA forces. Referring to the LRA leader, Joseph Kony, the army spokesman, Major Shaban Bantariza, said,

> We need close cooperation with the Arabs [Khartoum government]. Like now, Kony is in Nisitu. What is he doing there? ... They [Sudan] are giving him food, medicine. He sleeps on Sudan government mattresses. His greatest problem now is feeding well. There should be smooth exchange of information and understanding with each other at close range without ambassadors and ministers flying to Khartoum.[59]

It should be noted that Ugandan government's denigration of the Sudanese government for its support for the LRA may not have always been based on hard evidence of Sudanese sponsorship. Both its denigrations and its praise for Sudan for its cooperation in the fight against the LRA may have also been motivated by political expediency.

Then, the peace agreement between the SPLM and the Sudanese government brought further benefits to Uganda: in July 2006, the Ugandan government and the LRA entered into formal peace negotiation. These talks were hosted in Juba, Sudan, by the new "Government of Southern Sudan" that had been formed out of the leadership of the former the SPLM/A rebel organization.

In Somalia, the premier Islamist militia, Al Itihaad, which had been backed by Sudan and Al Qaeda, transformed into an Islamic Court based in Mogadishu with its own militia to enforce sharia. The Al Itihaad faction within the Union of Islamic Courts played a leading role in the UIC's 2006 expansion in much of southern and central Somalia. Al Itihaad leaders continued to play host to Al Qaeda in southern Somalia, which emerged as a major focus of jihadism in the Greater Horn of Africa region.[60]

NOTES

1. Barton Gellman, "U.S. Was Foiled Multiple Times in Efforts to Capture bin Laden or Have Him Killed: Sudan's Offer to Arrest Militant Fell through after Saudis Said No," *Washington Post,* October 3, 2001.
2. Ted Dagne, *Sudan: Humanitarian Crisis, Peace Talks, Terrorism, and U.S. Policy* (Issue Brief for Congress), January 23, 2003, http://www.fas.org/man/crs/IB98043.pdf. See also Mohamed Suliman, "The Nuba Mountains of Sudan: Resource Access, Violent Conflict, and Identity," in *Cultivating Peace Conflict and Collaboration in Natural Resource Management,* ed. Daniel Buckles (Washington, D.C.: IDRC/World Bank, 1999).
3. Nhial Bol, "Religion-Africa: Countries of the Horn Urged to Apply Sharia," *IPS,* April 15, 1998, http://www.oneworld.org/ips2/apr98/14_28_059.html.
4. "Sudan Augments Opposition NDA Representation in Unity Government," *Sudan Tribune,* November 21, 2005, http://www.sudantribune.com/article.php3?id_article=12662.
5. *Muslim Brotherhood Movement,* http://www.ummah.org.uk/ikhwan/; "Muslim Brotherhood — Egypt," *Encyclopaedia of the Orient,* http://i-cias.com/e.o/mus_br_egypt.htm; and "Muslim Brothers, Muslim Brotherhood, al-Ikhwan al-Muslimin, Jama'at al-Ikhwan al-Muslimun, Hizb al-Ikhwan al-muslimoon, al-Ikhwan ("The Brothers")," *Intelligence Resource Program,* http://www.fas.org/irp/world/para/mb.htm.
6. *Hassan al-Turabi: Profile and Biography,* http://atheism.about.com/library/FAQs/islam/blfaq_islam_turabi.htm.

7. Human Rights Watch, "Biography of Hassan al-Turabi," *Sudan: Human Rights Watch World Report 2002*, http://www.hrw.org/press/2002/03/turabi-bio.htm.
8. *The Muslim Brotherhood*, http://reference.allrefer.com/country-guide-study/sudan/sudan115.html.
9. Human Rights Watch, "Biography of al-Turabi."
10. *Hassan al-Turabi.*
11. Lawrence Wright, "The Man behind bin Laden: How an Egyptian Doctor Became a Master of Terror," *The New Yorker*, September 16, 2002, http://www.newyorker.com/fact/content/?020916fa_fact2a.
12. Hannah Wettig, *More Equal than Others: Hassan Al-Turabi Preaches the Virtues of the Islamic State*, http://www.cairotimes.com/content/region/turabi.html.
13. Gamal Nkrumah, *Home to Roost*, http://weekly.ahram.org.eg/print/2003/631/re2.htm.
14. Wettig, *More Equal than Others.*
15. *Sufism Casts a Spell of Moderation over Sudan*, http://www.internationalspecialreports.com/africa/01/sudan/arts_culture/.
16. Human Right Watch, *Sudan, Oil, and Human Right: The United States; Diplomacy Revived*, http://www.hrw.org/reports/2003/sudan1103/28.htm.
17. Nhial Bol, "Drawing the Line between Islam and Ethnicity," *IPS*, April 3, 1995, http://www.hartford-hwp.com/archives/33/191.html.
18. Alex de Waal, "The Politics of Destablisation in the Horn, 1989-2001" in *Islamism and its Enemies in the Horn of Africa*, ed. Alex de Waal (Bloomington, Indiana University Press, 2005), 194.
19. "Bin Ladin's Life in Sudan," *Al-Quds al-Arabi*, November 24, 2001, http://www.fas.org/irp/world/para/ladin-sudan.htm.
20. Alan Feurer, "Bin Laden Group had Extensive Network of Companies, Witness Says,' *New York Times*, February 12, 2001, http://www.vitrade.com/sudan_risk/laden/210213_extensive_bin_laden_company_network.htm; *Counts One Through Six: Conspiracies to Murder, Bomb and Maim, Count One: Conspiracy to Kill United States Nationals*, Indictment Kenyan Embassy Bombing in the Southern District of New York of Osama bin Laden *et alia*, http://www.terrorismcentral.com/Library/Incidents/USEmbassyKenyaBombing/Indictment/Start.html.
21. Praveen Swami, "Of Theology and Terrorism," *Frontline*, 17, no. 1 (January 8-21, 2000), http://www.flonnet.com/fl1701/17010140.htm.
22. Stephen Braun and Judy Pasternak, "Long before Sept. 11, bin Laden Aircraft Flew under the Radar," *Los Angeles Times*, November 18, 2001; Human Rights Watch, "Sudanese Government Military Support for

Armed Opposition Forces," *Annual Report,* 1998, http://hrw.org/reports98/sudan/Sudarm988-06.htm.
23. Ibid.
24. Global IDP, *Background of the Alliance for Democratic Forces, 1996-1999,* http://www.db.idpproject.org/Sites/IdpProjectDb/idpSurvey.nsf/wViewCountries/98DCFBCA069DBA7CC125692600484436.
25. Grace Matsiko, "Uganda, DRC in Rebel Arms Talks," *The Monitor,* June 4, 2004, http://allafrica.com/stories/200406040071.html.
26. Chris Kutschera, "Eritrea: Asmara-Khartoum: Hostility in the Horn," *Middle East Magazine,* May 1995, http://chris-kutschera.com/A?Asmara%20 Khartoum.htm.
27. Gerard Prunier, "Armed Conflict in the Heart of Africa: Sudan's Regional War," *Le Monde Diplomatique,* February 1997, http://mondediplo.com/1007/02/02sudan.
28. Minorities at Risk Project, *Ethiopia,* University of Maryland Center for International Development and Conflict Management, June 1998, http://www.bsos.umd.edu/cidcm/mar/ethiopia.htm.
29. Medhane Tadesse, Paul Watson, and Sidhartha Barua, "Somalian Link Seen to Al Qaeda, February 25, 2002, *Los Angeles Times,* http://latimes.com/news/nationworld/world/la-020502hawk.story.
30. David H. Shinn, "Ethiopia: Coping with Islamic Fundamentalism before and after September 11," *Africa Notes,* no. 7, February 2002.
31. Gamal Nkrumah, "The Lure of Africa," *Al-Ahram Weekly On-line,* August 13-19, 1998, no. 390, http://weekly.ahram.org.eg/1998/390/in5.htm.
32. "Sudanese Envoy Denies SPLA Allegations of Support for Kenyan Opposition," *SWB,* March 25, 1995 [KTN TV, Nairobi, in English, March 23, 1995], http://www.sas.upenn.edu/African_Studies/Newsletters/HAB395_SUD.html.
33. Ayre Oded, *Islam and Politics in Kenya* (Boulder: 2000), 149-152.
34. Stephen Engleberg, "One Man and a Global Web of Violence," *New York Times,* January 14, 2001.
35. Human Rights Watch, *Sudan, Oil, and Human Rights,* September 2001, http://www.hrw.org/reports/2003/sudan1103/.
36. Jack Kelley, "Saudi Money Aiding Bin Laden," *USA Today,* October 29, 1999, http://www.vitrade.com/who_is_who/991029_saudi_money_aiding_bin_laden.htm; Paul McKay, "Terrorism's Bagmen," *The Ottawa Citizen,* September 29, 2001, http://www.coperativesearch.org/timeline/2001/ottawacitizen09290.
37. Office for the Spokesman of the Secretary General, *Use of Sanctions under Chapter VII of the UN Charter* (Updated January 2002)*: Sudan,* http://www.un.org/News/ossg/sudan.htm.
38. Prunier, "Armed Conflict."

39. *Middle East Intelligence Bulletin*, http://www.meib.org/articles/9911_me4.htm.
40. Grace Matsiko, "Uganda, DRC in Rebel Arms Talks," *The Monitor*, June 4, 2004, http://allafrica.com/stories/200406040071.html.
41. Gerard Prunier, "Sudan: Irreconcilable Differences," *Le Monde Diplomatique*, December 2002, http://mondediplo.com/2002/12/06sudan.
42. Muhammad Ali Saeed, "Khartoum Closes Turabi's International Organization," *Middle East Times*, http://www.metimes.com/2Kissue2000-7/reg/Khartoum_closes_turabi/.
43. Ben Fenton, "Sudan Rounds Up bin Laden's Men," *News Telegraph*, September 28, 2001.
44. U.S. Department of State Office of the Coordinator for Anti-terrorism, *Patterns of Global Terrorism*, 2003, http://www.state.gov/s/ct/rls/pgtrpt/2003/31644.htm.
45. See Letter to President George W. Bush from Donald M. Payne and Thomas Tancredo, February 5, 2002, http://dehai.org/archives/dehai_news_archive/0189.html., n. a. February 2004 letter to President George Bush, U.S. Representatives Donald Payne and Thomas Tancredo asked the American administration to investigate the responsibility of Sudanese government officials in terrorist acts committed against U.S. interests and Egyptian President Mubarak. The Congressmen listed twelve individuals by name, including, First Vice President Ali Osman Mohammed Taha, Dr. Nafee Ali Nafee, Minister of Federal Government and former Minister of Interior (External Intelligence), Dr. Ghazi Salahadin, president advisor and one-time senior member of the NIF, and Dr. Awad Ahmed El Jaz, minister of energy and Mining.
46. Ken Silverstein, "Official Pariah Sudan Valuable to America's War on Terrorism, *Los Angeles Times*, April 29, 2005, http://www.globalpolicy.org/empire/terrorwar/analysis/2005/0429sudan.htm; U.S. Department of State Office of the Coordinator for Counterterrorism, *Country Reports on Terrorism*, April 28, 2006; "The U.S. Removes Sudan from Blacklist," *Xinhua News Agency*, May 19, 2004, http://www.china.org.cn/english/international/95863.htm.
47. Damien McElroy, "US Forces Hunt Down al-Qa'eda in Sudan," *Telegraph*, August 1, 2004.
48. "Al-Qaeda Leader Killed in Saudi Arabia," *BBC*, August 18, 2006, http://news.bbc.co.uk/2/hi/middle_east/4162084.stm.
49. Dagne, *Sudan: Humanitarian Crisis*.
50. Silverstein, "Official Pariah."
51. Alex de Waal, "Tragedy in Darfur: On Understanding and Ending the Horror," *Boston Review, A Political and Literary Forum*, http://www.bostonreview.net/BR29.5/dewaal.html.

52. "Al Turabi Denies Stirring up Darfur Conflict," *Al Jazeera*, December 31, 2003, http://english.aljazeera.net/NR/exeres/BDE0F12D-A1E8-40BA-A522-A214A30FA0CE.htm.
53. Gedab News, *Eritrea, Sudan & Their Opposition Groups*, July 11, 2004, http://www.awate.com/artman/publish/article_3465.shtml.
54. "No End in Sight to Congo Crisis, *The East African,* December 13, 2001, http://www.globalpolicy.org/security/issues/congo/2001/1213noend.htm.
55. Geoffrey Kamali, "Tabliq Leader Back from Exile," *New Vision,* October 20, 2001, http://allafrica.com/stories/200111220124.html.
56. "Papers Point to African Terror Link," *Sydney Morning Herald*, April 18 2003, http://www.smh.com.au/articles/2003/04/17/1050172711464.html.
57. The United States Mission to the European Union, *Fact Sheet: State Dept. Adds Nine to Terrorist Exclusion List*, November 6, 2002, http://www.useu.be/Terrorism/ECONNews/Nov0602TerroristExclusionListFactSheet.html.
58. Alfred Watsike, "LRA Kills over 100 Sudanese," *New Vision,* July 8, 2004, http://allafrica.com/stories/200407080243.html.
59. Grace Matsiko, "Kayihura Deployed in Sudan," *The Monitor*, July 13, 2004, http://allafrica.com/stories/200407121679.html.
60. Anton Christen, "Bin Laden's Shadow in Somalia: Islamist Activities Amid Crumbling Government and Clan Rivalries," *NZZ Online*, November 22, 2001, http://www.nzz.ch/english/background/2001/11/22_somalia.html.

Chapter Two

JIHADIST SOMALIA
Al Itihaad Al Islamiya

On July 9, 1989, Somalia's Italian-born Roman Catholic bishop, Salvatore Colombo, was gunned down in his cathedral in Mogadishu by an unknown assassin. Bishop Colombo, who ministered to what was largely an expatriate community of Catholics, had been a critic of the human rights violations of the government of military strongman, President Mohamed Siad Barre. The Somali government charged that the death of the Catholic prelate had been the work of a radical Muslim assassin, but one pervasive belief has lingered: that the gunman had fled from the scene of his crime to the nearby presidential palace, and that the assassination had indeed been orchestrated by President Siad Barre himself as a pretext to launch a massive repressive action against the growing Islamic political movement in Mogadishu.

The question of culpability in the murder of Salvatore Colombo aside, the government reacted quickly, rounding up a large number of Islamic clerics. And then came the July 14 massacre, when a dreaded elite unit, the Red Berets, recruited from among the president's Marehan clansmen, slaughtered

450 civilians demonstrating against the arrest of their spiritual leaders. More than 2,000 others were seriously injured.

The next day, forty-seven people, mainly from the Isaaq clan, were taken to Jasiira Beach west of the city and summarily executed.[1] Siad Barre had become known for his brutality against members of the Isaaq clan. His military dominance had become increasingly challenged by armed rebel movements, including the Somali National Movement, which drew its support largely among the Isaaq; and government forces meted out horrific punishment on the Issaq civilian population, including the aerial bombardment of the city of Hargeisa that killed thousands of civilians.

In January 1991, within a few years after the massacres in the Somali capital of Mogadishu and immediately after Siad Barre abandoned the city under pressure from rebel forces, *Al Itihaad Al Islamiya* (Islamic Union) emerged as a military force in the port city of Kismayo. Al Itihaad—an Islamist organization composed largely of intellectuals—had become increasingly popular in Mogadishu. Siad Barre's massacre of Islamist protestors in July 1989 had set the social and political context in which Al Itihaad transformed from an organization devoted to *Da'wa* — the Muslim responsibility to call or invite Muslims and non-Muslims to the faith—to a jihadist organization dedicated to advancing its version of Islam through military means. In 1992, military assistance from Sudan, Iran, and Al Qaeda began to flow to Al Itihaad's military wing, facilitating its emergence as a major military player in a Somali now devoid of a central government.

After the July 1989 massacres, the United States began to distance itself from Siad Barre's regime. Opponents of Siad Barre's brutal dictatorship, including Somalia's Islamists, regarded U.S. support for the Somali regime as critical to its survival in the 1980s. Support was part of Washington's cold war calculations to counter Soviet influence in neighboring Ethiopia and to reestablish a military presence near the Red Sea and the strategic Gulf of Aden — all considered vital to the flow of oil from the petroleum-rich Arabian Peninsula; military bases in Somalia also provided a military umbrella for the Persian Gulf area.

The United States prodded Siad Barre's government to improve its human rights record, but the measures that were taken largely amounted to window dressing. Washington's support for Siad Barre left a legacy of distrust and a bitter imprint among the regime's opponents, including Somalia's Islamists, and the distrust and bitterness have been ingredients flavorng Islamist perception toward the United States ever since.

The Horn of Africa had been an important theater in the cold war. After the 1969 military coup that brought General Siad Barre to power, Somalia allied itself with the Soviet Union, and the Siad Barre government espoused an official ideology that professed to reconcile Marxist scientific socialism and traditional Somali Islamic values in a country that was nearly 100 percent Muslim.

During Siad Barre's pro-Soviet period, the United States maintained its influence in the Horn of Africa in an alliance with Ethiopia, but the leaders of the 1974 revolution in Ethiopia turned increasingly friendly toward the Soviet Union. The 1977 irredentist decision of Siad Barre and his government to invade and annex the portion of Ethiopia inhabited by ethnic Somalis known as the Ogaden brought an end to Soviet influence in Somalia. The Soviets sided with Ethiopia in its effort to retake the Ogaden occupied by the Somali army, and Siad Barre tore up his friendship treaty with the Soviet Union. Somalia's army was decisively routed by a joint Ethiopian-Cuban expeditionary force, and desperate to find a strong external alliance to replace the Soviet Union, Somalia abandoned its socialist ideology and turned to the West for international support, military equipment, and economic aid.

The Somali-Soviet parting of ways became the opening that Washington needed. The United States government was eager to secure military bases closer to the Persian Gulf to counter the strategic advantage obtained by the Soviet Union when it occupied Afghanistan in 1979. So, between 1979 and 1980, the United States negotiated to take over the former Soviet naval and air facility in the Somali port of Berbera and proceeded to upgrade the runway and docks in a project costing $35 million. From 1982 to 1989, the United States viewed Somalia as an important partner in defense.[2]

As the cold war rivalries eased and then ended between 1985 and 1991, Somalia's strategic importance to the United States decreased, making it easier for Washington to take the decision to drastically scale down its support for Mogadishu in response to the gross human rights violations, especially after the July 1989 massacres. The decrease in United States support made Siad Barre's regime more desperate, as the forces of the Hawiye-dominated United Somali Congress, the Isaaq-dominated Somali National Movement, and other members of a loose rebel coalition increasingly threatened the viability of the regime. Siad Barre responded to the deteriorating military situation with more repression.[3]

With the complete collapse of the regime in January 1991, Al Itihaad Al Islamiya emerged as the most militant Islamist group in Somalia. Other Islamist organizations existed in Somalia, but none of them came close to Al Itihaad in its influence within Somalia and its impact on neighboring states, as it used military force, terrorist tactics, and ideological persuasion in a bid to realize its aim of a pan-Somali Islamic state. The details of Al Itihaad's initial transformation from a Mogadishu-based Islamist movement into a movement with a militia remain unclear, but Somali *mujahadin* veterans, who had fought the Soviet occupation of Afghanistan as holy Islamic warriors, played a decisive role in this.[4]

With the militarization of Al Itihaad, the organization became enmeshed with regional actors wishing to influence the course of events in strategically important Somalia; just as Somalia's recent history had been shaped by the cold war contest between the Soviet Union and the United States. Somalia was to become a theater of combat for those espousing a militant Islamist ideology as a counterforce to U.S. influence and military presence in the region. In this context, Al Itihaad received training, materiel, and financial support from Sudan, Iran, Al Qaeda, and other international jihadist groups. These external sources of support helped Al Itihaad become a major military player in Somalia, where diverse factional militias vied for power after the collapse of the Somali central government in 1991. This external backing also encouraged Al Itihaad to carry out attacks within Ethiopia that advanced Sudan's objective of destabilizing Ethiopia and conformed to Al Itihaad's stated irredentist aims of bringing all regions inhabited by Somalis into a single caliphate.

The Roots of Al Ittihad Al Islamiya

Somalia has a well-known history of Islamic resistance to Western occupation and influences: In 1899, Muhammed Abdullah Hassan (also known pejoratively as the "Mad Mullah") raised an army of "dervishes" that sought to consolidate an Islamic state among Somalis and to rid northern Somalia of British occupation and to oppose Ethiopian imperial hegemony over Somali populations. His movement's resistance to colonialism lasted until his death in 1921. Muhammed Abdullah Hassan had sought to organize Somalis across clan divisions and to introduce the reformist, purifying Islam of the strict Salihiyah *tariqa* (religious order or brotherhood) to a population practicing a generally more moderate tradition of that faith.[5] The combination of moral rectitude and aggressive tactics, including opposition to Ethiopian control of Somali populations that characterized this earlier movement, can be seen in the Al Itihaad movement that emerged in Somalia in the 1980's.

The immediate ideological roots of Al Itihaad may be found, however, in Islamic resistance to the socialist and secular government of General Mohamed Siad Barre. Postindependence Islamist groups first emerged in Somalia in the 1960s, and were inspired by the Muslim Brotherhood, which is the first modern Islamist organization that challenged secular rule in Egypt through revolutionary tactics. Graduates of Al Azhar University in Egypt — the premier center of Sunni learning — returned home to establish similar organizations in Somalia. One of these graduates, the late Sheikh Mohamed Moalam Hassan, is said to have laid the basis for the modern Islamist movement in Somalia.[6]

Even before the July 1989 Mogadishu massacres, Somali Islamist groups had been brutally suppressed by Siad Barre's government. In a 1975 incident, the Siad Barre regime executed ten prominent sheikhs and jailed dozens of others after their protest of a new family legislation. The anti-Siad Barre Islamic groups attempted to garner popular support for their opposition to the regime through an appeal to Islamic identity and values — a faith-based political strategy that contrasted sharply with movements vying for political support on the basis of a secular Somali nationalism or clan identity and loyalty.

Later, in the early 1980s, Islamic religious study groups consisting of young professional men, many of whom had experience studying or working abroad, merged to form Al Itihaad. The two groups were *Al-Jamaa Al-Islamiya* (the Islamic Association), based in the South and was led by Sheikh Mohamed Eissa; and *Wahdat Al Shabab Al Islam* (the Unity of Islamic Youth) based in the North (Somaliland) and led by Sheikh Ali Warsame. The corruption and repression of the Siad Barre regime had motivated these groups to look for political alternatives to the status quo, and they were inspired by the Islamist traditions that merged politics and religion. The ranks of Al Itihaad's top leadership reportedly graduated from Islamic universities in Pakistan, Saudi Arabia, and Kuwait. Somali Wahabists who had fought against the Soviet Union in Afghanistan as mujahidin in the 1980s helped shape Al Itihaad's political, military, and religious strategies.[7] In Mogadishu, Al Itihaad's growing popularity and its radical militant message soon began to attract attention. The movement's visibility grew as its membership expanded to include faculty and students at secondary schools, colleges, and Somali National University.[8]

The Afghanistan mujahadin connection may explain the genesis of Al Itihaad's association with Al Qaeda and other jihadist groups that also emerged out of the international Islamic resistance to the Soviet Union's invasion of Afghanistan. East Africa reportedly was the scene of a major U.S.-sponsored recruitment drive for anti-Soviet fighters in Afghanistan. There is evidence indicating that Siad Barre's government allowed his new patron — the United States — to airlift in the 1980s several hundred recruits from central Somalia to Afghanistan to fight the Soviet Union as mujahidin. This trafficking in Somali "mercenaries" reportedly proved to be a lucrative trade, from which government ministers profited.[9] To a certain extent, the country was exporting some of its aspiring Islamist radicals and was providing them with the opportunity to form a link with what would become an emerging international jihadist movement. In addition, according to Kenyan security sources, over 2,000 recruits for the mujahidin forces in Afghanistan came from the Mombasa area alone. They were recruited from the ranks of unemployed youth and in later years, demobilized former Somali government soldiers.[10]

Little has been known of Al Itihaad's organizational structure, and its leadership has a history of being very secretive. Its more visible leaders went underground after the U.S. launched the war on terrorism in late 2001 and labeled Al Itihaad an ally of Al Qaeda.[11] Al Itihaad appears to be organized into units variously referred to as cells, chapters, and branches. It has been difficult to determine how much of Al Itihaad activity could be ascribed to centralized decisionmaking and how much of it reflects decentralized initiatives. It also established branches among Somali communities in neighboring Ethiopia and Kenya as well as in a number of cities in the Middle East.

In its appeal to religion as a unifying political force among Somalis, Al Itihaad may be considered an innovative organization. Al Itihaad at times worked independently of clans and sought to cut across clan divisions in its political and military organizing. Clan identity is very strong among Somalis, as Somalis generally look first to their clan before religion as their main source of identity. Nonetheless, the pervasiveness of clan identity inevitably meant that Al Itihaad necessarily worked out local relationships with traditional clan leaders.

In occupied areas, it set up statelike structures, including Koranic schools and courts to enforce Islamic law in a country with rampant lawlessness and random violence. Moral rectitude, military aggressiveness, and ideological indoctrination emerged as hallmarks of its organizational ethos.

THE ISLAMIST LANDSCAPE

Al Itihaad was not the only Islamic fundamentalist organization operating in Somalia, but it has earned the reputation of being the most militant with clear substantive links to international jihadism and with an appetite for terrorist tactics. As previously noted, Al Itihaad leaders have assumed dominant positions in Somalia's Union of Islamic Courts and the story of UIC-Al Itihaad relationship will be told in the next chapter. Other prominent Islamic fundamentalist organizations such as *Al Islah* and *Al Wahda* have focused more exclusively on social and educational aims than Al Itihaad, although it too has a history of heavy involvement in social and charitable works. Al Itihaad, Al Islah and Al Wahda at times have worked together through a loosely united front called the "Supreme

Somali Islamic League," and reportedly have benefited from common international financing from Saudi Arabia and other Middle East states.[12]

Al Islah's leadership has largely been composed of young professional men who have worked or studied in the Gulf States or in Egypt. They have advocated the adoption of a strict Islamic state as the solution to their country's chronic problems. Like Al Itihaad, Al Islah became influential in the failed attempt to establish a Transitional National Government (TNG) in Mogadishu in 2000. The TNG was the child of a national reconciliation conference held in Arta, Djibouti, that received significant international support, save from the United States. The TNG, which both Al Itihaad and Al Islah supported, ultimately governed little more than Mogadishu due in part to opposition by other political factions that objected to the Islamist influence within the would-be Somali state. Approximately one-quarter of TNG's 245-member parliament were reportedly linked to Al Islah.[13]

Some of the clan-based factional leaders in Somalia have seen little distinction between Al Itihaad and Al Islah. Al Islah has advocated the creation of an Islamic state and in this regard its objectives have been similar to that of Al Itihaad, but Al Islah members have contended that their principle goal is national reconciliation and promotion of education and democracy. According to Dr. Ibrahim Disuki, an Al Islah leader, "Al Islah is a peaceful organization. That is the main difference between Al Islah and probably other organizations who have a militaristic or a violent attitude."[14]

Despite Al Islah's professed nonviolent aims, Somali factional leader Hussein Aidid said that forces under his control confiscated in March 2001 large shipments of arms at an Al Islah warehouse located in front of the main Mogadishu port. According to Aidid, these arms were destined for use by the TNG, Al Itihaad, and other Islamist allies of the TNG.[15] One report contends that many Al Itihaad members have become active in Al Islah.[16]

Al Islah has basically functioned as a Saudi-funded outreach program — operating numerous Islamic schools, health posts, and community centers throughout Somalia.[17] The number of externally funded Koranic schools in Somalia has grown since the collapse of the country's central authority. These schools have been inexpensive and have provided basic education in a country where no state existed to provide such services to the population. These schools reportedly often require the veiling of small girls and have promoted other conservative Islamic practices not normally found in the local culture. Mogadishu University, the University of East Africa in Bosaso, Puntland, and many secondary schools in Mogadishu have also been externally funded and have been administered through organizations affiliated with Al Islah. The growing influence of Wahabist mosques and schools funded by foreigners has alarmed many Somali political figures historically opposed to Al Itihaad.

The growing Islamist reform movement advanced by groups like Al Islah and Al Itihaad may represent a historic turning point in the Somali Islamic outlook — away from the inward-looking spirituality more in attune with the traditionally dominant Somali Sufism toward a puritanical and legalistic view of religious practice. The implications of this shift from an inward-looking spiritual tradition to one that posits religiosity in external relations and dictums are far reaching. The new religious order may be seen as undermining individual autonomy and capable of creating authoritarian dependency — thus creating the ideological and psychological precondition for acceptance of authoritarian solutions as well as a greater vulnerability among the faithful to calls for extremist action.

Other Somali Islamist political and paramilitary organizations include the Muslim Brotherhood, which is also known by other names such as *Harakat Al-Islah* or "Reform Movement" and *Al-Harakah Al-Islamiya* or "Islamic Movement." The leader of the Somali Muslim Brotherhood, Dr Ali Sheikh Abu-Bakr, has presided over Mogadishu University, and the movement is said to be financed by "Gulf Arab money," especially from Kuwait.[18]

AL ITIHAAD'S JIHAD AGAINST THE UNITED STATES

In 1992, Al Itihaad launched major campaigns to occupy territory in the North and South of the country, but soon it would become embroiled in an international effort to expel the U.S. military from Somalia. Under the command of Sheikh Ali Warsame, one of Al Itihaad founders and a Somalilander, its forces, estimated at about 1,000 fighters, occupied, in June 1992, the city of Garoe and the port of Bosaso in the northern regions of Bari and Nugaal, in what later became the self-administered region of Puntland. There, Al Itihaad established a large base near Qaw, some twenty kilometers (twelve miles) west of Bosaso. Known as Nasrudiin, the base was inspired by *mujahidin* training camps in Afganistan, and it rapidly became the hub of Al Itihaad activities that were designed to establish an emirate in the region.

The main armed faction on the ground in what became Puntland, the Somali Salvation Democratic Front (SSDF), which drew its support largely from the Majeerteen subclan, responded to Al Itihaad's sizeable military presence by driving its forces out of the cities. The SSDF decision to challenge Al Itihaad came at the urging of SSDF military commander, Abdullahi Yusuf Ahmed who would in 2004 become President of Somalia's Transitional Federal Government. The defeated and considerably weakened forces of Al Itihaad then moved further to the west in a bid to gain a foothold in the cities of Bormama, Burao, and Las Korah, in the breakaway Republic of Somaliland that the Somali National Movement declared independent in May 1991. The Somaliland government banned Al Itihaad activities within its territory because the Islamist forces posed a threat to its authority.[19]

Hassan Dahir Aweys, a former colonel in the Somali army, commanded Al Itihaad forces in the South. Earlier in 1991, Aweys had switched his allegiance from the United Somali Congress's military wing, led by General Mohamed Farah Aidid, to join Al Itihaad militia in Kismayo.[20] Under the command of Aweys, Al Itihaad forces moved into the Gedo region in August 1992 near the Kenyan and Ethiopian borders with Somalia to set up an emirate.

Foreign military assistance for Al Itihaad began at least as early as August 1992. According to Yossef Bodansky, the author of *Bin Laden: The Man Who Declared War on America*, an Iranian-Sudanese delegation arrived in the port city of Marka [also written as Merca] to consult with Al Itihaad commanders on its future operations. The Iranians were led by Rahimi Safari and the Sudanese by Ali Uthman Taha, who would become first vice-president of Sudan in 1998. The Sudanese-Iranian delegation set about determining the materiel and training needs of Al Itihaad and ordered the implementation of an assistance plan upon its return to Khartoum. In Bodansky's account, which is presumably based on U.S. intelligence sources, he relates that the Iranians supplied the arms destined for Al Itihaad that were retransported to Somalia by Osama bin Laden.[21]

The visit of the Sudanese-Iranian delegation to Marka came as U.S. President George H. W. Bush, ordered a humanitarian relief airlift to Somalia in response to UN reports of growing starvation in southern Somalia, with infants, nursing mothers, and the elderly as the chief victims. The airlift, which used the Kenyan port city of Mombasa as a hub, was successful in alleviating food shortages around some of the major Somali airports such as Baidoa.

In late 1992, U.S. military involvement in Somalia expanded in response to the enormity of the humanitarian crisis. According to then U.S. Assistant Secretary of State for Africa Herman Cohen,

> ... in situations of major famine, airlifts are invariably insufficient because of the cargo limitations of aircraft. It was clear that the only solution to the problem of mass starvation (5000 Somalis were dying per week as of October 1992) was massive delivery by ship and overland truck transport. This could only take place, however, with military protection of the shipments against the predatory warlords who controlled Mogadishu's seaport and airport.

President Bush ordered a U.S.-led military operation to stop the starvation, if three conditions could be met: (1) that the UN Security Council agreed, (2) that there were troops of other countries to accompany U.S. forces, and (3) that the United Nations take over the relief operation within six months. Once these agreements were in place, the first U.S. forces arrived in Somalia in early December 1992 in what the U.S. military called Operation Restore Hope. A number of other countries also sent troops to Somalia, including the African countries of Botswana and Nigeria. Pakistan already had peacekeeping troops on the ground.[22]

The presence of the U.S. military in Somalia was of concern to Islamist Sudan and Iran, both of which feared a growing U.S. hegemony in the region. The year before, the United

States, with the blessings of the United Nations, had successfully protected Saudi Arabia from potential Iraqi aggression and repulsed Iraq's occupation of Kuwait in a vast effort that was first known as Operation Desert Shield and eventually Desert Storm. The military operation deployed hundreds of thousands of U. S. and allied forces and untold amounts of military equipment into Saudi Arabia with the consent of the Saudi government. The United States continued to maintain military bases in Saudi Arabia after the operation, and the removal of U.S. forces from the Islamic holy land became a key objective of Al Qaeda.

Osama bin Laden issued a *fatwa* to Al Qaeda members in response to the U.S. military presence in Somalia. A fatwa is normally a legal pronouncements by a Muslim scholar capable of issuing judgments on sharia. Bin Laden used fatwas to justify the decision to take a strategic direction and to compel compliance with the policy.

In trial testimony in 2001, the former Sudanese member of Al Qaeda, Jamal Al Fadl, explained the position of international jihadist organization toward the arrival of U.S. forces in Somalia.

> We got another fatwa because they say the American army come to the Horn of Africa in Somalia. Also I was in the guest house [in Khartoum] of Abu Ubaidah al Banshiri [Al Qaeda's second in command and cofounder]; he talk that...He says the American army [is] in the Horn of Africa in Somalia and now they already took off Gulf area and now they go to Somalia, and if they [are] successful in Somalia the next thing it could be [the] south of Sudan and [other] Islamic countries.
>
> In the big guest house [bin Laden] say about American army now they come to the Horn of Africa, and we have to stop the head of the snake. He said that the snake is America, and we have to stop them. We have to cut the head of the snake.[23]

Al Itihaad leaders reportedly met in 1992 with bin Laden in Khartoum, where the two organizations consolidated their alliance.[24] Both the Sudanese government and bin Laden became allies in an effort to make the region a radical Islamic state and to oppose U.S. actions in the region. At this same time, Bin Laden and his strategists reportedly were also giving assistance to the Eritrean Islamic Jihad in its efforts to establish an Islamic state in Eritrea, from whence Al Qaeda planned to take its jihadist revolution to Yemen and to Ethiopia. Somalia likely constituted a southern beach head in this regional strategy of Al Qaeda.

Also according to Yossef Bodansky, the Sudanese and Iranians advisors, who had gone to Marka for consultation with Al Itihaad commanders, directed them not to confront U.S. forces until the time was ripe. In spite of this advice to Al Itihaad, Al Qaeda seems to have acted on its own, dispatching operatives to Somalia about a month before the arrival of U.S. troops to force a confrontation. Al Qaeda attacked U.S. forces, but the Americans did not engage them, according to bin Laden.[25] Then, in what was its first known terrorist bombing, Al Qaeda also attempted to strike against U.S. military personnel in Yemen. On Al Qaeda's instructions, the affiliated Yemeni Islamic Jihad detonated bombs at the Aden Hotel and at the Golden Moor Hotel in Aden that was customarily frequented by American military personnel en route to Somalia. This occurred on December 29, 1992. American military personnel were not in the hotels at the time, but a number of civilians were killed in the blasts.[26]

Bin Laden dispatched a number of Al Qaeda operators to Somalia to train Al Itihaad and other factional militias in their battle against the U.S.-led forces. They were the first in a sizeable body of mujihidin who had served in Afghanistan and who were now mobilized to support Al Qaeda and Al Itihaad in their fight against UN and U.S. forces. Al Qaeda's number two man, Ayman al-Zawahiri, assumed command of the operation, and he was said to have personally traveled at some point to Somalia. Mohammed Saddiqi Odeh, a Palestinian born in Jordan, was among those dispatched to Somalia,[27] and an Afghanistan-trained member of the team that would later bomb the U.S. embassy in Dar es Salaam, the Tanzanian, Khalfan Khamis Mohamed, traveled by fishing boat from Kenya to Somalia to give military training to Al Itihaad.[28]

According to British government information, Mohamed Atef, the now-deceased Al-Qaeda operative who had been in charge of its training and organizing of military and terrorist operations, was also dispatched to Somalia in both 1992 and 1993 to instigate actions against U.S. and UN forces.[29] Another Al Qaeda leader who trained Somali militia members was Abdullah Ahmed Abdullah. He was among 480 Arab combatants who joined bin Laden when he moved from Afghanistan to Sudan in 1991. From Sudan, Abdulla moved to Somalia, and in 1998 he moved to Kenya, where he arranged and paid for travel of the Al Qaeda operatives who planned the August 7, 1998 embassy bombings in Kenya and in Tanzania.[30]

The banned Pakistani militant group *Jaish-e-Mohammed* (The Army of Mohammed), associated with the killing of *Wall Street Journal* reporter Daniel Pearl, helped play Al Qaeda's hand in Somalia. The leader of Jaish-e-Mohammed, Maulana Masood Azhar, admitted to having traveled to Nairobi, Kenya, in 1993 to meet with leaders of Al Itihaad. Azhar said Al Itihaad asked for assistance and got recruits and money from the ranks of a Pakistani militant group, which Washington later designated as part of bin Laden's terrorist network. Azhar told Indian intelligence that Al Itihaad leaders complained to him that Pakistan's army, which was taking part in the UN mission in Somalia, was working on behalf of the United States in what they considered the American effort to establish its dominance there. According to Indian intelligence sources, Azhar visited Somalia three times and became a key player in Al Qaeda's operation in Mogadishu.

Also according to Azhar, Al Itihaad benefited from Pakistan's decision in 1993, under international pressure, to expel between 400 and 500 foreign veterans of the Afghan war. Most of these went to Sudan, where bin Laden was then based, and from there to Somalia. Azhar also helped to bring mercenaries from Yemen to Somalia with the help of Yemeni militant leader and Afghanistan war veteran, Tariq Nasr al-Fadhli.[31] Members of the Eritrean Islamic Jihad also went to Somalia to join in the fight.[32] According to U.S. officials, bin Laden spent $3 million to recruit and to airlift elite veterans of the Afghan jihad to Somalia via third countries such as Yemen and Ethiopia.[33]

In late 1992, Aweys's Al Itihaad forces first came into contact with U.S. soldiers who had arrived as part of Operation Restore Hope. According to Colonel Fred Beck, the Marines spokesman in Mogadishu: "A group of the American Marines seized one of the strongholds of the Somali Islamic

Unity in the city of Merca [Marka] 90km south of Mogadishu on December 31, 1992." Consistent with the advice provided by the Sudanese and Iranian delegation, Al Iithaad forces avoided direct contact with U.S. forces. According to Mohammed Othman, Al Itihaad's representative for the United States and Europe,

> Our forces withdrew from Merca in order to avoid total confrontation with the U.S.A.; we do not want, at present, any military confrontation yet we have not given up our weapons nor did we give in to any power.[34]

Whether by design or through defeat, as occurred in Al Itihaad's northern campaign, Al Itihaad forces had abandoned its military presence in Somali cities. Then, it moved to consolidate its positions in the countryside, and it was there that Al Qaeda began to stockpile weapons for later use by Al Itihaad against the UN and U.S. forces.[35]

Under Aweys' command, Al Itihaad took Luuq and Bula Hawa in Gedo and occupied this area until the Ethiopian military invaded Somalia in 1996 and drove Al Itihaad out. From the Gedo region, Al Itihaad followers frequently crossed over into Kenya's North Eastern Province where they recruited Kenyan Somalis for their militia and laid the ideological groundwork for the establishment of an all Somali caliphate.[36] As will be shown later, the Gedo bases were also used for operations against Ethiopia.

Al Itihaad's next step toward the UN and U.S. forces appears to have been planned in Khartoum. In February 1993, four Somali Islamist organizations, including Al Itihaad, met there to discuss strategy for expanding fundamentalism in Somalia.

Sometime thereafter, Aweys' forces took the Wadajir section of Mogadishu; and in March, a U.S. military spokesman in Mogadishu announced that U.S. troops had found a cache of arms at a compound belonging to Al Itihaad. Then about midyear, Al Itihaad launched an anti-Western and anti-U.S. propaganda effort, calling for jihad against the United States.[37] It appears that the time was now ripe to confront U.S. forces.

In March 1993, Mohamed Farah Aidid also traveled to Sudan, where he met with Hassan al-Turabi, leader of the ruling National Islamic Front. Al-Turabi, reportedly, offered Aidid help in training his forces on the condition that Sudanese support would remain anonymous. A flow of more sophisticated arms, including remote-controlled mines that were used to kill dozens of United Nations peacekeepers, followed. Training in the use of these weapons was conducted in camps inside Sudan.[38]

These bases in Sudan, according to U.S. State Department spokesman Michael McCurry, were used to train the supposedly "untrained militia" of General Aidid. "In actuality, warlord Mohamed Farah Aidid's men are a well-trained and motivated light infantry force that operates with support from Iran and elsewhere in the same way that previous Somali factions took arms and money from successive European, Arab, American and Soviet governments."[39]

Al Itihaad's move into Mogadishu, its call for jihad against the United States, and Mohamed Farah Aidid's talks with al-Turabi in Khartoum coincided with a further expansion of the UN's role in Somalia. On March 3, 1993, the UN Secretary-General Boutros Boutros-Ghali submitted to the UN Security Council his recommendations for effecting the transition of the humanitarian operation to a much more ambitious mission known as United Nations Operation in Somali II (UNOSOM II). It aimed to establish a secure environment throughout Somalia and to achieve national reconciliation so as to create a democratic state. The U.S.-led relief operation was turned over to UN control in May 1993, as originally planned. U.S. forces were reduced from 28,000 to 2,500 troops who would serve in a reserve capacity.

At the Conference on National Reconciliation in Somalia held on March 15, 1993 in Addis Ababa, fifteen Somali parties agreed to the terms set out to restore peace and to promote democracy. Yet, by May it became clear that, although signatory to the March agreement, General Mohammed Farah Aidid's faction, now with secret Iranian, Sudanese, and soon to be Al Qaeda and Al Itihaad support, would not cooperate in the agreement's implementation. General Aidid had been suspicious of the UN's interest in Somalia from the beginning; he believed the UN secretary general had a secret plan to make Somalia a UN trusteeship and to restore Siad Barre to power. The role of UNOSOM II was too close to the reality of a trusteeship for Aidid's comfort. In addition, Aidid believed

Jihadist Somalia: Al Itihaad Al Islamiya

that the United Nations had favored and provided arms to General Aidid's chief rival in Mogadishu, Ali Mahdi, who had in October 1991 declared himself president of Somalia. When the United Nations began to implement a disarmament of factional leaders, all hell broke out in Mogadishu, as factional leaders became fearful of losing their power to the United Nations and the United States or to their rivals. These factions refused to disarm and resorted to violence in an attempt to resist this. On June 5, violence reached an all time high when twenty-five Pakistani soldiers trying to close down Aidid's radio station were killed by militiamen loyal to General Aidid. The Security Council then gave Boutros-Ghali authority to deal with Aidid, and the United Nations put a bounty on his head. An attempt by U.S. forces to bring in Aidid commanders led to the famous Black Hawk Down incident of October 3, 1993.

British intelligence reported that Al Qaeda operative Mohamed Atef trained Somalis to fight UN forces, and Al Qaeda operatives participated in the October 3 attack against U.S. forces.[40] In a 1997 interview with CNN, bin Laden gloated that Al-Qaeda had trained and organized the Somali fighters who did the actual fighting against the U.S. forces.[41] Al Qaeda members are suspected of teaching General Aidid's militia how to shoot down U.S. helicopters by altering the fuses of rocket-propelled grenades so that they exploded in midair. This tactic, developed by the Afghan mujahidin in their war against the Soviet Union, was the same one Al Qaeda forces used to bring down two U.S. helicopters near Gardez, Afghanistan, during Operation Anaconda in early March 2002.[42] Some reports also say that Al Itihaad commander Hassan Dahir Aweys led the October 1993 attack against U.S. forces. Aweys belongs the same Ayr subclan of Hawiye Habr Gedir clan as Mohamed Farah Aidid.[43]

In the battle's aftermath, bodies of dead American soldiers were dragged through the streets of Mogadishu, and the grisly images of this were shown on international news reports. The visuals shocked the U.S. public, and this created the public opinion context in the United States that influenced President William Clinton's decision to pull all U.S. forces out of Somalia and to close down the UN operation. In early 1994 the Security Council set a deadline for the mission of March 1995.

In a series of letters to its "Africa Corps," that is, Al Qaeda operatives in Africa, an Al Qaeda analyst named Hasan commented on some of the strategic lessons learned from the organization's experience in Somalia.

> The Somali experience confirmed the spurious nature of American power and that it has not recovered from the Vietnam complex. It fears getting bogged down in a real war that would reveal its psychological collapse at the level of personnel and leadership. Since Vietnam, America has been seeking easy battles that are completely guaranteed. It entered into a shameful series of adventures on the island of Grenada, then Panama, then bombing Libya, and then the Gulf War farce, which was the greatest military, political, and ideological swindle in history. . . .
>
> America wanted to continue this series of farces. It assumed that Somalia was an appropriate space for another ridiculous act. But the Muslims were there—so the great disaster occurred. They fled in panic before their true capabilities could be exposed.[44]

From its confrontation with U.S. forces in Mogadishu, Al Qaeda may have learned additional lessons, and the Mogadishu experience may have informed the urban warfare and propaganda tactics that Al Qaeda would later deploy in Baghdad and in other Iraqi cities during the U.S. occupation of Iraq that began in 2003. An example of this occurred in the Iraqi city of Fallujah, located thirty miles west of Baghdad, on March 31, 2004. Exactly one week after assuming responsibility for the city in a troop rotation, the California-based 1st Marine Expeditionary Force suffered the loss of five soldiers when a bomb exploded under their vehicle in a village near Fallujah. Inside the city, gunmen attacked two civilian cars carrying four U.S. civilian contractors. The cars were torched by a dancing lynch mob that dragged the bodies through the city, dismembered and decapitated them and hanged them by their feet. This sequence of events reportedly was calculated and carried out by Al Qaeda to influence U.S. public opinion in a way reminiscent of the battle of Mogadishu in October 1993.[45]

Jihad Against Ethiopia

With the departure of U.S. troops from Somalia, Al Itihaad turned its jihadist ambitions against Ethiopia and entered into a loose coalition with Ethiopian rebel movements, Somali militia factions, Sudan, Al Qaeda, and eventually Eritrea in its new jihad. The strategic objectives of Sudan and Al Itihaad coincided in this regard. The ambitions of Sudan's National Islamic Front to create a greater Islamic state in the Horn of Africa coincided with Al Itihaad's own objective of establishing a "strong Islamic State in the Horn of Africa." Al Itihaad started its political activities on the basis of the "Greater Somali Nation" agenda, and as such maintained the ambition to unite territories in Ethiopia, Kenya, and Djibouti inhabited by Somali populations into a greater Somalia. Sudan was also engaged in a number of wars by proxy in the region to undermine support for the armed rebel movements operating from the South, and as had been previously noted Ethiopia was a target of Sudan's aggressive policies.

The concept of a pan-Somali state was not new. In the 1960s, the Shifta rebels in Kenya had sought to unite Kenya's North Eastern Province with Somalia, and later in 1977, the Siad Barre government waged an unsuccessful war with Ethiopia to annex the Somali-populated Ogaden region of Ethiopia. However, Siad Barre's vision was based on a secular state. Al Itihaad advocated an Islamic caliphate for all Somalis.

Within Somalia, after the departure of U.S. forces, Al Itihaad retained a military presence in Mogadishu, a camp on a small island near the coastal town of Ras Komboni near the Kenya-Somali border, and a stronghold in the Gedo region. In addition, a faction of Al Itihaad was actively operating in Ethiopia's Ogaden region. In Mogadishu, Al Itihaad maintained an uneasy and shifting relationship with more powerful factions led by Ali Mahdi and General Aidid. Even though Al Itihaad and Al Qaeda furnished critical support to General Aidid in the October 1993 battle of Mogadishu, General Aidid moved to ally himself with the more traditionalist Muslim organization, *Majima al-Ulama*. General Aidid made this move to counterbalance what was the recent Al Itihaad entry into the military-political equation in the capital, where opposing political factions continued to fight over neighborhood control.

Then, for a short while, Al Itihaad came to be supported by Aidid's nemesis, Ali Mahdi, and during this period reportedly received financial support from some Saudi sources. At the same time, North Mogadishu, where Ali Mahdi was based, began to return to some semblance of normalcy, or at least did not suffer complete lawlessness, due largely to the harsh implementation of the sharia by the Islamic Court that made an association with Al Ithaad's militias. But distrust of Al Itihaad led Ali Mahdi to expel its militias from North Mogadishu.[46]

At Ras Kamboni, Al Itihaad established a base after militias of the Somali Salvation Democratic Front ended Al Itihaad's efforts to establish an emirate in the northwestern part of the country. One remnant of Al Itihaad's defeated combat forces headed south and established a base under the command of Hassan Abdullah Hersi al-Turki on an island near Ras Kamboni. This base has been described as a joint Al Qaeda-Al Itihaad camp. UN officials reported that components of bombs that exploded at the American embassies in Nairobi and Dar es Salaam in 1998 may have been made at this camp. UN observers added that bin Laden visited the camp shortly after the bombings, presumably to offer congratulations.[47] For some time, U.S. officials were concerned that Ras Kamboni was being used as a transit point for movement of personnel by al Qaeda and Al Itihaad.[48] Local residents reported that after the September 11, 2001 Al Qaeda attacks in the United States, the U.S. military placed sophisticated electronic devices on the island to detect possible terrorist movements.[49]

In 1999, Al Itihaad fighters fled from Ras Kamboni in southern Somalia into Kenya (crossing at the border town of Kolpio) after fighting with a local Ogadeni subclan, that was attempting to seek revenge for the killing of a U.S. aid worker. Al Itihaad members had shot and killed Deena Umbarger, who was a consultant for the United Methodist Committee on Relief, while she was taking tea with town elders in Ras Kamboni.[50]

Al Itihaad fighters from this southern sector of operations are known to have engaged in international maritime piracy. On January 4, 1999, Al Itihaad gunmen commandeered near Kismayo the *MV Sea Johana,* a large commercial ferry and its twenty-one-member crew. The vessel was en route from Mombasa to India and apparently experience mechanical problems. The gunman took the ship to the port of Bur Gabo, south of Kismayo, and demanded an initial ransom of $6.5 million and later reduced it to $150,000. The gunmen eventually set the ship adrift, and it was found in April 1999, unmanned, off the coast of Mombasa.[51]

It was in the Gedo region that Al Itihaad established, with Al Qaeda support, camps from which the two organizations made incursions into Ethiopia and trained jihadists for operations throughout the Greater Horn of Africa. Strategically located near both Kenya and Ethiopia, the camps afforded potential for strikes into both Kenya and Ethiopia. Al Itihaad had first established its presence in August 1992, about the time that it adopted a strategy of abandoning its military presence in the cities. In the Gedo districts of Bay and Bakol, Al Itihaad began to erect the structures for an emirate. The organization filled the void created by the lack of government—offering assistance to the poor, building schools, and enforcing sharia laws in areas under its control. Al Itihaad encountered resistance, however, from within the local population mainly because of its strict interpretation of Islam and its effort to ban the consumption of *khat*, a mild "recreational drug" used widely in Somalia.[52] Nonetheless, Gedo has reportedly remained a region where Islamist sentiment continues to have a popular following.

Two Al Qaeda front organizations based in Nairobi under the guise of Islamic charities—Help Africa People and Mercy International Relief Agency (MIRA)—provided support for Al Itihaad humanitarian activities after 1994. (See chapter 5 on Kenya.) Al Qaeda also used MIRA to channel support for Al Itihaad militia camps located in the Gedo region.[53] In these camps, Al Itihaad and Al Qaeda trained recruits from Eritrea, Ethiopia, Kenya, Tanzania and Uganda in a wide range of skills used in direct warfare and terrorist operations. The two Kenya-based charities were also supporting Al Itihaad activities in Kenya's North Eastern Province across the border from Gedo at this time.

According to Hussein Mohamed Dires, the police chief in Bula Hawa, a small village near El Wak in the Gedo region, Al Itihaad had set up military training camps around El Wak, where followers were trained by "Arab foreigners" in preparation for a global Islamic jihad. Dires and other regional leaders said that Al Qaeda supported Al Itihaad's activities, supplying both weapons and cash, and that Osama bin Laden himself once visited.[54] When Al Itihaad launched its operations inside Ethiopia from its base in the Gedo region, about a dozen "Afghan Arabs" were reported to have been among its fighters. In June 1995, Al Itihaad forces also occupied Beledweyne located near the Ethiopian border in the Hiraan region.[55]

From these bases and with Sudanese and Al Qaeda support, Al Itihaad carried out small-scale actions in Somali-inhabited regions of Ethiopia: the Ogaden region by the end of 1993 and the Somali region a year later. The Ogaden National Liberation Front (ONLF), which is a separatist rebel group fighting to make the region of Ogaden an independent state, was also militarily active inside Ethiopia at this time.

A faction of Al Itihaad had already been operating inside Ethiopia from at least 1990. This faction registered as an official political party after the Ethiopian People's Revolutionary Democratic Front (EPRDF) overthrew the dictatorship of Mengistu Haile Mariam. In Ethiopia, Al Itihaad participated in the new, more liberal political disposition that the EPRDF allowed; but while Al Itihaad was enjoying the more open political system, it also was developing its military wing, building a fleet of gun-mounted four-wheel-drive vehicles (known as "technicals").[56] At some point, Ethiopian government forces made a surprise attack on one of Al Itihaad's militia training camps in the Ogaden, that of Tareq Bin Ziyad. According to a spokeperson for Al Itihaad's Ethiopian faction,

> This attack aimed to put a stop to the successful Islamic education of the people which was highly popular as they attended lectures and talks and conferences and many Islamic schools and colleges were opened as were a number of humanitarian aid organizations in the area.
>
> The treachery of the enemy was evident in their ambush late at night where they attacked and killed the leader of the movement, his deputy, and some of the best men, leaders and teachers. The brothers were not forewarned of this ambush and had no weapons to defend themselves.[57]

The Al Itihaad account is not clear as to the exact date of this reported surprise attack. So, there is some question as to whether it occurred before or after the overthrow of Mengistu.

The Ethiopian government responded to the Al Itihaad and ONLF operations by sending reinforcements to contain the situation,[58] and in 1994 at the invitation of the Ethiopian government, the Al Itihaad faction in Ogaden and the ONLF met the government at Qabri Dharhar in central Ogaden for peace talks. When talks broke down, hostilities resumed. According to Al Itihaad, the parties had observed a truce for sixteen months.[59]

Al Itihaad also launched a terrorist campaign inside Ethiopia. In early January 1995, Al Itihaad bombed a hotel in Addis Ababa; in May 1995 it exploded a bomb in a busy marketplace in Dire Dawa, Ethiopia's second-largest city, killing eighteen people. It also bombed the government-owned Ghion Hotel in Addis Ababa in January 1996, followed a month later by a bombing of the Ras Hotel in Dire Dawa. Al Itihaad claimed responsibility for the bombings and for the assassination of General Hayelom Araya, head of operations of Ethiopia's Ministry of Defense. Al Itihaad also claimed responsibility for the July 1996 assassination attempt on then Ethiopian Minister of Transport and Communication Abdulmejid Hussein, himself an Ethiopian Somali. The minister was wounded but survived. Al Itihaad said it would continue targeting senior Ethiopian officials and would pursue its guerrilla attacks in the Ogaden until the latter became independent of Ethiopia.[60]

Many Somalis saw Al Itihaad's military and terrorist actions inside Ethiopia as evidence that Al Itihaad was playing Khartoum's hand and had become a foreign puppet. Sudan's backing of Al Itihaad fit into Khartoum's wider regional strategy that included support for armed opposition groups fighting against the governments of Eritrea, Ethiopia and Uganda, as was discussed in the previous chapter.

The link between Sudan and Al Itihaad in aggression against Ethiopia was direct. In late 1996, during a meeting with supporters of Al Itihaad, the Sudanese *chargé d'affaires* in Mogadishu called publicly for a jihad against Ethiopia.[61] In its war by proxy with Ethiopia, the Sudanese government supported Ethiopia's armed opposition which included the Oromo Liberation Front (OLF) and the Ogaden National Liberation

Front. However, the secular OLF was uncomfortable with Sudan's ideological orientation, so Khartoum promoted an Islamic Oromo alternative, the Islamic Front for the Liberation of Oromiya (IFLO).[62] In the mid 1990's, IFLO based its operation out of Somalia and with Sudanese support worked in alliance with Al Itihaad to carry out actions inside Ethiopia. IFLO military actions were reportedly intermittent and relatively ineffective.

The containment of Al Itihaad and its Islamist aggression emerged as a national security priority of the Ethiopian government. While Abdulmejid Hussein, who survived an Al Itihaad assassination attempt, was serving as Ethiopia's ambassador to the United Nations in 2003, he underscored his government's commitment to containing the Islamist threat posed by Al Itihaad: "If you allow these people to infiltrate Somalia, our multicultural, multireligious and multiethnic country will pay a price....If the Somalis don't solve their problems, then we will do it for them.... We won't wait forever."[63]

In August 1996, a month after the assassination attempt on Abdulmejid Hussein and two months after Osama bin Laden was forced to leave Sudan for Afghanistan, Ethiopia intervened in Somalia to eviscerate Al Itihaad of its military and terrorist capabilities. Its first military incursion inside Somalia occurred in the Gedo region against the Al Qaeda-supported Al Itihaad camps in Luuq and Bula Hawa, and it has intervened on an "as needed" basis since then.[64] Ethiopia concomitantly elaborated a policy of building local alliances with military and political factions inside Somalia in opposition to Al Itihaad and its political allies, which included the Transitional National Government in Mogadishu and the Jama Ali Jama-led faction in Puntland. In 2001, Jama Ali Jama challenged the continuing presidency of Abdulahi Yusuf Ahmed; Puntland forces loyal to Abdulahi Yusuf fought with Al Itihaad militias that were supporting Jama Ali Jama; and Ethiopian troops reportedly aided the Puntland forces of Abdulahi Yusuf.

In response to the 1996 rout of Al Itihaad forces in the Gedo region, Aweys issued a statement condemning the Ethiopian attacks and labeling the United States the number one enemy of Muslims and accusing its government of seeking to place the entire Horn of Africa under Ethiopian, Christian rule (though Ethiopia's Muslims constitute a majority of the country's population). Aweys called on Muslims worldwide to show solidarity with Al Itihaad by resisting American aggressions and by sending aid to their suffering Somali brethren. His statement was issued on behalf of a previously unknown group: *Jama'at al-I'tisaam Bil-Kitaab Wa Sunna* (The Group for Adherence to the Book and the Sunna).[65]

Inside Somalia, the Ethiopian intervention provided Al Itihaad with a new supporter in the form of Hussein Aidid, the son of General Mohamed Farah Aidid. After the general's death in 1996, Hussein assumed control of his father's political and military machine. In an expression of Somali nationalism, he then allied himself with Al Itihaad to oppose Ethiopian incursions into Somalia.[66]

The losses that its forces suffered at the hands of the Ethiopian military appear to have provoked a strategic shift for Al Itihaad. Executive committee member Sheikh Aweys announced in Mogadishu at the beginning of 1997 that his organization would become an Islamic political party. He said that Al Itihaad had abandoned military actions and was seeking to assume power by political means, and that it would support any Islamic leader who might undertake to declare the Somali Islamic Republic. At his press conference which he held in Mogadishu, Aweys said,

> From now on the Islamic Union movement has been transformed into a political organization that seeks to hold power in Somalia, but our target is not only power, but to work towards the attainment of a Muslim president to run the country based on the Islamic law (sharia). We will announce our allegiance to any leader selected by the people who undertakes to establish the Somali Islamic Republic."[67]

Aweys went on to publicly distance his organization from Al Itihaad attacks inside Ethiopia, denying that Al Itihaad in Somalia had any connection with attacks by Al Itihaad supporters in Ethiopia. Others later suggested that the Al Itihaad actions inside Ethiopia were the work of the Ogadeni faction of the Al Itihaad and had not been planned by Al Itihaad inside Somalia.[68] These distinctions within the Al Itihaad structure, however, did not dissuade Ethiopia from further pursuing its interventionist policy inside Somalia. Indeed, in July 1998, four gunmen assassinated Al Itihaad commander Colonel Abdullahi Irad outside a mosque in Mogadishu, and a separate attempt was reportedly made on the life of Sheikh Aweys. Al Itihaad charged Ethiopia with the assassination of Colonel Irad who was widely believed to have organized the raids inside of Ethiopia. Between May and August 1998, Ethiopia claimed that it killed or captured more than 1,000 Oromo Liberation Front and Al Itihaad militia members near the Somali border,[69] and in August 1998 Ethiopian forces once again occupied the town of Bula Hawa in the Gedo region to quash a peace agreement between the Somali National Front and Al Itihaad, which Sheik Mohamud Moallin Nur, deputy chairman of Al Itihaad, had negotiated.[70]

After Al Itihaad's 1998 rout in Gedo by a coalition of local ethnic militias and Ethiopians, leaders in the town of El Wak told a *Christian Science Monitor* reporter that the organization had disbanded. "Those days are gone," says District Commissioner Yussuf Haji Osman. "We did not welcome them; we would not do so now." Others said that the fighters went into hiding but could reemerge.[71]

EXTERNAL SUPPORT FOR AL ITIHAAD SHIFTS

Al Itihaad experienced both the loss of Sudanese backing and a lessening of support from Al Qaeda. As already noted, under pressure from the United States and Saudi Arabia, in May 1996, Khartoum expelled bin Laden and much of his forces from Sudan, from whence they set up residence in Afghanistan.[72] Bin Laden's departure from Sudan deprived Al Itihaad of an immediate and major ally and financier in the rough Horn of Africa neighborhood. Then, also in 1996, the Ethiopian interventions inside Somali became an additional set back to Al Qaeda's ambitions in the region, certainly undermining its effort to train regional jihadist fighters at camps in the Gedo region. Although bin Laden still had a well-established and well-heeled network of cells and allied organizations in Tanzania, Kenya, Somalia, and Uganda, with the 1998 embassy bombings in Nairobi and Dar es Salaam, the Al Qaeda cells in East Africa dispersed; and their once robust operations ceased. Al Qaeda was left only able to operate with impunity in a reduced area of Somalia, mainly in Mogadishu.

Bin Laden's flight from Sudan also marked an important turning point in the unraveling of Sudan's increasingly discredited policy of regional destabilization and of its plans for regional Islamic hegemony, and became an important step in a long drawn out process of moderation by Khartoum. The outbreak of the border war between Ethiopia and Eritrea in 1998 then provided Khartoum with an opportunity to reduce tensions with Ethiopia. With a costly war waging on its northeastern border with Eritrea, Addis had ample reason to seek *détente* and normalization with Khartoum in a bid to protect its southeastern Somalia flank from armed actions. In the deal, Ethiopia withdrew support for southern Sudanese rebels, and Sudan quietly curbed its support to both Al Itihaad and the armed Ethiopian opposition based in Somalia.

Al Itihaad and the Ethiopian separatist groups based in Somalia found, however, a new backer to replace Sudan. Eritrea began supplying arms to various groups in Somalia in a bid to undermine Ethiopia by waging a proxy war from Somalia. Inside Somalia, factional leader and self-proclaimed Somali President Hussein Aidid became a direct recipient of Eritrean military support, and he channeled some of this support to Al Itihaad and the Oromo Liberation Front in their fight against the Ethiopian government. Hussein Aidid acknowledged the presence of about 700 "politically organized" Oromos at Qoryooley in Somalia.[73]

Eritrea may have also been behind the resurgence of military actions by the Islamic Front for the Liberation of Oromia (IFLO). Eritrean radio reported in 2001 that IFLO rebels killed over sixty-eight Ethiopian government soldiers when IFLO forces attacked the town of Aweday and ambushed a military convoy along the Dire Dawa-Finfine road near the town of Alemaya.[74]

Ethiopia set out to find new allies in Somalia and to build a coalition among various Somali faction in a bid to further blunt its armed opposition and Al Itihaad operating out of Somalia. In October 1999, Somali factional leaders, including Aidid, Osman Hassan Ali Atto, and Umar Haji Masaleh, held talks with Ethiopian officials. Ethiopian Foreign Minister Seyoum Mesfin called upon Aidid to stop its support of Al Itihaad and Oromo rebel groups based in Somalia. Aidid replied that Ethiopia should end its military intervention in Somalia.[75]

But in 1999, Hussein Aidid would reverse himself when Al Itihaad, once again launched a military operation in southern Somalia. Sheikh Aweys had transformed his Al Itihaad militia into an Islamic Court operating in Mogadishu; and despite his disavowal of militarism for his organization two years earlier, Al Itihaad militiamen cum Islamic Court took the cities of Marka and Qoryooley and entered Kismayo, where they became influential. The forces of Hussein Aidid and those of Al Itihaad engaged in combat in Marka, Qoryooley, and Mogadishu.[76] These events pushed Hussein Aidid to become an ally of Ethiopia against Al Itihaad and later the Al Itihaad-influenced Transitional National Government (TNG) based in Mogadishu.

Ethiopia's efforts at coalition building among various Somali factions ultimately paid big dividends. In March 2001, following several meetings in Ethiopia, Somali factional leaders opposed to the TNG and Al Itihaad set up the Somali Reconciliation and Restoration Council (SRRC). The SRRC included a presidential council, consisting of five co-chairmen, each presiding on a monthly basis, and a first secretary. The five cochairmen were: Hussein Aidid, Somali National Alliance; Hilowle Iman Umar from northern Mogadishu; General Adan Abdullahi Nur 'Gabyow', Somali Patriotic Movement; Dr. Hassan Mohammed Nur 'Shaatigaduud', Rahanweyn Resistance Army, and Abdullahi Sheikh Ismail, Southern Somalia National Movement.

Immediately the SRRC announced its commitment to lead "the nation towards an all inclusive reconciliation conference and the establishment of a legitimate transitional representative government of National Unity." The factional leaders called upon all political movements in Somalia including the TNG, civil society, clan and religious leaders, the business community, and Somalis in the diaspora to join them for an immediate and unconditional national reconciliation conference aimed at establishing a representative and a broad-based national government.[77] SSRC members then came to play a central role in the IGAD-sponsored reconciliation talks that took place in Kenya that resulted in the formation of the Transitional Federal Government.

Notes

1. Jama Mohamed Ghalib, *The Cost of Dictatorship:The Somali Experience* (New York: Lilian Barber Press, Inc., 1995), 204-207.
2. Herman J. Cohen (former U.S. Assistant Secretary of State for Africa), "Somalia and the United States: A Long and Troubled History," *allAfrica.com*, January 21, 2002, http://allafrica.com/stories/200201210455.html.
3. Controversy over the Siad Barre government's human rights policies had clouded U.S. military cooperation with Somalia. The U.S. government had pressed Somalia's government to improve its human rights record. Siad Barre's policy of repression aroused criticism of his regime in the United States Congress, where the Foreign Affairs Committee of the House of Representatives held extensive hearings during July 1988 on human rights abuses in Somalia. In 1989, under congressional pressure, the administration of the first President George Bush terminated military aid to Somalia, although it continued to provide food assistance and to operate a small international military education and training program. In 1990, Washington revealed that Mogadishu had been in default on loan repayments for more than a year. Therefore, under the terms of the Brooke Amendment, this meant that Somalia was ineligible to receive any further United States aid.
4. International Crisis Group, *Somalia's Islamists*, 4.
5. Douglas James Jardine, *The Mad Mullah of Somaliland* (New York: Negro University Press, 1969); Abdi Sheikh-Abdi, *Divine Madness: Mohammed Abdulle Hassan (1856-1920)*, (London: Zed Books Ltd., 1992).
6. "Somalia between the Fire of the United States, The Allegations of Bin Laden and the Obscurity of El Itihad El Islami (Islamic Union)," *Al-Hayat* (Cairo), December 10, 2001, in translation, http://www.somaliawatch.org/archivedec01/011222601.htm.
7. Ejara Amante, *Defending the Nation against Terrorist Organizations*, http://www.ethioembassy.org.uk/articles/articles/march-00/Ejara%20Amante%20-%201.htm; David H. Shinn, *Somalia: Another Foreign Policy Challenge for the United States*, May 21, 2002, http://www.waltainfo.com/Conflict/Articles/2002/May article4.htm.
8. International Crisis Group, *Somalia's Islamists*, 4.
9. *Setting the Historical Record Straight*, n.d., http://www.arlaadi.com/Abuse.htm.
10. "Bombing Probe Turns to Kenya's Soldiers for Hire," *The East African*, October 19-25, 1998, http://www.nationaudio.com/News/EastAfrican/1910/Regional/Regional22.html.
11. International Crisis Group, *Somalia: Countering Terrorism in a Failed State*. Africa Report no. 45, 13.

12. Medhane Tadesse, 'Islamic Fundamentalism in Somalia: Its Nature and Implications," *WIC*, April 10, 2001, www.somaliawatch.org/archivesep01/011128401.htm.
13. International Crisis Group, *Somalia*, 13, http://www.crisisweb.org/library/documents/report_archive/A400662_23052002.pdf.
14. Jeff Koinanage, "U.S. Takes Closer Look at Somalia as Possible Target in War on Terror," *CNN*, January 29, 2002, http://www.cnn.com/TRANSCRIPTS/0201/19/cst.12.html.
15. "Hussein Aidid Accuses Asmara, Tripoli and Djibouti - Calls for Air Embargo on Somalia," *The Daily Monitor* (Addis Ababa), March 19, 2002, http://allafrica.com/stories/200203190399.html.
16. Johnathan Clayton, "In Mogadishu, They Wonder if Americans Will Come Kill Them," *San Francisco Chronicle*, January 20, 2002, http://www.dehai.org/archives/dehai_news_archive/jan02/0318.html.
17. André le Sage, "Prospects for Al-Itihaad and Islamist Radicalism in Somalia," *Review of African Political Economy*, 27, no. 89 (September 2001).
18. Gamal Nkrumah, "Somalia: Next on the Block?" *Al-Ahram Weekly Online*, December 27, 2001-2 January 2002, no.566, http://weekly.ahram.org.eg/2001/566/war5.htm.
19. Hussein Ali Soke, "Is Somalia a Safe-haven for Terrorists?" *africanconflict.org*, http://allafrica.com/stories/printable/2000201090390.html; International Crisis Group, *Somalia's Islamists*, 5.
20. *Somalis Fully Support Forthcoming Government*, 1999 Security Council Committee Concerning Afghanistan, Press Release AFG/163, SC/7206, September 11, 2001, http://www.un.org/News/Press/docs/2001/afg163.doc.htm.
21. Yossef Bodansky, *Bin Laden: The Man Who Declared War on America* (Roseville, Calif.: Prima Publishing, 2001), 68; Bodansky provides a fascinating account (pp 70 —80) of a number of the internationalist jihadist interventions on the side of Al Itihaad and Mohamed Farah Aidid in 1993, including the participation of Hezbollah fighters in the fight against U.S. forces. Bodansky's information is not sourced, and I have used his information where corroboration could be obtained.
22. Herman J. Cohen, *Somalia and the United States, AllAfrica.com*, January 21, 2002, http://allafrica.com/stories/200201210 455.html.
23. Peter L. Bergen, *The Osama bin Laden I Know: An Oral History of al Qaeda's Leader* (New York: Free Press, 2006), 137.
24. Adrian Blomfield, "Banks-to-terror Conglomerate Faces US Wrath" *Telegraph* (Nairobi), September 28, 2001, http://news.telegraph.co.uk/news/main.jhtml?xml=/news/2001/09/28/wsom28.xml
25. Ibid., Bin Laden related this incident to Abdel Bari Atwan, editor of the Egyptian newspaper, *A Quads al Arabi*.

26. David A. Phillips, "The Yemen Bombing: Another Wake-up Call in the Terrorist Shadow War," *The Heritage Foundation Executive Bulletin*, no.703, October 25, 2000, http://www.heritage.org/Research/Middle East/EM703.cfm; Asaf Maliach, *The Global Jihad - The Yemeni Connection: An updated Perspective*, March 20, 2006, http://www.ict.org.il/articles/articledet.cfm? articleid=559#_edn5.
27. Karl Vick, "Embassy Plotter Undone When Suicide Bomber Lived," *Washington Post*, November 23, 1998, http://www.library.cornell.edu/colldev/mideast/nairobi.htm.
28. Mark Huban, "Bankrolling Bin Laden," *Financial Times*, November 28, 2001, http://specials.ft.com/attackonterrorism/FT3FJ5RJMUC.html.
29. David H. Shinn, "Ethiopia: Coping with Islamic Fundamentalism before and after September 11," *Africa Notes*, no. 7, February 2002, http://mailgate.supereva.it/soc/soc.culture. somalia/msg02561.html.
30. Global Witness, *For a Few Dollar$ More: How Al Qaeda Moved into the Diamond Trade*, April 2003, 43, http://www. globalwitness.org/reports/show.php/en.00041.html.
31. Paul Watson and Sidhartha Barua, "Somalian Link Seen to Al Qaeda," *Los Angeles Times*, February 25, 2002, http://latimes.com/news/nationworld/world/la-020502hawk.story.
32. Bodansky, *Bin Laden*, 69.
33. Richard Sale, *"*Yemen: Rocky Road to Terror Cooperation,*" United Press International*, December 11, 2001.
34. "Somalia between the Fire of the United States, The Allegations of Bin Laden and the Obscurity Of 'El Itihad El Islami' (Islamic Union)," *Al-Hayat* (Cairo), December 10, 2001 in translation, http://www.somaliawatch.org/archivedec01/011222601.htm.
35. Bodansky, *Bin Laden*, 68.
36. See chapter 5 for discussion on Kenya.
37. Shinn, "Ethiopia: Coping with Islamic Fundamentalism."
38. "Sudan and Iran Suspected of Assisting Aidid," *Somalia News Update*, October 12, 1993, http://www.etext.org/Politics/Somalia.News.Update/Volume.2/snu-2.28.
39. Christopher Whalen, "In Somalia, the Saudi Connection," *Washington Post*, October 17, 1993.
40. Shinn, "Ethiopia: Coping with Islamic Fundamentalism."
41. J.T. Caruso, *Al-Qaeda International*, Testimony of J. T. Caruso, Acting Assistant Director, CounterTerrorism Division, FBI, Before the Subcommittee on International Operations and Terrorism, Committee on Foreign Relations, United States Senate, December 18, 2001, http://www.fbi.gov/congress/congress01/caruso121801.htm.

42. "Bin Laden, "Millionaire with a Dangerous Grudge," *CNN*, September 12, 2001, http://www.cnn.com/2001/US/09/12/binladen.profile/index.html.
43. "Somalia's New Warlord Abdiqasim Salad," *The Republican*, no. 129, September 23, 2000, http://www.somalilandforum.com/news/the_republican/Republican-Editorials2.htm.
44. *The Al Qaeda Documents: Al Qaeda Operations in Somalia, Thoughts about Chechnya, Plus a View of Bill Clinton*, http://austinbay.net/blog/?p=947.
45. "In Fallujah Al Qaeda Reminds Americans of Mogadishu," *DEBKA-Net-Weekly*, March 31, 2004, http://www.debka.com/article.php?aid=818.
46. Marc-Antoine Perouse de Montclos, "Des ONG sans gouvernement: mouvements islamiques et velleites de substitution a l'Etat dans la Somalie en guerre," (paper presented at the UNESCO Colloquium, ONG et Gouvernance dans le Monde Arabe, Cairo, March 29-31, 2000), http://www.mafhoum.com/press4/119P1.htm#_ftn6; Jeffrey Krutz, *Africa, Islam, and Terrorism - Meeting Summary*, Carnegie Endowment, posted December 21, 2001, http://www.somaliawatch.org/archivedec01/011221601.htm.
47. Blomfield, "Banks-to-terror Conglomerate Faces US Wrath."
48. Jeffrey Donovan, "Reports Say Somalia Next Target in U.S. War on Terrorism," *Radio Free Europe/Radio Liberty*, January 4, 2002, http://truthnews.com/world/2002_01_somalia.html.
49. "Somalia: Al-Ittihad's US assets frozen," *IRIN*, http://www.cidi.org/humanitarian/irin/hafrica/01b/ixl12.html.
50. "Somalia: Armed Group Flees to Kenya," *IRIN*, April 17, 1999, http://www.africa.upenn.edu/Hornet/irin_41799.html.
51. Scott Coffen-Smout, *Pirates, Warlords and Rogue Fishing Vessels in Somalia's Unruly Seas*, http://www.chebucto.ns.ca/~ar120/somalia.html.
52. Ali Soke, "Is Somalia a Safe Haven?"
53. International Crisis Group, *Somalia's Islamists*, 7.
54. Danny Harman, "Somalis Wary of Growing US Scrutiny," *The Christian Science Monitor*, January 8, 2002, http://www.csmonitor.com/2002/0108/p1s3-woaf.htm.
55. Perouse de Montclos, "Des ONG sans gouvernement."
56. International Crisis Group, *Somalia's Islamists*, 15.
57. "Nida'ul Islam Interviews the Spokesman for the Islamic Union of the Mujahideen of Ogadin," *Nida'ul Islam*, July-August 1997, http://www.islam.org.au.
58. Tadesse, "Islamic Fundamentalism."
59. International Crisis Group, *Somalia's Islamists*, 9.

60. David Shinn, "Ethiopia Coping with Islamic fundamentalism before and after Sept. 11," www.somaliawatch.org/archivemar02/020316601.htm.
61. Shinn, "Ethiopia: Coping with Islamic Fundamentalism."
62. Gerard Prunier, "Armed Conflict in the Heart of Africa: Sudan's Regional War," *Le Monde Diplomatique,* February 1997, http://mondediplo.com/1007/02/02sudan.
63. *IRIN,* February 26, 2002.
64. Mohamed Guled, "Ethiopia Crosses Border into Somalia—Witnesses," *Reuters,* August 6, 1998, http://www.geocities.com/~dagmawi/News/News_Aug7_Somalia.html.
65. International Crisis Group, *Somalia's Islamists,* 10.
66. Perouse de Montclos, "Des ONG sans gouvernement."
67. "Somalia Between the Fire of the United States."
68. Interview, June 30, 2004.
69. Shinn, "Ethiopia: Coping with Islamic Fundamentalism."
70. Guled, "Ethiopia Crosses Border.
71. See chapter 5 for discussion on Kenya.
72. Barton Gellman, "Sudan's Offer to Arrest Militant Fell Through after Saudis Said No, *Washington Post,* October 3, 2001, http://www.library.cornell.edu/colldev/mideast/ladnsudx.htm.
73. "Horn of Africa: Armed Factions and the Ethiopia-Eritrea Conflict," *IRIN,* May 14, 1999, http://www.sas.upenn.edu/African_ Studies/Hornet/irin51499e.html; Amante, "Defending;" Assistant US Secretary of State Susan Rice, *The Ethiopian-Eritrean War; U.S. Policy Options,* (Testimony to the House Africa Subcommittee), May 25, 1999, http://www.geocities.com/~dagmawi/NewsMay99/May27_SusanRice.html.
74. BBC Monitoring. Source: Voice of the Broad Masses, Asmara, May 12, 2001, http:lists.sn.apc.org/pipermail/pol.ethiopia/2001-May/000587.html.
75. "Somalia: Aidid has "Difficult"Talks in Addis," *IRIN,* October 26, 1999.
76. Perouse de Montclos, "Des ONG sans gouvernement."
77. "Faction Leaders Establish Somali Reconciliation and Restoration Council," *Addis Tribune,* March 2001, http://www.addistribune.com/Archives/2001/03/23-03-01/Faction.htm.

Chapter Three

JIHADISM IN SOMALIA'S ISLAMIC COURTS

In January 2005, a militia closely associated with the Ifka Halane Islamic Court entered a colonial-era Italian cemetery on Imperial Road in Mogadishu and disinterred more than 700 bodies of Italian nationals — soldiers, traders, and missionaries — who lived in the city early in the twentieth century when southern Somalia was still an Italian colony. The desecration became public when Somali residents noticed young children playing with skulls and other human remains that had been dumped on a garbage heap near the Mogadishu airport.

The Italian public was outraged at the news of the desecration of the graves as were many residents of Mogadishu, including traditional clan leaders and Muslim religious figures, and a popular demonstration was held in Mogadishu to protest the defiling of the cemetery. According to the Italian daily, *Corriere della Sera*, the Islamic fundamentalist militants justified their action by saying there was no reason "for the tombs of the unfaithful to exist under Somali soil."

Initial reports attributed the desecration to real estate developers who employed the Islamist militia to empty the cemetery in anticipation of rising land values that would occur when the new Transitional Federal Government (TFG) was to set up in Mogadishu.[1] But there was much more to this story. The act itself was the work of what was probably the most radical Somali jihadist group, and the cemetery desecration was rife with symbolism. Perhaps, the defilement represented an attempt to control the future of Somalia by seeking to control its past and in so doing to find release from the perceived humiliations of the colonial experience.

The commander of the militia that came to occupy the cemetery was Hasan Adan 'Ayro, a young protégé of Sheikh Hasan Dahir Aweys. 'Ayro had emerged in 2006 as a senior commander of the UIC forces when they consolidated their control of Mogadishu and other areas of southern Somalia, and he was one of the two Al Qaeda-affiliated commanders who led UIC forces when it took over the city of Kisymayo in October 2006.[2]

'Ayro was the leader of a Somali jihadist terrorist cell.[3] Hasan Adan 'Ayro received training at Aweys's Ifka Halane Islamic Court. Along with other youths, 'Ayro reportedly was then assigned by Sheikh Aweys to guard Al Qaeda operatives in Mogadishu, and the young body guards, including 'Ayro, became greatly influenced by the Al Qaeda members.[4] 'Ayro was then selected for further training in Afghanistan in the 1990s. According to one account, 'Ayro also traveled there on the eve of the October 2001 American offensive against Al Qaeda and the Taliban, which was the U.S. response to Al Qaeda's September 11 attack. Sheikh Aweys reportedly accompanied 'Ayro to Afghanistan and returned to Somalia several months later. If true, this account may in part explain the whereabouts of Sheikh Aweys during the period when he had gone underground after the designation by the United States and the United Nations of Al Itihaad as an ally of Al Qaeda, and it also seems to corroborate reports that Al Itihaad had sent young recruits to join the Taliban and Al Qaeda in the fight against the U.S.-led intervention in Afghanistan. 'Ayro's role in the international jihadist movement was once again confirmed when in July 2006 he led more than 700 Islamic militants from Somalia who traveled to Lebanon to fight alongside the Shi'a Islamist militant and political organization Hezbollah in its war with Israel, according to a UN report.[5]

'Ayro heads an extensive, highly organized network that assassinated four foreign humanitarian workers in Somaliland in 2003 and 2004, and his organization is suspected to have been behind other assassinations, including that of Somali Police General Youseff Ahmad, the TFG police commander who began an official investigation of the cemetery desecration.[6] 'Ayro's network seemed to be particularly dedicated to the destabilization of Somaliland, and terrorist action of this type would be a fitting tactic for the Islamic Court's Al Itihaad faction, which has not had the capacity to pose a military challenge to Somaliland since it rebuffed Al Itihaad in the early 1990s.

Two of the captured suspects in the Somaliland assassinations had been affiliated with Al Itihaad since the early 1990s, and one of them, a businessman from Burao in eastern Somalia, an Islamist stronghold in Somaliland, had landed a job as deputy manager of the local office of the Saudi-based charity Al Haramain. As discussed later in this chapter, Al Haramain has provided support for Al Itihaad and Al Qaeda. Like 'Ayro, both of these assassination suspects had trained with Al Qaeda inside Afghanistan. The three other suspects were hired gunmen.

When news of the Italian cemetery desecration ceremony became public, leaders of the Habar Gedir 'Ayr subclan summoned Aweys and 'Ayro separately in an attempt to stop the affront, but to no avail. 'Ayro kept up his occupation of the cemetery. According to eyewitnesses at the meetings with the subclan leaders, Aweys insisted 'Ayro was beyond his control; 'Ayro defended his actions, saying they were consistent with the teachings of Islam. But when challenged by learned sheikhs from the subclan, 'Ayro was unable to justify himself.[7]

Yet, another source has indicated that Aweys and 'Ayro had both given the orders to the militia to dig up the Italian bodies.[8] Despite Aweys's disavowal of 'Ayro, 'Ayro was appointed commander of the Ifka Halane court militia in July 2005 with Aweys's likely approval. In a 2006 interview, Sheikh Aweys reconfirmed his confidence in 'Ayro. Asked by a reporter about U.S. concerns that Ayro was responsible for the killing of the four foreign aid workers and Abdul Qadir Yahya, the internationally respected founder of the Center for Research and Dialogue in Mogadishu, Aweys said:

> Adan 'Ayro is a Somali man, he is a good man, he is part of the Islamic Courts, a member of the Islamic Courts, and if they have evidence that he is a criminal, it has to be tried in court. But I want to ask them, how are the domestic affairs of Somalia a concern of America?[9]

After the Italian cemetery take over by 'Ayro and his 'Ayr-lineage militia, the site became one of the most fortified compounds in Mogadishu. Few people have been able to visit the compound, but several people who reportedly have been on the inside described having seen men from Saudi Arabia, Yemen, and Pakistan leading the training of young Somali men, some of them reportedly orphans, who had been recruited to join 'Ayro's militia.[10]

Sheikh Aweys's strong support for the suspected terrorist, 'Ayro, gives credence to the alert issued by U.S. government in response to purported calls by Aweys on Somali web sites to carry out suicide bombings in Kenya and in Ethiopia. In November 2006, the U.S. embassies in Nairobi and Addis Ababa warned of the threat of suicide attacks against "prominent" targets in those countries and urged Americans to use "extreme caution" in the two countries. "These threats specifically mention the execution of suicide explosions in prominent landmarks within Kenya and Ethiopia." These threats came at a time when the UIC was decrying Ethiopian and Kenyan support for the Transitional Federal Government.

The UIC denied the U.S. allegations that Sheikh Aweys had authorized any such suicide bombings. UIC's deputy defense minister, Sheikh Mukhtar Robow, said:

> We know that America never favors Islamic movements anywhere in the world and such statements are part of an incorrect Zionist-inherited ideology. Islam does not harm people. The warnings issued by the American embassy are baseless, and we never attack neighboring countries. America misleads its own people by giving such baseless warnings but we will never falter because we stand ready to defend our religion and people from the enemy of Allah.[11]

By Fall 2006, Sheikh Aweys, 'Ayro, and other Somali jihadist with ties to Al Qaeda had assumed commanding positions within the Islamic Courts movement. The roots of the Islamic Courts may very legitimately be viewed as a local Islamist response to the lawlessness of stateless Somalia, but that the movement also became the expression of an international agenda to bring a jihadist revolution to all Somalis, and perhaps to all Muslims, in the Horn of Africa seems irrefutable.

The Origins of the Islamic Courts

Somalia's Islamic Courts movement arose after the collapse of the country's central government in 1991. The Courts were established to provide a system of justice in a society devoid of government as a way to bring order to the lawless streets of Mogadishu, and they were later extended to other areas of southern Somalia. The Courts have been largely subclan-based and typically apply Somali customary law (*xeer*) and/or sharia.[12] Of the eleven courts operating in Mogadishu in mid-2006, ten of them were associated with subclans of the Hawiye clan.[13] Each court typically has held judicial proceedings, maintained a prison, and fielded a militia. The court militias have acted as a local police force and have been mobilized to rein in abusive practices of secular subclan factional militias, many of which have a history of victimizing local residents through violence and extortion.

Outside the structure of Mogadishu's Islamic Courts, justice has been administered in other areas of Somalia in different ways. In areas controlled by factional leaders, also referred to as warlords, the clan-based factional leaders have not usually been involved in matters of jurisprudence, which remained the jurisdiction of clan elders. When elders have not been able to address a problem, usually when it involved an action by a militia member, the factional leader would then weigh in. In the breakaway Republic of Somaliland and in the self-administered region of Puntland, the governments have set up formal judiciaries.[14]

The ideological orientations of Mogadishu's Islamic Courts have varied, ranging from Somali's historic tradition of Sufi moderation to a Wahabist reformism with a strong jihadist bent. The Al Itihaad-associated court, Ifka Halane, represents perhaps the most militant of the courts. Al Itihaad's ideological orientation has been present in the Islamic Courts movement since its beginnings in 1993, when an Al Itihaad splinter group, *Al Ansar Al Sunna* (Defenders of the Tradition) organized the first court in Mogadishu's Madina District.[15]

For its part, Al Itihaad has a history of setting up sharia courts in its occupied territory such as in the Gedo region, and it also supported Islamic Courts in Mogadishu. When Hassan Dahir Aweys first deployed his forces to Mogadishu in 1993, for instance, he received support from his fellow Haber Gedir subclansman, General Mohamed Farah Aideed. However, this powerful factional leader reportedly grew wary of Al Itihaad, and he began to patronize a less militant and more traditional Islamic organization, *Majima Al Ulama*. Aweys then switched his allegiance to Aidid's crosstown rival, Ali Mahdi, whose stronghold was located in North Mogadishu. There, in 1994, Al Itihaad reportedly supported the setup of a court under the direction of Sheikh Ali Dheere. Dheere's court was known for its harsh sharia punishment which included amputations. It succeeded, however, in bringing relative order to the unruly streets of North Mogadishu and reportedly achieved some popularity among the local population for this. Sheikh Ali Dheere continued to chair the North Mogadishu court after Al Madhi, who became distrustful of Al Itihaad, expelled its militia from territory under his control.[16]

Other subclans in Mogadishu saw the positive results that these early courts were achieving, especially in reducing militia and other gang-related violence and crimes, and they began to institute their own courts. In 2000, the chairman of the Islamic Courts in Mogadishu, Hassan Sheik Mohamed Abdi, explained how the Courts viewed their role in Somali society.

> We have a very large responsibility in Somalia, because when the central government disappeared and everything broke down and failed, people despaired. They were without any help. It was a very good chance for the gangs and the criminals to do whatever they wanted. The wise men and religious men, the intellectuals and the elders came together and thought of how they could save themselves and their property. That was the way we started — to use the Islamic courts to solve that problem.[17]

Hassan Sheikh Mohamed Abdi advocated the establishment of an Islamic state to solve the country's problems, but also took pain to stress that he wanted to have good relations with the United States and Europe.

Eager to end the lawlessness that was hurting commerce, the Mogadishu business community saw value in the Islamic Courts and often helped finance their operations. The Islamic Courts had some success in improving the business environment of the city—curtailing, for example, the system of extortion by armed gangs that hampered business life.

Somali human rights activists came to address the harsh punishments administer by Dheere's court and human rights abuses committed by other courts and promoted higher criminal justice standards. In an interview in 2000, Hasan Shire Sheikh, codirector of the Dr. Ismail Juma'le Human Rights Center explained:

> We have had a difficult relationship with the Islamic Courts. In May 1997 we stopped the mutilation of limbs in Sheikh Ali Dheere Court (north Mogadishu) through strong public pressure. Then the Islamic Courts in south Mogadishu were established on a clan basis. They were more concerned in protecting the clan from the activities of the clan militias. Their jurisdiction did not go beyond the individual clan. I see them more as places where delinquent youngsters are rehabilitated, than as serious courts. They don't have capital punishment and do not amputate limbs. We monitor every three months the conditions of the Islamic Courts' prisons, where they keep the delinquent children (the young gunmen), and issue a report. We see whether they are complying with international standards. Sometimes we offered training in the prisons, and there has been some response. Recently, we have lively debates in Horn Afrik Radio and television with the court representatives; we both come there and talk about human rights issues.[18]

Aweys's Al Itihaad Becomes an Islamic Court

At the beginning of 1997, after Al Itihaad had been seriously weakened militarily by Ethiopian military interventions, Sheikh Aweys appears to have been searching for alternative ways of keeping his jihadist movement alive. He revealed a strategic shift for the jihadist organization, announcing that Al Itihaad would function as an Islamic political party, and henceforth it intended to achieve its Islamist aims by working through existing organizations rather than by force of arms.

Shortly thereafter in 1998, Sheikh Aweys became a central figure in the establishment of the Ifka Halane court located in western Mogadishu, which came to resemble less a court than an armed camp, brisling with gun-mounted vechicles known as "technicals."[19] Sheikh Aweys's court benefited from the practice of Haber Gedir businessmen providing financial support to Islamic Courts dominated by fellow Haber Gedir clansmen who had been part of the Al Itihaad leadership, and Sheikh Aweys transformed, or perhaps reidentified, his militia as one of the Islamic Courts.

Al Itihaad cum Islamic Courts cultivated relationships with the Mogadishu business communities that paid Aweys's Court for their law enforcement services. Al Itihaad also began to invest directly in business ventures, including banking, telecommunications, export-import, transport and religious schools.[20] The tactic of investment in business enterprises to finance its military and political activities was reminiscent of the practice of Al Qaeda cells in East Africa that sought to become self-financing entities through investment in a number of "legitimate" business concerns.

One of Aweys's business supporters also allegedly supported the Al Qaeda network. A Somali-owned money transfer company, *Al Barakat,* (meaning "holiness" in Arabic), was an apparent conduit of funds to Al Itihaad and one of its financial backers, for instance, reportedly paying the salaries of Al Itihaad officials. At the time, *Al Barakat*—through its telecommunications, banking and other holdings—was the largest employer in Somalia.[21]

The U.S. government accused Al Barakat of transferring funds on behalf of Osama bin Laden and his Al Qaeda network. In November 2001, U.S authorities ordered the immediate closure of Al Barakat and the seizure of its worldwide assets, although the United States never charged Al Barakat for its alleged crimes in a court of law. According to the United States, Al Barakat's network had moved tens of millions of dollars a year to Al Qaeda. Allegations were also made that Al Barakat skimmed off money from its transfers and made millions of dollars from this practice available to Al Qaeda. The

U.S. government claimed that Al Barakat had been formed for the specific purpose of aiding terrorists. "By shutting these networks down, we disrupt the murderers' work," said U.S. President George W. Bush.[22]

According to one source, the U.S. Federal Bureau of Investigation and the Immigration and Naturalization Service had investigated large overseas money transfers by Somali immigrants who had recently arrived in Minneapolis, Minnesota. The Somali immigrants had reportedly sent $75 million outside of the United States in sums averaging between $2 million and $4 million per month. U.S. authorities were concerned that some of this funding may have been going to support Al Itihaad.[23]

Ahmad Ali Jimale, Al Barakat's founder and chairman, has insisted that his company had no links whatsoever with bin Laden and Al Qaeda, although some sources suggest Jimale fought alongside bin Laden in Afghanistan as an anti-Soviet mujahidin. Al Barakat had come to operate in forty countries worldwide after the outbreak of civil war in Somalia in 1991 and the collapse of the country's banking system. Its customers were largely Somalis who had fled the country as refugees who needed a way to transfer much-needed funds to relatives back home. At the time when Al Barakat was closed down in November 2001, an estimated total of $750 million entered Somalia annually from remittances of Somalis working and living abroad.[24] As the country's largest employer and largest transferor of emigrant remittances,[25] the closure of Al-Bakarat seriously setback Somalia's struggling economy, and many Somalis lost money as a result of the freezing of Al Barakat's assets. Other money transfer services gradually moved in to fill the void created by Al Barakat's closure, but the closure and the losses that obtained from it reportedly created ill-will among many Somalis toward the U.S. government.

The advent of Al Itihaad as an Islamic court, with its international jihadist rhetoric and ties to Al Qaeda, began to worry clan-based factional leaders in Mogadishu. In February 1999, representatives of the Islamic Courts met with clan-based factional leaders, including Ali Mahdi and Hussein Aidid, to discuss their concerns about possible U.S. actions within Somalia. Noting the August 1998 U.S. cruise missile attack on the Al Shifa pharmaceutical plant in Khartoum after Al Qaeda's bombing of the U.S. embassies in Nairobi and in Dar es Salaam, Aidid warned the Islamic Courts not to go to the extremes. According to Aidid, it was "their collective responsibility to avoid giving their enemy the pretext of attacking Somalia with missiles...."[26]

AWEYS ON THE MARCH AGAIN

While the Islamic Courts were proving their value to business by returning Mogadishu and surrounding areas to a sense of normalcy, including an end to the practice of extortion, those courts in Mogadishu under Al Itihaad influence also proved to be something of a Trojan Horse for secular factional leaders. In 1999 and 2000, Sheikh Aweys came to serve as chairman of the Islamic Courts in southern Mogadishu. Under his influence, the Islamic Courts launched by October 1999, a military operation to take control of an area from Mogadishu up to the lower Shabelle region and from Marka to Brave. Its militias succeeded in taking control of key facilities of Marka port, an important Indian Ocean facility, and began both to appoint local administrators and Islamic Courts' officials and to recruit additional militia members.[27]

In early 2000, Peter Maas of the *New Republic* interviewed the leader of the Islamic Courts' militia that had occupied Marka, Sheikh Hassan Ainte. Maas likened the Islamic Courts to the Taliban and indicated that the goal of the courts was "to sweep through the country, much as the Taliban did in Afghanistan, and unify it under Islam." Ainte expressed his commitment to spreading sharia to all of Somalia and contended, nonetheless, that there were "very big differences" between the Islamic Courts and the Taliban. "We are all Muslim. They came to power by shedding blood, but we don't want to do that. They killed a lot of people. We don't want that. We came here at the request of the people. Everyone is happy with us."

Despite Sheikh Ainte's claim, not everyone in Marka was happy with the presence of the Islamic Courts. A prominent Marka businessman, Isse Haji Ismaile, regrettably pointed out:

> There are two ways this can go. One way is evolution. We tell them how grateful we are that they have brought us security...and that it is time for them to go home. The other way is that, at the same time, we get our own

[armed] groups ready, and, if they will not leave when we ask them, we will fight them.[28]

Factional leaders in southern Somalia fearing that the growing power of the Islamic Courts would deprive them of political power began resisting the militias under Sheikh Aweys's control. Haber Gedir subclan rivals, Osman Hassan Ali Atto and Hussein Aidid, who frequently fought over control of South Mogadishu, joined forces against Aweys's militias. Also at stake was control of the lucrative trade passing through the port of Marka — made all the more profitable because of the volume of humanitarian relief passing through the port to southern Somalia, which at the time was stricken by drought.[29]

Radio Pacification, operated by factional leader Ali Atto, denounced the offensive by the Islamic Courts.

> We are surprised by the move of the Islamic courts...if they are fighting banditry, we would have joined them, but their intention is to create a permanent occupation in the area without the blessing of the people.... A tribal army should not claim Islamic responsibility of battling banditry, they should leave the areas captured by their gunmen immediately.[30]

Court officials vowed to remain in control of Marka port and urged relief agencies to continue using the port facilities.

The resurgence of Al Itihaad through the Islamic Courts pushed Hussein Aidid and other factional leaders into Ethiopia's camp, resulting in the formation of the Somali Reconciliation and Restoration Committee (SRRC) discussed in the previous chapter. The Ethiopian government actively worked with one member of the SRRC, the Rahanwein Resistance Army, based in central Somalia, to oppose the expansion of the Islamic Courts to that region.[31] The SRRC also opposed the Mogadishu-based Transitional National Government (TNG) in large measure because of the latter's strong Islamist backing, charging that Al Itihaad was taking over the TNG.

NATIONALIZATION OF THE COURTS

In August 2000, a so-called Transitional National Government (TNG) was installed in Mogadishu, and through the Islamic Courts it offered Al Itihaad an opportunity to become institutionalized within the new government. The TNG was the child of a national reconciliation conference held in Arta, Djibouti, that as has been previously noted, received significant international support, save from the United States. Al Itihaad commander and Islamic Courts leader Sheikh Aweys participated in the conference. He welcomed the formation of the new government: "The best choice would be an Islamic government, but anything that would get Somalia out of this mess is one hundred percent acceptable."[32]

The conference assembly elected Abdiqasim Salad Hassan as president. However, significant Somali political figures boycotted the gathering—including some Mogadishu factional leaders and the representatives of Somaliland and Puntland—and their opposition undercut the TNG's objective of becoming a new central government for Somalia. As a result, the TNG never came to control more than parts of Mogadishu and its environs by the end of its three-year mandate.[33] Soon after his selection, TNG President Abdiqasim announced a plan to recruit at least 4,000 police officers to bring law and order back to Mogadishu, and the Islamic Courts were ready to play their hand.

In early 2000, Court leaders from Mogadishu formed a new umbrella organization, the Sharia Implementation Council (*Golaha Fulinta Sharee'ada Islaamka*), in order to better coordinate activities of the diverse courts in the city. Its assembly (*Majlis*) of 63 members elected as its Chairman Ali Dheere with historic ties to Al Itihaad, and Sheikh Aweys was appointed secretary general. According to the International Crisis Group, "The Council's primary functions included prisoner exchanges and occasional joint militia operations, but it also served as a political vehicle for the ambition of Aweys and other court leaders."[34]

As secretary general of the Sharia Implementation Council, Aweys backed the TNG's plans for policing Mogadishu, stating that "we must strengthen the new government and be wary of actions of nonbelievers who want us to follow their leadership."[35] Courts and their paramilitary forces were maneuvering to become the backbone of the TNG law enforcement and judicial system at the urging of the Sharia Implementation Council. Leaders of clan-based militias such Hussein Hoji Bod in northern Mogadishu, Osman Hassan Ali Atto, and Musa Suli Yalahow opposed the formation of the police force.[36] The factional leaders had already offered resistance to Islamic Courts' expansion to the South of Mogadishu, and a TNG force formed from the ranks of Islamic Courts militias would likely pose an additional challenge to the authority of these factional leaders.

In June 2001, the TNG announced that it had "nationalized" the Mogadishu Islamic Courts. The TNG said it had set up its justice ministry in an attempt to reinstitute the judicial system and to tackle issues of law and order. Sheikh Hasan Muhammad, the former chairman of the Mogadishu Islamic Courts, said that the dual function of the Islamic Courts had been reallocated, with their policing role placed under the Ministry of Interior and hearing of cases and issuing decrees under the Ministry of Justice.[37]

The TNG never established an effective administration even in Mogadishu, and after the end of its mandate in August 2003, it faded into complete irrelevance. The incorporation of the sharia courts into the TNG weakened the Islamic courts movement considerably. When the TNG took over the militias of the courts, the Islamic Courts lost the financial backing of the business community, so that when the TNG ended, few of Mogadishu's courts were operational.[38]

During the period of its mandate, however, the TNG reportedly succeeded in attracting considerable funding from Saudi Arabia and sources in other Arab countries. One report said that the TNG received at least $50 million in 2000, from Qatar, Saudia Arabia and the United Arab Emirates.[39] Reports that the TNG had acquired weapons with this overseas funding raises the question as to whether the arms contributed to the building up of arsenals of the Islamic Courts.

Diverse Arab backing for the TNG and the nationalization of the Islamic Court reinforced the perception among many Somali political figures in southern Somalia, in Puntland, and in Somaliland that the TNG was dominated by Islamist, if not jihadist forces, including Al Itihaad. This view of the TNG, which was not without merit, was one factor preventing the TNG from achieving a broader base of support from factional leaders.

In April 2002, the TNG security chief, Ahmad Jilow Adow, offered his fledgling government's support in the war on terror at a time when the TNG had absorbed, at least on paper, the

Islamic Courts into its state apparatus as judiciary and as police including Aweys's Court. At that time, the security chief said:

> We are sure that there are no al Qaeda training bases or garrisons here. But there are some elements who come to Somalia from time to time and there must be an exchange of information about them to enable us to track them down. ... Al Qaeda was very new to me, and we never heard that name before September 11.[40]

At best, Ahmad Jilow Adow's statement appears to have been an underestimation of Al Qaeda's activities in the Mogadishu area and elsewhere in Somalia. According to informants, the intensive links between Al Qaeda and Al Itihaad leaders were well known within Mogadishu military and political elite, and by the time of Al Qaeda's November 2002 terrorist attacks in Mombasa, Mogadishu had replaced Nairobi as Al Qaeda's "nerve center" in East Africa.[41]

An Israeli-based intelligence subscription newsletter made the uncorroborated claim in 2002 that 150 Al Qaeda and Egyptian Islamic Jihad fighters were stationed southwest of the Somali city of Xagar. According to the newsletter, a coalition of Somali supporters of Osama bin Laden sheltered the Xagar fugitive community. "It is made up of local warlords, who receive money, weapons and orders from Colonel Barre Aden Share, known locally as Barre-Hiralle. The colonel reportedly received money, support and fighters from Sheikh Bashir of the fundamentalist Jama Islamiya and Abdulqassim Salaad Hassan, the transitional president of Somalia." According to this source, members of the Al Qaeda team that carried out the 2002 attacks in Mombasa escaped from Kenya by flying to this camp.[42] This report on the flight of Al Qaeda operatives from Kenya differs from the UN's investigation findings.

According to the UN report on the Mombasa attacks, the bombers of the Paradise Hotel used converted fishing boats for transport on at least two occasions, including their escape back to Somalia from Lamu. Weapons used in the Mombasa attacks were smuggled into Kenya by sea from Somalia. Weapons shipped from Somalia to Kenya generally originated in, or were routed through, Djibouti, Eritrea, Ethiopia, United Arab Emirates, and Yemen. The missiles and launchers used in the attempted downing of the Israeli airliner came from either Yemen or Eritrea *via* Somalia.[43] Most of the Al Qaeda operatives who made it back to the Somali capital remained there for several months, living on cash allowances provided by a Sudanese financial controller, the UN panel reported.[44]

In March 2003, Suleiman Abdalla Salim Hemed, one of the Mombassa terrorists, was captured in Mogadishu with the assistance of Somali factional leader Mohamed Dheere. Kenya's national security minister, Chris Murungaru, claimed credit for Hemed's capture and said Hemed had been turned over to U.S. authorities. Hemed's whereabouts are not known at the time of the writing of this book. Somali sources said there were rumors that the U.S. has paid substantial sums of money to the factional leader for handing over Al Qaeda suspects. They said U.S. counterterrorism agents were believed to be operating from a house in Bosaso in Puntland. Gunmen close to Mohamed Dheere also said U.S. agents regularly visited Dheere at his Mogadishu home, and an *Associated Press* reporter saw two of the alleged agents, dressed in regular Western clothing, moving through Mogadishu with a team of bodyguards belonging to Bashir Rageh, a wealthy businessman closely associated with Dheere.[45]

After the Mombasa terrorist attacks, Al Qaeda's small number of cadre in Mogadishu likely functioned more as liaisons between Somali jihadists and the wider international jihadist movement rather than as a force on its own to be reckoned with. Since the Mombasa attack, Somalia has also been used to transit operatives into Kenya, and Kenyan authorities have apprehended a number of suspected terrorists who entered from Somalia or have been linked to Somalia.

CONFRONTATION IN PUNTLAND

Al Itihaad cum Islamic Courts also took its military campaign to Puntland during this period. With Ethiopian support, however, Abdullahi Yusuf's administration succeeded in repulsing what were described as Al Itihaad fighters in January 2000, but later Abdullahi Yusuf also accused Al Itihaad of taking sides in a power struggle over the presidency of Puntland. With the expiration of Abdullahi Yusuf's mandate, Jama Ali Jama, a former military officer under Mohamed Siad Barre and an ally of the TNG, challenged Abdullahi Yusuf as president by convening a conference of elders in Garowe that would seek to replace Yusuf. Abdullahi Yusuf accused Al Itihaad of being behind the conference, and he welcomed Ethiopian military support to keep Al Itihaad and Jama Ali Jama at bay.[46] Al Itihaad reportedly sent fresh recruits to Puntland and with another newly armed group named the Total Somali Liberation Tigers occupied the port city of Bosaso on the Gulf of Aden in 2001. The jihadist coalition claimed that their victory at Bosaso marked the beginning of a new jihad, not only in the northeastern region but in all other parts of Somalia as well as those areas in Kenya and Ethiopia with Somali-speaking populations.[47]

In 2002, Abdullahi Yusuf told the BBC that more than three hundred of his militia had been killed by Al Itihaad forces attempting to overthrow his administration and introduce Islamic rule. He contended that despite defeats on the battlefield the Islamists were taking over civilian life: "They dominate the economic sector, they dominate educational services. They melt into the civic society. They are so powerful that no weak government can challenge them."[48] Indeed, there is evidence to suggest that the business community in Puntland has been supporting Al Itihaad, and that the Al Itihaad had set up Islamic Courts there.

Alarmed by the growth of radical Islam in Puntland, Abdallahi Yusuf decreed in 2002 that only Shafi'iyah, a more traditional form of Islam followed by many Somalis, would be tolerated in Puntland. Several days later, Puntland security forces entered several mosques in Bosaso to compel compliance.[49]

In the post-September 11 environment, claims of Al Itihaad's association with Al Qaeda increased. For instance, Allpuntland.com, a website linked to Abdullahi Yusuf, accused the "extremists of the Itihaad and bin Ladin's al-Qaida," in conjunction with the TNG, of deliberately working toward toppling Abdullahi Yusuf and the dissolution of Puntland as an autonomous region. The website reported that later, after the start of the U.S. campaign against Al Qaeda in Afghanistan, Al Itihaad had opened military training bases in Puntland and had sent reinforcements from Mogadishu via Bosaso in order to hasten a coup in Puntland.

Local Somali leaders in Galkayo said that they had captured 119 young Al Itihaad recruits en route to Bosaso, and that 400 other young men had been sent to Bosaso to travel to Afghanistan to support Al Qaeda after Sepember 11.[50] Another report said that Al Itihaad commander Sheikh Aweys had sent more than 300 Al Itihaad militia men to Afghanistan to fight the United States.[51]

Adbdullahi Yusuf's opponent Jama Ali Jama denied the existence of Al Itihaad training camps in the region or of any links to bin Laden and accused Abdhullahi Yusuf of making false and exaggerated statements in a bid to draw international attention to himself to benefit from the prevailing international antiterrorism mood.[52] But statements by a former Al Itihaad member, Abdi Ahmed Hussein, appear to confirm the allegations of Al Qaeda and Al Itihaad cooperation during this period. Abdi Ahmed Hussein, who had been an Al Itihaad member for five years in the 1990s, said that Al Qaeda operatives successfully recruited some members of Al Itihaad to fight against American forces in Afghanistan. According to him, right after the United States began the war on terror against Osama bin Laden's Al Qaeda network and the Taliban in Afghanistan, Al Qaeda asked many Al Itihaad members to join and help in the fight. Abdi Ahmed Hussein said that most Al Itihaad men declined, but some eventually went to Afghanistan.[53]

Also, after September 11, Hussein Mohamed Aidid accused Eritrea, Libya, and Djibouti of supplying arms to Al Itihaad, Al Tabliq, Al Islah, and the Al Qaeda network, as well as to Jama Ali Jama. According to Aidid, arms arrived by ship in Bosaso, and by air and ship in Mogadishu, some of which were confiscated by the SRRC at an Al Islah warehouse in Mogadishu.[54]

Sources of Funding

The fluctuation of financial support for Al Itihaad may help explain the changing tactics and the shifting alliances of the organization. In the early 1990s, when Sudanese and Al Qaeda support was strong, Al Itihaad engaged in anti-Ethiopian and anti-United States campaigns. When Ethiopia and Eritrea began their border war in 1998, Al Itihaad found a new patron in Eritrea. Al Itihaad appeared to have been most successful in attracting foreign patrons than in establishing a popular base of support. But as these backers waned in importance, Al Itihaad as an Islamic Court then drew support from elements of the local business community with its promise of restoring law and order as a way of improving the business environment. Al Barakat's contribution was apparently a substantial portion of the business community's support. When factional leaders began to see the Islamic Courts as a rival, Al Itihaad as an Islamic Court merged with the TNG to gain new legitimacy and funding through the nascent state structure.

All the while the abovementioned sources of support have been at play, a mysterious international network of private and public organizations that support Islamic charities also appear to have been active in funding Al Itihaad. Much of this funding reportedly comes from wealthy families and ruling elites in Saudi Arabia, United Arab Emirates, and Kuwait. It should not be forgotten that the Al Qaeda-front and Nairobi-based charities, Mercy International Relief Agency and Help African Peoples, supported both Al Itihaad training camps and its humanitarian work in the mid-1990s.

One Saudi charity that appears to have been a major supporter of Al Itihaad activities, whether in Kenya's North Eastern Province or in Somalia, was the Al Haramain Islamic Foundation, which had a close association with the Saudi government. Al Haramain functioned as a private, charitable, and educational organization dedicated to promoting Islamic teaching throughout the world. A growing amount of its funding derived from grants from other countries, individual Muslim benefactors, and special campaigns that selectively sought donations from Muslim-owned business entities around the world.

In March 2002, the United States and Saudi Arabia joined forces to block funds to Al Haramain's Somalia branch because of its support to Al Itihaad, and in 2003 the charity's Kenyan and Tazanian operations also closed. The Kenyan branch of the foundation had a history of extensive charitable activities in Kenya's North Eastern Province and appears to have been promoting an Al Itihaad agenda there. Al Haramain also allegedly plotted to carry out terrorist attacks against Zanzibar's tourist industry catering to Westerners, and it financed the group that bombed the Western-oriented tourism industry in Bali, Indonesia.

To justify the decision to shut down Al Haramain, the U.S. Department of the Treasury reported that the branch offices of Al Haramain in Somalia were clearly linked to terrorist financing.

> The Somalia office of Al-Haramain is linked to Usama bin Laden's al-Qaida network and Al-Itihaad Al-Islamiya, a Somali terrorist group. Al-Haramain Somalia employed Al Itihaad members and provided them with salaries through Al-Barakaat Bank, which was designated on November 7, 2001 under E.O. 13224 because of its activities as a principal source of funding, intelligence and money transfers for Usama bin Laden.
>
> Al-Haramain Somalia has continued to provide financial support to Al Itihaad. In late December 2001, Al-Haramain Somalia was facilitating the travel of Al Itihaad members in Somalia to Saudi Arabia where the Al Itihaad members planned to apply for residency permits.[55]

In January 2004, the United States reported that Al Haramain branches in Kenya and Tanzania had provided support or had acted on behalf of Al Itihaad and Al Qaeda. A U.S. Department of Treasury press release indicated that Al Haramain was used to transfer funds and that Al Itihaad had also invested in the "legitimate" business activities of Al Haramain.[56]

The Saudi government in 2003 ordered Al Haramain to close all of its overseas branches. Al Haramain stated it had closed branches in Indonesia, Kenya, Tanzania, and Pakistan, but continued monitoring by the United States and Saudi Arabia indicated that these offices and/or former officials associated with these branches continued to operate or had other plans to avoid closure.

COURT REVIVAL AND GROWING CONFRONTATION

After the lapse of the TNG, the Islamic Courts movement reorganized itself into the Union of Islamic Courts and experienced an unprecedented expansion of its authority over Mogadishu. Representatives of ten courts elected Sheikh Sharif Ahmed as chairman of the confederation, and Sheikh Aweys became one of his deputies.[57] Sheikh Sharif Ahmed has been characterized as a cleric associated with the more moderate

Sufi association *Ahlu Sunna wal Jama'a*, and is said to disapprove of the jihadism within the UIC. Ahlu Sunna wal Jama'a was created in 1991 to counter the influence of the most radical Islamist trends. The movement is home to politically motivated sheikhs whose primary goal is to unify the Sufi community under one unified leadership capable of consolidating the powers of the three primary Sufi Tariqas—the Qadiriyya, Salihiyya and Ahmadiyya—into one front whose sole mission is the rejuvenation of the "traditionalist" interpretation of Islam and the de-legitimization of the beliefs and political views of Al Itihaad and other radical Islamic movements.[58] Two courts, the Ifka Halane (closely associated with Aweys) and the Lugeeye, have been associated with jihadist militancy. On various occasions, both moderate and militant UIC leaders have made known their opposition to the TFG seated in Baidoa.

After a group of factional leaders, including some TFG officials, set up the Alliance for the Restoration of Peace and Counter-Terrorism (ARPCT) in Jowhar, Somalia, in February 2006, the contempt of UIC leadership for the TFG appears to have hardened. The United States had reportedly promoted the formation of the grouping and supplied it with covert financial assistance. UN experts monitoring the arms embargo on Somalia had been told that "financial support was being provided to help organize the structure of a militia force created to counter the threat posed by the growing militant fundamentalist movement in central and southern Somalia." The United States also apparently wanted the antiterrorism militia to capture and turn over to U.S. officials Al Qaeda operatives in Somalia who had taken part in terrorist bombings of the U.S. embassies in Nairobi and in Dar es Salaam. By May 2006, the ARPCT had engaged UIC militia's in Mogadishu in heavy fighting. The UIC forces routed the ARPCT fighters and consolidated their authority over Mogadishu and expanded it to other areas of southern Somalia.[59]

International media attention focused on these development, but the truth of the matter is that the conflict between factional militias and the Islamic Court militias, especially the Aweys faction, had been underway for some time, and there is little wonder as to why factional leaders would see the growing power of the UIC as a threat. The failed ARPCT campaign may have only accelerated a process of confrontation that was

Jihadism in Somalia's Islamic Courts

already well underway. The gulf between the TFG and the UIC only widened, and the TFG, which many considered to be weak militarily, expressed its concern that the then more powerful UIC would launch an attack on its headquarters in Baidoa.

In reaction to the ARPCT offensive, UIC chairman Sheikh Sharif Ahmed said,

> Our view is that the TFG has failed to save the country. It is a government established outside the country. It was set up by the government of Ethiopia. The people invited and the manner in which they were invited, was decided by IGAD and the biggest influence and interference came from the Addis Ababa government....
>
> Apart from that, we see that they [TFG] have now added to the country's problem. They now want to bring foreign [Ethiopian] troops into the country. Government ministers were among those responsible for initiating fighting in Mogadishu. In truth, we see that they are not capable of meeting the needs and aspiration of the Somali people.[60]

Ethiopian troops had reportedly been dispatched in July 2006 by Addis to Baidoa to protect the TFG from what appeared to be an imminent assault by UIC forces.

INTERNATIONALIZATION OF THE CONFRONTATION

An internationalization of the conflict had taken place. Clandestine U.S. military assistance was being channeled to the ARPCT. Ethiopia troops were reported to have arrived in Baidoa in July 2006, although the Ethiopian foreign minister Seyoum Mesfin denied this. On the other side, Eritrea, with whom Ethiopia had fought a border war from 1998 to 2000, was supplying weapons to armed Ethiopian opposition fighters inside Somalia as well as to Sheikh Aweys's forces, whose Al Itihaad has a history of actions against Ethiopia. An alliance between Ogaden National Liberation Front (ONLF) and Aweys's forces only spelled troubled for Ethiopia, as both the ONLF and the Al Itihaad wanted to separate the Ogaden, or what Al Itihaad calls Western Somalia, from Ethiopia. Fighters of another Ethiopian armed opposition group, the Oromo Liberations Front, were also reported to be supporting the UIC in its 2006 campaign. There was a real threat that the Somali's internal conflict would once again become regional, and Al Itihaad figures once again were playing a central role in widening conflict.

An array of foreign forces were reportedly backing the UIC forces in its offensive against factional militias in the summer of 2006. There were reports of fighters from both OLF and the ONLF assisting UIC forces. Eritrea also transported 270 trained and equipped ONLF fighters from Eritrea to Dhusamareeb, Somalia, in May 2005.[61]

International jihadists were also engaged on the side of Aweys's forces. A July 2006 video seen on an international jihadist website showed images of non-Somali jihadist fighters, thought to be Arabs, supporting UIC forces in combat against factional militias.[62] Days earlier, in an audio tape attributed to Osama bin Laden, the Al Qaeda leader called on the Somali people to support the UIC and to reject the TFG. Bin Laden warned foreign forces against intervening on Somali soil: "We pledge that we will fight your soldiers on the land of Somalia and we will fight you on your own land if you dispatch troops to Somalia."[63]

The TFG prime minister, Ali Mohamed Gedi, reacted angrily to Bin Laden's audio statement on the conflict in Somalia, saying that "the Somali People were practicing Islam before the birth of Osama bin Laden and his ancestors, so Osama should leave the Somali affairs to the Somalis."[64]

As these Somali and international forces faced off, Sheikh Aweys reportedly moved within the UIC to consolidate control of the UIC forces. On June 24, 2006, he was appointed head of the Majlis Al Shura Council, a policy-making body that oversees the UIC,[65] and within days his jihadist allies within the UIC reportedly had pushed aside moderate leaders. Sheikh Aweys is said to have installed like-minded lieutenants to other key posts and undermined the authority of moderates such as Sheikh Sharif Ahmed. Sheikh Aweys's growing authority seemed to place him both on the brink of a regional war and in a position to continue his military quest to create a pan-Somali caliphate. His actions and those of his followers seemed to breathe new life into the jihadist dream of dominating the Horn of Africa region.

NOTES

1. Sabina Castelfranco, "Islamic Militants in Somalia Vandalize Italian Cemetery," *VOANews.com*, January 20, 2005, http://www.voanews.com/english/archive/2005-01/2005-01-20-voa32.cfm?CFID=72973265 &CFTOKEN=78870319; "Somalia: Militamen Dig Up Colonial Cemetery," *New York Times*, January 20, 2005; "Somalis Build Mosque on Cemetery," *BBCNews*, January 26, 2005, http://news.bbc.co.uk/2/hi/africa/4208771.stm.
2. "Thousands Crowd Camp: A Struggle to Keep People and Hope Alive," *The Toronto Star*, October 22, 2006, http://www.thestar.com/NASApp/cs/ContentServer?pagename=thestar/Layout/Article_Type1& call_pageid=971358637177&c=Article&cid=1161467438938.
3. International Crisis Group, *Counter-Terrorsim in Somalia: Losing Hearts and Minds?* Africa Report no. 95, July 11, 2005, and International Crisis Group, *Somalia's Islamists*.
4. Bruck Shewareged, "It Was Obvious from the Start that Al-Ithihad was in a Position to Exploit the Chaos in Somalia (Interview with Ato Medhane Tadesse, Center for Policy Research and Dialogue)," *The Reporter* (Addis Ababa), July 17, 2006.
5. "Nations Arming Somali Factions, U.N. Report Says," *Reuters*, November 13, 2006; Robert F. Worth, "U.N. Says Somalis Helped Hezobollah Fighters," *New York Times*, November 15, 2006.
6. "Command of the Somali Police Killed in Mogadishu," *Arabicnews.com*, January 25, 2005, http://www.arabicnews. com/ansub/Daily/Day/050125/2005012508.html.
7. International Crisis Group, *Counter-Terrorism in Somalia*, 6.
8. Chris Tomlinson, "Is Somalia a Haven for al-Qaeda?," *Associated Press*, June 20, 2006.
9. Rod Norland, "Heroes, Terrorists and Osama," *Newsweek*, July 22, 2006
10. Tomlinson, "Is Somalia a haven for al-Qaeda?"
11. "Somali Islamists Deny Suicide Order, Vow to Fight Enemies of Allah," *Agence France-Presse (AFP)*, November 4, 2006.
12. André Le Sage, "Stateless Justice in Somalia: Formal and Informal Rule of Law Initiatives," *Center for Human Dialog Report*, July 2005, 14.
13. "Understanding Somalia," *Addis Fortune*, n.d., http://www.addisfortune.com/Understanding%20Somalia-6.htm.
14. Ibid, 49.
15. International Crisis Group, *Somalia's Islamists*, 19.
16. Mogadishu Political Report, October 26, 1996, http://www.netnomad.com/garcadde3.html.

17. "Somalia: IRIN Interview with Islamic Courts Chairman Hassan Sheik Mohamed Abdi," *IRIN,* August 25, 2000, http://irinnews.org/webspecials/somalia_npc/20000825.asp.
18. Somalia: IRIN Interview with Hasan Shire Sheik, Co-director of Dr Ismail Juma'le Human Rights Centre, Mogadishu, *IRIN,* October 2, 2000, http://www.irinnews.org/webspecials/somalia_npc/20001002b.asp.
19. International Crisis Group, *Somalia's Islamists,* 20.
20. Shinn, "Ethiopia: Coping with Islamic Fundamentalism."
21. "Somalia Gets New Telecoms," *BBC News,* April 30, 2002, http://news.bbc.co.uk/1/business/1959540.stm.
22. The Office of the Coordinator for Counter Terrorism, U.S. Department of State, *Comprehensive List of Terrorists and Groups Identified under Executive Order 13224,* December 31, 2001, http://www.state.gov/s/ct/rls/fs/2001/6531.htm.
23. Yehudit Barsky, "Prime Suspects: Osama Bin Laden and Al Qaeda," *The Review,* Australia/Israel Jewish Affairs Council, October 2001, http://www.aijac.org.au/review/2001/2610/prime_suspect.html.
24. "Disaster Beckons as US Cuts Lifeline," *IRIN,* November 8, 2001, http://allafrica.com/stories/printable/200111080274.html.
25. "Somalia Gets New Telecoms Firm," *BBC News,* April 30, 2002, http://news.bbc.co.uk/1/hi/business/1959540.stm.
26. "Mogadishu Factions Meet to Narrow Gap," *Xinhua,* February 25, 1999.
27. Ibid.
28. Peter Maas, "Court Martial: An Islamic Militia Gains Ground in Somalia," *The New Republic,* March 13, 2000, http://www.petermaass.com/core.cfm?p=1&mag=18&magtype+1.
29. Somalia's Islamic Courts Goad Arch-rivals into Rare Alliance," *AFP,* 1999, http://www.metimes.com/issue99-46/reg/somalia_s_islamic.htm.
30. *AFP,* December 12, 1999, http://www.reliefweb.int/w/rwb/nst/0/00a663878fb4334f885256879005b10c8?OpenDocument.
31. Maas, "Court Martial."
32. "Somalis Fully Support Forthcoming Government," n.d., http://www.banadir.com/fully.htm.
33. Ken Menkhaus, *Somalia: A Situation Analysis,* Center for Documentation and Research, UNHCR, November 2000, WRITENET Paper no. 07/2000.
34. International Crisis Group, *Somalia's Islamists,* 20.
35. "Somali Warlords Oppose Police Force," *BBC,* September 11, 2000, http//:news.bbc.co.uk/1/hi/world/africa/919883.stm.
36. Ibid.

37. "TNG Announces Islamic Courts "Nationalised," *IRIN*, June 23, 2001, http://allafrica.com/stories/printable/200106230048.html; "Al-Ittihad's US Assets Frozen," *IRIN*, September 25, 2001, http://allafrica.com/stories/printable/200109250252.html.
38. Le Sage, "Stateless Justice," 47; Le Sage, "Prospects for Al Itihad and Islamist Radicalism in Somalia," *Review of African Political Economy* 27, no. 89 (,September 2001).
39. "Somalia's New War Lord Abdiqasim Salad," *The Republican* (Hargeisa), September 23, 2000, http://www.somalilandforum.com/news/the_republican?Republican-Editorials2.htm.
40. "Somali Security Chief Seeks Help in Terror Fight," *Business Recorder*, April 4, 2002, http://www.paksearch.com/br2002/Apr/4/INTERVIEW-Somali.
41. "Two Terror Suspects Deported," *The Standard*, May 20, 2004, http://allafrica.com/stories/200405200460.html; Stephen Muiruri, "Suspect Terrorists Sent Back to Kenya," *The Nation*, December 4, 2002, http://allafrica.com/stories/200212040045.html; "State Links Two to Al Qaeda Cell," *The East African Standard*, July 6, 2004, http://allafrica.com/stories/200407061166.html.
42. "Mombasa Bomber Fazul's Secret Hideaway," *Debka-Net-Weekly*, December 13, 2002, 2, issue 18, http://archives.econ.utah.edu/archives/a-list/2002w51/msg00009.htm.
43. "The Journey of Haroun Fazul," *Frontline*, http://www.pbs.org/wgbh/pages/frontline/shows/saudi/fazul/.
44. Kevin J. Kelley, "How Al Qaeda Carried Out Paradise Hotel Bombing," *The East African*, November 11, 2003, http://allafrica.com/stories/200311111068.html; James Macharia, "Somalia Says Qaeda Suspect Handed to U.S. Agents, *Reuters*, March 19, 2003, http://www.intellnet.org/news/2003/03/19/18151-1.html.
45. Declan Walsh, "Al-Qa'ida Used War-torn Somalia as a Base to Plan and Launch Mombassa Hotel Bombing" *Saylac.com*, November 2003, http://www.saylac.com/news/war-torn.htm; Chris Tomlinson, "Somali Network Aids Hunt for Terrorists," *Associated Press*, November 6, 2003, http://www.boston.com/news/world/articles/2003/11/06/somali_network_aids_hunt_for_terrorists?mode=PF.
46. Hussein Ali Soke, "Is Somalia a Safe-haven for Terrorists?," *africanconflict.org*, http://allafrica.com/stories/printable/2000201090390.html; David Shinn, "Ethiopia," *Africa Notes*, no. 7, February 2002, http://mailgate.supereva.it/soc/soc.culture.somalia/msg02561.html.
47. Joint British-Danish Fact-finding Mission, *Report on Political, Security and Human Rights*, September 1-24, 2001.

48. Mike Thomas, "Terrorism in Somalia," *BBC News,* November 30, 2002, http://www.bbc.co.uk/radio4/today/reports/archive/international/somalia_terrorists.shtm.
49. U.S. State Department, Bureau of Democracy, Human Rights and Labor, *International Religious Freedom Report, 2003*, http://www.state.gov/g/drl/rls/irf/2003/23752pf.htm.
50. Press Release, DGPL, Galkayo, October 9, 2001.
51. "The Elements in the Somali Equation: TNG, Al-Ittixad, USA, UN, etc.?" *Qandala,* 2002, http://www.qandalo.tripod.com/id114.htm.
52. Anton Christen, "Bin Laden's Shadow in Somalia: Islamist Activities Amid Crumbling Government and Clan Rivalries," *NZZ Online*, November 22, 2001, http://www.nzz.ch/english/background/2001/11/22_somalia.html.
53. Alisha Ryu, "Somalia Terror," *VOANews*, February 23, 2004, http://www.help-for-you.com/news/Feb2004/scripts/39e7dd62.html.
54. "Hussein Aideed Accuses Asmara, Tripoli and Djibouti—Calls for Air Embargo on Somalia," *The Daily Monitor* (Addis Ababa), March 19, 2002, http://allafrica.com/stories/200203190399.html.
55. U.S. Department of the Treasury, *Press Release: Designations of Somalia and Bosnia-Herzegovina Branches of Al-Haramain Islamic Foundation*, March 11, 2002, http://www.fas.org/irp/news/2002/03/dot031102fact.html.
56. Ibid., *Treasury Announces Joint Action with Saudi Arabia Against Four Branches of Al-Haramain in the Fight Against Terrorist Financing*, JS-1108, January 22, 2004, http://www.ustreas.gov/press/releases/js1108.htm.
57. Le Sage, "Stateless Justice," 47.
58. Anouar Boukhars, "Understanding Somali Islamism," *Terrorism Monitor*, 4, no. 10 (May 18, 2006), http://www.jamestown.org/terrorism/news/article.php?articleid=2369999&printthis=1.
59. The factional leaders included Musa Sudi Yalahow, Omar Mohamoud Finish, Botan Issa, Bashir Raghe Shirar, and Mohamed Afrah Qanyare. "Somali Warlords Hold 'Secret Anti-Terrorism' Talks with US Agents: Witnesses," *AFP*, February 28, 2006; Emily Wax and Karen DeYoung, "U.S. Secretly Backing Warlords in Somalia," *Washington Post*, May 17, 2006.
60. "Interview with Shaykh Sharif Shaykh Ahmed, Union of Islamic Courts Chairman," *IRIN*, June 22, 2006.
61. The UN report further said Eritrea maintained its contact with the groups through its envoy based in Mogadishu. Elias Haite Talaze, who is reported to operate through informal local networks, is predominantly engaged in "dealings with dissident Ethiopian ethnic groups who are concentrated in Banaadir and the Lower Shebelle regions." "UN Report Implicates Eritrea in Support for Al-Itihaad," *The

Reporter (Addis Ababa), June 17. 2006, http://allafrica.com/stories/200606190149.html.

62. Chris Tomlinson, "Video Shows Arabs Fighting in Somalia," *Associated Press*, July 5, 2006.
63. "Leave Somalia Alone, Alleged bin Laden Tape Says," *CBC News*, July 1, 2006, http://www.cbc.ca/story/world/national/2006/07/01/binladen-tape.html?print.
64. "Somali PM Slams Osama bin Laden," *Shabelle Media Network* (Mogadishu), July 2, 2006, http://allafrica.com/stories/200607030679.html.
65. Rod Norland, "Heroes, Terrorists and Osama," *Newsweek*, July 22, 2006, http://ethiomedia.com/carepress/aweys_interview.html.

Chapter Four

ERITREAN ISLAMIC JIHAD/ ERITREAN ISLAMIC SALVATION FRONT

The Eritrean Islamic Jihad (EIJ) has been the principal Eritrean jihadist organization since the late 1980s. The EIJ has adhered to a Wahabist view of Islam, has advocated the establishment of an Islamic state in Eritrea and has engaged in an armed struggle to achieve it. During the course of its history, the EIJ received support from the National Islamic Front (NIF) government in Sudan and from Al Qaeda when Sudan was hosting bin Laden. However, in the fall of 2004, under the name of the Eritrean Islamic Salvation Front (EISF), the EIJ abandoned its goal of creating an Islamic state, most likely as a way of aligning its objectives with that of the Eritrean National Alliance (ENA), of which it is a member. The ENA is an umbrella organization of opposition political groups formed in 1998 against the Eritrean government led by President Isaias Afwerki.

According to EIJ's secretary general, Sheikh Mohamed Amer, the movement changed its name to the Islamic Salvation Front (*Harakat al Khalas al Islami*) during its August 1998

Congress held in Khartoum, Sudan. The name change followed closely on the heels of the U.S. cruise missile attack on a Sudanese pharmaceutical plant after Al Qaeda's bombing of the U.S. embassies in East Africa and also came in the context of the formation of the ENA. At a news conference Sheikh Amer explained that the change of his organization's name stemmed from the need to appear different from other movements that used the term jihad—an apparent reference to terrorist organizations such as the Egyptian Islamic Jihad of Ayman al-Zawahiri and the Islamic Jihad (Palestine), both of which, like the EIJ, had also been hosted by the NIF government in Sudan. Sheikh Amer reiterated, nonetheless, the movement's objective of forcibly overthrowing the government of Eritrean President Isaias Afwerki and replacing it with an Islamic government.[1] Many observers continue to use the "Eritrean Islamic Jihad" appellation for the EISF, and for the sake of simplicity the organization will be identified below by combining the acronyms of the two names as the EIJ/EISF.

The umbrella ENA, which has received backing from both Ethiopia and Sudan, has espoused a strategy of armed action against strategic targets such as radio and TV stations inside Eritrea.[2] However, the EIJ/EISF has a history of being much more aggressive militarily than the ENA in general and has engaged in an intermittent armed conflict with the Eritrean government since late 1992. The intensity of EIJ/EISF's military actions seemed to reflect the state of relations between Asmara and Khartoum and has underscored the EIJ/EISF dependence on Sudan for rear bases and material support. This dependency on Sudan, however, has also created the impression that in such actions the EIJ/EISF has acted more as a surrogate of Sudan than a force waging a war on behalf of its own Islamist objectives for Eritrea. At times, the EIJ/EISF has targeted civilians, especially foreign civilian targets. In 1998, for instance, it boasted of destroying many joint Eritrean-Israeli ventures. At the height of its military operation in 1995, the EIJ/EISF was estimated to have a fighting force of 500.[3]

Another Islamist organization, the Eritrean People's Congress, has also been member of the umbrella Eritrean National Alliance and is believed to possess an armed wing called the Eritrean Reform Movement, which operates outside the framework of the umbrella organization.[4] There is little information in the public domain about either the Eritrean People's Congress or the Eritrean Islamic Reform Movement, although in March 2006 the Eritrean Islamic Reform Movement issued a statement saying that it had carried out actions inside Eritrea against government forces.[5]

The base of support for the Eritrean Islamist organizations lies in the Gash Barka region of Eritrea and among Eritrean refugees living in Sudan. Gash Barka, located along the Sudanese and Ethiopian borders, has been the area of Eritrea most ravaged by the wars of Eritrean independence between 1962 and 1991, and most recently during the 1998-2000 border war between Eritrea and Ethiopia. The impact of these wars on the people of Gash Barka created a set of cultural and economic grievances that have provided fertile soil for Islamic radicalization.

ISLAMIC POLITICAL EXPRESSION IN ERITREA: BACKGROUND

The roots of recent Eritrean Islamist political movements are traceable to the 1981 collapse of the Eritrean Liberation Front (ELF) as an effective military and political force; it was the first movement to call for the independence of Eritrea from Ethiopia. With the ELF's defeat at the hands of the rival Eritrea People's Liberation Front, many Eritrean Muslims lost the one secular nationalist organization that represented their interests. Eritrean Islamists, who had been held in detention by the ELF and were freed after the collapse of the ELF, sought to fill the political vacuum, and created various Islamist organizations that rivaled the weakened ELF.[6]

In Eritrea, the characteristics of political movements since the 1950s have been shaped by the existence of relatively distinct Christian and Islamic communities. Eritrean Muslims dominated the ELF from its formation in 1958 until its demise as an effective organization in 1981. Young Eritrean Muslims attending Al Azar University in Cairo had formed the ELF in 1958, and throughout its existence the ELF continued to draw its leadership largely from Eritrean Muslim intellectuals and drew popular support largely from Eritrea's Muslim communities, most of which were located in Eritrea's lowland areas.

The ELF followed a secular line, and unlike the Eritrean Islamic Jihad, never advocated the establishment of an Islamic state in Eritrea, despite efforts by the then Ethiopian government to portray it as an Islamic extremist organization. This portrayal by the Ethiopian government was part of a divide-and-rule tactic that preyed on the fears of Christian populations, and that helped sow the seeds of mistrust between the two religious groups.[7]

The ELF leadership defined its independence struggle against the Ethiopian government in anticolonial and nationalist terms. The Italians had ruled Eritrea from 1890 until World War II, when the British captured the Italian colony. It later was administered as a UN Trust Territory. Then in 1952, Eritrea became federated with Ethiopia and enjoyed substantial autonomy, including its own parliament; but the Ethiopian government eroded Eritrea's political freedoms and political autonomy. Ethiopia annexed Eritrea as a province in 1962 in violation of the UN agreement. This annexation gave rise to the ELF's armed struggle.

Support for Eritrean independence had historically been stronger among Eritrea's Muslim communities. The country's population is about evenly divided between Christians and Muslims. Eritrea's Muslim populations live largely in the lowland regions of the country and are pastoralists. They consist of various ethnic groups, including the Tigre, the Afar, and the Kunama.[8]

Eritrea's Orthodox Christian population is composed largely of Tigrinyan-speaking peoples who occupy much of the agriculturally fertile Kebessa Plateau in the central region of the country, and are historically agriculturalists. Historically and culturally the Christian population has close ties to the Tigray region of Ethiopia. Throughout the independence war against Emperor Haile Selassie's Ethiopia, the Tigrinyan Christians in Eritrea for the most part continued to support union with Ethiopia. Only when the pro-Soviet military junta, known as the Derg, overthrew the emperor in a bloody coup in 1974 and launched its "Red Terror" of Marxist-Leninist reforms, did Eritrea's Christians begin to support the independence struggle in large numbers.

A splinter group from the ELF composed mainly of Tigrinyan intellectuals who had attended the University of Addis Ababa and led by the present Eritrean president, Isaias Afwerki, formed the rival Eritrean People's Liberation Front

(EPLF). Although the EPLF contained a grouping of Muslims from the Northern Red Sea Region in its leadership, the EPLF's political strategy overall concentrated more on organizing its support among Eritrea's Tigrinyan-speaking Christians and eschewed what it considered the tradition-bound backwardness of the mainly Muslim ELF.

Fighting between the ELF and EPLF hastened the demise of the ELF as a political and military force, and it splintered into several competing organizations. In the vacuum created by the ELF's breakup, Muslim political figures in the Gash Barka region turned to Islam as an organizing tool to redress their grievances, and the success of the mujahidin in Afghanistan inspired many into believing that Islam could be a powerful political organizing tool. The Sudanese government and groups within Saudi Arabia attempted to support the Islamist movements in Eritrea. The Sudanese government was particularly active in developing Islamist support among the large Eritrean refugee population in Sudan.[9]

The EPLF's military forces helped bring down the Derg government in Ethiopia in 1991. After the 1993 UN-sponsored referendum that gave independence to Eritrea, the EPLF took over governance of the country. In 1994, the EPLF changed its name to the People's Front for Democracy and Justice (PFDJ).

THE GASH BARKA CONTEXT AND MUSLIM GRIEVANCES

Historically, the EIJ/EISF has enjoyed a base of support among the Tigre population of Gash Barka. The Tigre people comprise about 35 percent of the country's total population. The Gash Barka Region, which borders both Sudan and Ethiopia's Tigray Province, has been the part of Eritrea most affected by the 30-year independence war and most recently by the 1998-2000 border war between Eritrea and Ethiopia. During the period of independence, hundreds of thousands of its residence abandoned their traditional lands for safe havens in Sudan or became internally displaced. Tigre Muslims from Gash Barka comprised the vast majority of Eritrean refugees in Sudan; their numbers have been estimated as 600,000 in 1994 and 328,000 in 1997.[10]

As large segments of the Gash Barka population became displaced, over the years the region witnessed an increasing influx of Tigrinyan-speaking Christian settlers from the highlands. This immigration created conditions for an economic clash in Gash Barka, as Christian farmers moved into areas once used by displaced Muslim pastoralists. Some of the returning refugees and the internally displaced had to confront the reality that some of the most fertile lands were now in the hands of the Christian farmers. In its refugee reintegration program, the Eritrean government reportedly placed conditions on the returnees to prevent the settlers from being displaced. This policy reinforced the perception that the government with its history of Christian support was favoring the Christian population and fueled Muslim opposition. The secretary general of the Islamic Salvation Front, Sheikh Amer, said in January 2004, "We are for liberty, justice, democracy and individual rights and the return of land to its rightful owners."[11]

The arrival of the Christian settlers also provoked what may be described as cultural resentment within Gash Barka's Muslim community, which largely subscribes to traditional Muslim values. Because of the Islamic prohibition of alcohol consumption, many Gash Barka Muslims took exception to the appearance of bars catering to Christian settler communities. For the first time, many Muslims also had to come to terms with the existence of non-Muslim schools in their traditional areas. In the words of EIJ/EISF Deputy Amir Abul Bara' Hassan Salman, "Supporting Jihad and the Mujahideen is the way to remove the nightmare of degradation and humiliation which has rested on the chests of our community in its various forms."[12]

Eritrean government linguistic policies since independence have also contributed to a growing sense that Tigrinyan Christian cultural colonization was occurring in predominately Muslim areas. Arabic had a strong presence in the region—a presence that was fortified by the large number of refugees living in the Sudan and by the sizeable Eritrean migrant-worker population in Arab-speaking Middle East countries. Many Muslim leaders had anticipated a return to the policy of the 1940s, 1950s and 1960s when both Tigrinyan and Arabic enjoyed status as the two official languages of Eritrea under British and UN rule. Much to their disappointment, the EPLF government adopted a "no official language policy" after independence, which, according to Muslim activists, has had the practical result of Tigrinyan becoming the *de facto* official language in business and government.[13]

The opposition ENA, of which EIJ/EISF is a member, has accommodated Muslim grievances on language and the judicial system in its political program. It acknowledges the right of Muslims to apply sharia in matters that guide their lives, as Christians have the right to order their daily lives in accordance to their religious beliefs. As for the issue of national languages, it declares that Tigrinya and Arabic shall be the official languages of Eritrea, adding that the nationalities of Eritrea retain the inalienable right to use and develop their languages.[14]

Even prior to independence distrust of the EPLF among Muslims hailing from Gash Karba had been high. Particularly decisive in creating Muslim enmity in Gash Karba toward the EPLF had been the conscription campaign of Muslim youth, especially girls, which the EPLF carried out in 1983 when it was still an armed rebel movement. The conscription met with resistance by the Muslim traditionalists who objected especially to the call up of girls, and, according to the EIJ/EISF, this led to the death of many Muslim civilians. In the words of EIJ/EISF Deputy Amir Abul Bara' Hassan Salman, "...the regime pointed its guns to the hearts of the unarmed Muslim citizens in order to forcibly conscript Eritreans into the army. Hundreds of Muslim civilians were killed by the regime in this process of conscription."[15]

The severe restrictions that the Eritrean government imposed on independent political organizations also created a problem for many returnees who could not legally bring their organizations, formed in exile, back with them to Eritrea after independence from Ethiopia was achieved. This meant that such political organizations could only operate underground, as the authoritarian nature of the Eritrean regime did not provide an outlet for democratic aspirations.[16]

JIHAD AND THE COUNTER ATTACK

After the EPLF occupied Eritrea's capital, Asmara, in May 1991, the EIJ/EISF, which had been formed in 1988, launched an armed struggle against what it termed the "Christian regime" governing Eritrea with the aim of establishing an Islamic state. The first serious incidents of guerrilla warfare occurred at the end of 1992. EIJ/EISF members laid mines on desert tracks near the Sudanese border and infiltrated small groups of fighters inside Eritrea. In September 1993, new clashes took place, and the government captured several EIJ/EISF members who confessed they had been trained in camps inside Sudan. The government also said its forces killed several EIJ/EISF fighters from Afghanistan, Morocco, and Yemen. These foreign fighters were most likely part of bin Laden's Al Qaeda network then operating from Sudan.[17]

The fledgling Eritrean government had to contend with a hostile neighbor, Sudan, bent on its Islamist expansionism and on undermining what Khartoum regarded as growing U.S. influence in the region. In response to the aggression, Eritrea broke off relations with Sudan,[18] and countered Sudan's hostility by hosting Sudanese armed opposition groups within its borders. When the first EIJ/EISF commando from Sudan was intercepted on Eritrea territory in January 1994, the Asmara government reacted strongly and threatened reprisals against the Sudanese. As the skirmishes escalated throughout the year, the Sudanese opposition, particularly the northern Muslim opposition, began arriving in Asmara. The following year, the presence of the Sudanese opposition in Eritrea became official when the Eritrean government finally broke off diplomatic relations with Khartoum and installed the Sudanese opposition in Sudan's embassy in Asmara.[19]

The government of President Isaias also took harsh measures domestically to ferret out its militant Islamic opponents and to undermine what it perceived as a growing Islamic fundamentalist threat. The harshness of these measures gave the EIJ/EISF further justification for its jihad against the "Christian regime," and the EIJ/EISF characterized its jihad as a defense of the Muslim populations of Eritrea.

After independence, Islamic schools and religious institutions in Gash Barka became increasingly fundamentalist. In reaction, the Eritrean government closed many of these institutions and sought to curtail their external financial support, reportedly Islamic charities based in Saudi Arabia. The EIJ/EISF called this "intellectual terror against the Muslims." According to EIJ/EISF, "the regime regards every Muslim who practices his religion and adheres to its obligations and cares for his honor as a danger, so they filled their prisons with the pious Muslims, teachers and students, politicians, leaders, and the common people...."[20]

The government's repressive actions appear to have been designed to quash support for the EIJ/EISF. According to an investigative report by the opposition Awate.com, beginning in 1994, a number of schoolteachers in areas of EIJ/EISF support were jailed and disappeared. "Mobile squads under the command of Brigadier General Tekheste, aka, Shaleq Tekheste, instilled fear among the citizenry."[21] In late 1996 and 1997, there were a number of skirmishes between government forces and those of the EIJ/EISF. Each blamed the other for several attacks against civilian targets and murders of foreign nationals. The government reportedly rounded up and executed scores of civilians from Seber, Sheab, Gedged and Shebah. According to the opposition, the government used its campaign against "jihadist sympathizers" as a cover for a larger campaign against all of its political opponents.[22]

The EIJ/EISF has complained of the general repressive character of the Eritrean government, and not only measures directed against Muslims. These complaints included political detentions, politically motivated killings, and lack of due process. The EIJ/EISF Deputy Amir Abul Bara' Hassan Salman described such actions as "the broad political terror against the entire Eritrean population that is stopping them from expressing their views, opinions, or thoughts with respect to the widespread corruption or with respect to their right to participate in the administration of the country."[23]

The EIJ/EISF has also been critical of the mismanagement of the economy by the ruling PFDJ. The EIJ/EISF has claimed that the PFDJ has imposed unreasonable foreign trade restrictions and promotes the ruling party's control of businesses. It has accused the ruling party of enriching itself at the expense of the rest of the country.

No information has been found on EIJ/EISF military operations inside Eritrea during the period of the 1998-2000 Ethiopian-Eritrean border war, when Eritrea and Sudan were in a period of *détente*. Sudan's support for EIJ/EISF military actions inside Eritrea seems to have been sacrificed on the altar of Khartoum's political expediency. However, with Ethiopian acquiescence, the ENA reportedly attempted to mobilize support in Eritrea's western regions after the Ethiopian military wrested control of that from the Eritrean government.[24]

In 2003 and in 2004, the EIJ/EISF appears to have returned to its tactics of intermittent warfare against the Eritrean government, as Eritrea returned to its policy of supporting elements of the Sudanese opposition. In September 2003, the ENA, which claimed its members were carrying out minor guerrilla attacks against President Isaias Afewerki's government, announced that they would launch a joint armed action to end "dictatorship" in Asmara. According to Huroy Tadle Beyrow, ENA secretary general: "Each of the 13 organizations forming our alliance, having their troops on the ground, believe now in uniting our efforts in one army and moving for action inside Eritrea."[25]

Asmara accused Khartoum of backing the EIJ/EISF once again, saying that the EIJ/EISF has been carrying out attacks on its territory from eastern Sudan. Khartoum denied the charges.[26] Operating from positions within Sudan, EIJ/EISF planted mines in the buffer zone separating Eritrea and Ethiopia monitored by the United Nations Mission in Ethiopia and Eritrea. In March 2004, a mine blast killed five members of an Eritrean militia, including a colonel.[27] The Eritrean government implicated the EIJ/EISF in the killing of three civilians as a result of a bomb blast at a hotel in the town of Tesseney. Eritrea's government also said an unspecified jihadist organization based in Sudan was responsible for a May 2004 bomb blast in Barentu that killed five people and wounded another ninety.[28] The umbrella Eritrean National Alliance that included the EIJ/EISF claimed responsibility for the Barentu blast.[29] The government also accused the EIJ/EISF of being behind the 2003 murder in western Eritrea of a British geologist and two local staff members of the international relief organization Mercy Corps; but the EIJ/EISF denied involvement in these incidents.[30]

The EIJ/EISF's on-again, off-again military actions appear to reflect the state of relations between Khartoum and Asmara. When relations between the two governments have gone sour, reports of EIJ/EISF operations appear, and in periods of warming relations, EIJ/EISF military actions subside. So, after 2004, when most Sudanese opposition groups either signed agreements with Khartoum or entered into peace negotiations, reports on EIJ/EISF military operations also faded.

INTERNATIONAL JIHADISM

During the period of his influential presence in Sudan in the 1990s, the EIJ/EISF maintained close relations with Osama bin Laden and his paramilitary organization. Bin Laden gave the EIJ/EISF a seat on his advisory council that consisted of several jihadist organizations. In this period, Sudanese government support to the EIJ/EISF appears to have closely tracked that provided by bin Laden. He provided financial support and military training to the EIJ/EISF; and the Sudanese government provided safe houses and arsenal.

A source close to the Eritrean government suggested that Al Qaeda supported the EIJ/EISF for its potential strategic value as a launching pad to export the Islamist struggle to Yemen and Ethiopia. In this view, once an Islamist state was established in Eritrea, Eritrea would be the staging ground for similar struggles in Yemen and Ethiopia.[31] This interpretation is consistent with the overall of strategic vision of Al Qaeda at the time which regarded the Horn of Africa region as a base of operations for ultimately taking Saudi Arabia.

Evidence exists that documents bin Laden's involvement with the EIJ/EISF. One Eritrean informant has made the uncorroborated claim that in 1994 bin Laden narrowly escaped an Eritrean attack on an EIJ/EISF training camp inside Sudan near the Eritrean border.[32] During the trial of Al Qaeda operatives for the 1998 bombings of the U.S. embassies in Kenya and in Tanzania, Jamal al-Fadl, a former close associate of bin Laden's, testified that he delivered $100,000 to the EIJ/EISF sometime in the early 1990s,[33] adding that the Sudan office of the Qatar Charitable Society, which supported Al Qaeda operations by funneling funds from Persian Gulf states, provided $20,000 to EIJ/EISF to carry out actions outside of Sudan.[34] During this period, the EIJ/EISF reportedly sent fighters to Somalia to assist the Al Qaeda ally, Al Itihaad, in its jihad against the United States. One of the bin Laden-financed training camps in Sudan was located near Hamesh Koreb near the Eritrean border. In 1997, Sudanese rebels launched an attack from Eritrean territory and overran the Hamesh Koreb camp that trained EIJ/EISF mujahidin.[35]

The EIJ/EISF has placed its struggle in a global and regional context, and has asserted that the United States is leading the current "Christian onslaught" against Muslim populations in the Horn of Africa and Red Sea regions in alliance with what it describes as "Christian minority" governments of Eritrea and Ethiopia. The EIJ/EISF linked Israeli support for the new Eritrean government in the 1990s to a wider strategy of regional domination by Jews and Christians. From its independence in 1993 until 1998, Eritrea maintained close relations with Israel and was widely believed to have harbored an Israeli submarine facility and a telecommunications surveillance operation on the Dahlak Islands near Masawa.

The EIJ/EISF had regarded the Eritrean government as an ally of Israel and saw Israel as working "to destroy the current Islamic strategy which aims at making the Red Sea an Islamic Sea." However, Eritrea began to court Arab countries as a way of seeking new allies once its war with Ethiopia broke out in 1998. As a result, Eritrea's previously close relationship with Israel began to cool, and Eritrea reportedly denied Israeli naval ships access to its ports.[36] In its rhetoric about the threat that Israel and the United States pose to the Islamization of the region, the EIJ/EISF strongly echoed the position of its one-time historic external backers: Sudan and Osama bin Laden. The EIJ/EISF's 2004 abandonment of its goal of establishment of an Islamic state marked a substantive shift in its jihadist agenda.

OPPOSITION SUSPICIONS OF THE EIJ/EISF

Despite its abandonment in 2004 of its strategic objective of establishing an Islamic state in Eritrea, some Eritrean Muslims advocating the separation of religion and state as well as Christian opposition activists have remained wary of the EIJ/EISF and its ultimate motives. At the heart of this suspicion lies not only its jihadist roots, including past backing from NIF Sudan and Al Qaeda, but also an ideological conundrum of sorts that exists for the EIJ/EISF and perhaps for many other Islamist organizations operating in multireligious contexts. On the one hand, Sheikh Amer has observed, "Islam is a religion and a state (*Islam Deen we Dewla*); on the other, he has also noted from the teachings of the Koran that "there is no compulsion in religion." In a 2004 interview, the organization's secretary general Sheikh Amer sought to reassure those suspicious of his organization's intentions:

> There are rights for me, as there are for you, when we all return to Eritrea. We have to work together based on trust. We have to stop being suspicious of each other. Eritrea is for me and for you. If you have reasons to be afraid of me, I too have reasons to be afraid of you. We discuss, we negotiate, we co-exist, we tolerate each other. Secularists, Christians, even communists. This is our land; it belongs to all of us.[37]

The ENA's advocacy of the application of Islamic law in matters of daily life and of the family may have been the compromise that the EIJ/EISF needed to reconcile its apparently conflicting ideological positions of seeing Islam as a religion and state and of believing that there should be no compulsion in religion, thus allowing the EIJ/EISF to switch from its policy of establishing an Islamic state to its present goal of seeking political pluralism as a solution for Eritrea's political ills.

Notes

1. "Islamists Change Name," *The Indian Ocean Newsletter*, no. 823, September 5, 1998.
2. "New Rebel Force in Eritrea," *BBC News/Africa*, May 2, 2003, http://news.bbc.co.uk/1/low/world/africa/2995673.stm.
3. Awate Team, "The Gedab Investigative Report," *The "Executed": No Smoking Gun, but Plenty of Circumstantial Evidence*, March 13, 2003, http://www.awate.com/cgi-bin/artman/exec/view.cgi/11/1090/printer.
4. "Interview: Khalil M Amer/Eritrean Islamic Salvation Front, January 11, 2004, http://www.awate.com/artman/publish.htm.
5. Summary of the statement appeared in the Site Institute web site, March 28, 2006, http://www.siteinstitute.org.
6. Awate Team, "The Gedab Investigative Report."
7. Interview by phone with Eritrean Muslim journalist, March 15, 2004.
8. Patrick Gilkes, *Ethiopia—Perspectives of Conflict, 1991-1999*, Swiss Peace Foundation, Institute for Conflict Resolution, 1999, 7-8, http://www.isn.ethz.ch/publihouse/fast/crp/gilkes_99.html.
9. Interview by phone with Eritrean Muslim journalist, March 15, 2004.
10. U.S. Committee for Refugees, *Getting Home Is Only Half the Challenge: Refugee Reintegration in War-Rvaged Eritrea*, Washington, D.C., 2002, 5.
11. Awate Team, "The Gedab Investigative Report."

12. Interview: Abul Bara' Hassan Salman, "The Governing Regime is a Terrorist Regime Which Acts with Enmity against the Eritrean People, *Nida'ul Islam,* February—March 1998, http://www.islam.org.au.
13. Nair Fesseh, *Healing the Land through a Federal Structure,* http://www.gabeel.com/ARTICLES/ENGLISH/NAIRARTC1.HTM.
14. Eritrean National Alliance official website, July 2006, http://www.erit-alliance.com/Info/organstruct.asp.
15. Interview: Hassan Salman Abul Bara.
16. Interview by phone with Eritrean Muslim journalist, March 15, 2004.
17. Chris Kutschera, "Eritrea: Asmara-Khartoum: Hostility in the Horn," *Middle East Magazine,* May 1995, http://chris-kutschera.com/A?Asmara%20Khartoum.htm.
18. U.S. Committee for Refugees, 11.
19. Gerard Prunier, "Armed Conflict in the Heart of Africa: Sudan's Regional War," *Le Monde Diplomatique,* February 1997, http://mondediplo.com/1007/02/02sudan.
20. Interview: Abul Bara' Hassan Salman.
21. Awate Team, "Gedab Investigative Report."
22. Ibid.
23. Ibid.
24. Patrick Gilkes, "Free Rein for Eritrean Opposition," *BBC News,* May 23, 2000.
25. "Eritrean Opposition Groups Plan Armed Struggle against Asmara," *PANA,* September 2003, http://www.erit-alliance.org/News/September%202003/eNAPLANARMEDSTRUGGLE.asp.
26. "Eritrean Forces on Alert for the Mujahideen Fierce Operations, *From Around the World,* 9, Issue 3 (October—November 2002), http://www.islam.org.au/editions/nov2002/english/aroundthe world/index.htm#news.5; "Eritrea/Ethiopia: Islamic Group Says It Planted Mines," *IRIN,* March 22, 2003 http://dehai.org/archives/dehai_news_archive/mar03/0426.html.
27. "Sudan Peace and the Region, *IRIN,* April 2, 2004, http://allafrica.com/stories/200404020001.html.
28. "Eritrea Bomb Suspect Admits '*Jihad*' Attack Planned from Sudan," *AFP,* June 23, 2004, http://www.sudantribune.com/article.php3?id_article=3560.
29. "Eritrean Opposition Claims Barentu Bomb Blast Responsibility," *Sudan Tribune,* June 4, 2004.
30. "Sudan: The Neglected East," *IRIN,* March 24, 2004, http://allafrica.com/stories/200403240229.html.
31. Interview, April 2, 2004.
32. Ibid.

33. Judy Aita, "Bin Laden Associate First Witness in Embassy Bombing Trial," *Washington File*, February 6, 2001, http://usinfo.state.gov/topical/pol/terror/01020708.htm.
34. Steven Emerson, *Fundraising Methods and Procedures for International Terrorist Organizations,* Testimony before the House Committee on Financial Services Subcommittee on Oversight and Investigation, February 12, 2002, http://64.233.161.104/search?q=cache:rnpwTRakSZoJ:financialservices.house.gov/media/pdf/021202se.pdf +%22Help+Africa+People%22+Somalia&hl=en.
35. Human Rights Watch, "Sudanese Government Military Support for Armed Opposition Forces," *Annual Report,* 1998, http://hrw.org/reports98/sudan/Sudarm988-06.htm.
36. Patrick Gilkes, "World: Africa Analysis: The War's Bitter Legacy," *BBC News*, March 2, 1999, http://news.bbc.co.uki/1/hi/world/africa/289111. stm); Douglas Davis, "Report: Eritrea Denies Israel Use of Strategic Islands," *The Jerusalem Post*, July 18, 2000, http://www.jpost.com/Editions/2000/07/18/News/News.9763.html; "Close Intelligence Relations between Israel and Ethiopia, Eritrea," *ArabicNews.com*, Sept. 26, 1998, http://www.arabicnews.com/ansub/Daily/Day/980626/1998062608.html.
37. Awate Team, *Interview: Khalil M. Amer*, January 11, 2004.

Chapter Five

KENYA
JIHADISM IN AN OPEN SOCIETY

Kenya has figured prominently in the international jihadist agenda to achieve Islamist hegemony in the Horn of Africa. From his base in Khartoum, Osama bin Laden established a large Al Qaeda cell in East Africa that was centered in Kenya. The cell supported activities of the jihadist Al Itihaad organization in Somalia and in Kenya's North Eastern Province, worked to challenge the U.S. military presence in Somalia, and conspired to hobble U.S. diplomatic and intelligence capacities in the region that Al Qaeda thought to be thwarting ambitions of the international jihadist movement. The devastating 1998 bombing of the U.S. embassy in Nairobi was but one of several Al Qaeda plans to hit American targets in Kenya. Al Qaeda's bombing in 2002 of the Israeli-owned Paradise Hotel near Mombasa and the simultaneous but failed missile attack on an Israeli civilian jetliner, however, appear to have been more an action of propaganda value designed to bolster Al Qaeda's anti-Zionist and pro-Palestinian credentials than operations intending to promote its strategic objectives in the Horn of Africa. From 1992 to 1998, the cell used Kenya as a gateway to support its activities in Somalia through financial transactions, the hosting of meetings in Nairobi, the shipment of arms, the facilitation of travel by its operatives, and other activities. In turn, Somalia's premier jihadist movement, Al Itihaad, provided support for Al Qaeda operations in Kenya as well as in Tanzania.

Al Itihaad, too, has been active in Kenya, as it sought to gain a foothold both within Kenya's Somali community in North Eastern Province and among the large community of refugees there, who had fled from neighboring Somalia after the collapse of the Somali state in 1991. During the period under study, North Eastern Province witnessed the growth of Islamic fundamentalism, in part promoted by Al Qaeda-front charities and by the Saudi-based charity Al Haramain, which enjoyed strong links to both Al Qaeda and Al Itihaad. The growing adherence to fundamentalism in the Somali refugee camps has also been attributable to the preaching of Al Itihaad activists. North Eastern Province has also seen some active recruitment of Kenyan youth into the Al Itihaad forces by militiamen based in neighboring Somalia. Kenyan authorities have reported the capture of suspected foreign jihadist terrorists using the Somalia-North Eastern Province transportation corridor to enter Kenya.

For its part, Sudan, under the National Islamic Front, sought to promote Islamism in Kenya through support for the Islamic Party of Kenya (IPK), a homegrown movement based in Coast Province. The successful emergence of multiparty politics, however, enabled IPK's leadership to channel its issues into electoral politics and away from radical Islamic nationalism. Nonetheless, Sudanese support appears to have helped steer the political discourse of some IPK followers into a more radical direction. Foreign Islamic charities, especially those funded by Saudi Arabian sources, have actively been promoting Islamism by gaining control and ownership of mosques and schools to teach a Wahabist brand of Islam. This has created a sense among some Muslim communities that their traditional religious practices have been under attack.

Overall, however, the introduction of multiparty politics and a political culture that has been relatively tolerant of diverse political discourse appears to have helped channel Kenyan Muslim political, social, and economic grievances away from radical solutions and into the established political system.

Muslim dissatisfactions have remained high though, and the Kenyan government's aggressive antiterrorism campaign following Al Qaeda bombings in the country has compounded the sense of grievance within the Muslim community and has even created a backlash that fostered ill-will and certain anti-Americanism. In this context, prominent Kenyan Muslim leaders have expressed concern about the vulnerability of young Muslims both to the seductive rhetoric of Osama bin Laden and to the recruitment efforts of Al Qaeda and Al Itihaad.

MUSLIM ECONOMIC AND POLITICAL GRIEVANCES

Kenya's Muslim community has articulated a set of common grievances that found vocal expression in multiparty politics. The return of multiparty politics to Kenya in 1992 led to often-raucous political competition and the emergence of political actors ready to exploit the country's real or perceived social injustices and economic inequalities as a way to appeal to voters and/or to seek the redress of legitimate grievances. The Muslim community proved no exception to this rule, as many Muslim leaders believed that Kenya's minority Muslim population has been at a political and economic disadvantage since Kenya achieved independence in 1963. They have contended that the second-class status of Muslims resulted from the fact that Kenya African National Union (KANU)—the party that ruled Kenyan politics from independence through 2002—largely reflected a shifting coalition of political elites from various "inland" ethnic communities that are overwhelmingly Christian, although it should be noted that KANU also enjoyed support from elements of the Muslim community.

According to this perspective on Muslim disadvantage, which is not without merit, the country's development has favored the largely inland regions that have predominately Christian populations; and those regions with largely Muslim populations, namely Coast, North Eastern and Eastern Provinces, remained more marginal in terms of education, economic development, and political access. Within North Eastern and Coast Provinces, there has been a generalized perception that residents, regardless of religion, have enjoyed fewer opportunities than people of other provinces. They feel that they are less well integrated into the modern economy and have benefited less than other peoples of Kenya during the postindependence era.

Muslims constitute a minority population in Kenya, and estimates of the size of the Muslim community typically range from 10 percent to 20 percent of the country's total population that in 2006 was estimated at around thirty million people. Of the total population, Protestants comprise the largest religious group, at around 45 percent of the population and Roman Catholics are often estimated to be around 30 percent. Hinduism is practiced by about one percent of the population, and the remainder follows various traditional African religions.[1]

Kenya's Muslim population is concentrated in Coast, Eastern and North Eastern Provinces. The overwhelming majority of Muslims follow a Sunni tradition of Islam that goes back many centuries and is heavily influenced by the teachings of the Sufi brotherhoods. The small community of Kenyan Shiite Muslims is largely composed of descendants of immigrants from India and Pakistan.

Coast Province remains predominately Muslim. Its Muslim population may be categorized as ethnically Swahili, Arab, and Mijikenda. The Bantu-speaking Mijikenda communities, which are overwhelmingly Muslim, are a cluster of nine ethnic groups. The Swahili culture resulted from the interaction of African Bantu-speaking peoples in East Africa and Arab-speaking peoples largely from the Arabic peninsula. The Swahili culture zone stretches along Africa's Indian Ocean coast from northern Mozambique to southern Somalia and includes the adjacent islands of Unguja, Pemba, and the island nation of Comoros. Swahili, which is a Bantu language with considerable importation of vocabulary from Arabic, has become the official language and/or *lingua franca* for many countries in East and Central Africa. Kenya's Arab Muslims have historically regarded themselves as being of "pure" Arab heritage as opposed to the mixed Swahili and the "African" Mijikenda. For many from the Swahili community, who are of mixed Arab and African descent, there has been a certain ambiguity about their African and Arab identities. The Sultan of Zanzibar once ruled the coastal region that is now part of Kenya and Tanzania, and there remain strong cultural affinities and sympathies among the communities throughout the region's coastal zone.

North Eastern Province and the northern section of Eastern Province are vastly Muslim and ethnically Somali. The Somali-speaking peoples are divided among the countries of Djibouti, Ethiopia, Kenya, and Somalia.

COASTAL GRIEVANCES

The influx of Kenyans from other regions to Coast Province in search of employment and business opportunities has compounded feelings that Muslims have been at a disadvantage. These largely Christian "outsiders" have created competition and resentment among some elements of the Coastal Muslim population. The feeling of alienation has been particularly strong among both unemployed Muslim and non-Muslim youth along the coast who have seen the wealth and economic prosperity, whether of Kenyans from inland regions or the tourists, all around them.[2]

With the re-adoption of a multiparty system in December 1991, the Coast became host to the emergence of a strong political reformist movement that has championed land rights as one of its primary issues. There were two basic land issues: the rights of so-called squatters and public landgrabbing as a form of political patronage.

Many Coastal inhabitants, especially the Mijikenda and the descendants of African former slaves, have been squatters with no title deeds to the lands that their ancestors lived on, and in some cases find themselves threatened by eviction. They settled, often for generations, on unused land titled to Arab and Swahili owners. The occupants engaged in both subsistence and cash crop agriculture and have relied on local ecological niches for fuel, building materials, and medicine. When the tourism industry expanded during the 1980s and as immigration by "inlanders" grew, the price of land skyrocketed with the result that titled owners often drove squatters off the land that they wished to sell to take advantage of the favorable land market conditions.[3] Those evicted were left landless and impoverished, and those who continued to toil the land, to which they did not possess title, felt vulnerable and insecure. Both remaining squatters and the dispossessed were often attracted to politicians willing to champion their cause.

Under the KANU government, party supporters were often given public land as a form of political patronage, and given the rising price of land near the coast, these transactions were often very lucrative. Squatters living on public land could be readily dispossessed of their homes and means of livelihood through this form of political appropriation of land. In some cases, the disputed land in question held religious significance, for example, the *Kaya*, or sacred forest stands of the Mijikenda.[4] The Kayas serve as ceremonial areas, burial grounds for prominent Mijikenda elders, and as places of worship. Trees and plants taken from them are used for traditional herbal medicine.

An attempted appropriation of a Kaya occurred in 1998: the Kenyan government sought to decertify one of the sacred forest stands, Kaya Tiwi, as a protected area, which would have made it available to forest speculators. This attempt was met with strong resistance by local Mijikenda leaders, who warned of bloodshed if anyone moved into the kaya to develop it. The government's order to decertify was rescinded within two weeks.[5]

ISLAMIC PARTY OF KENYA

The Islamic Party of Kenya (IPK), which was formed to compete in the 1992 multiparty parliamentary elections, effectively tapped into the political alienation, resentment, and economic disenfranchisement of Kenya's Coastal Muslim youth. Radical street preacher Sheikh Khalid Balala rose to prominence during the waning years of the single-party era as a result of his fiery religious sermons in Mombasa's Wembe Tayari marketplace. As an IPK leader, Sheikh Balala came to command a sizeable following among the youth in Coast Province, some of whom were known to have advocated the establishment of an Islamic state in Coast Province and the full application of sharia. This appears not to have reflected, however, the mainstream policies of the IPK, whose political platform was more concerned with reforming the political and economic order in Kenya rather than one promoting the establishment of an Islamic state for predominately Muslim areas of the country. Although the Kenyan government did not allow the IPK to register as an official party because of its religious orientation, its candidates won, nonetheless, three of Mombasa's four parliamentary seats in 1992.

Sheikh Balala was born in Mombasa in 1958 to a father originally from Yemen. As a boy, Balala studied the Koran and Arabic in local schools. At the age of seventeen, he traveled to Saudi Arabia to fulfill the Muslim duty of pilgrimage to Mecca, and he remained there for more than ten years, studying Islam at Medina University while making a living selling religious books. He then visited various countries in Europe and Asia. In Britain he completed a course in business management, and in India he studied Islam and comparative religion. According to Balala, he decided to combine the knowledge he had acquired of Islam and of business management in order to "sell," that is, to disseminate, the Islamic religion.[6]

During the period when Sheikh Balala became *de facto* head of IPK, external support helped the IPK to effectively mobilize a mass following. The Sudanese and the Iranian governments reportedly played key roles in this regard. Sheikh Balala cemented his relationship with Sudan's radical National Islamic Front regime during his several trips to Khartoum.[7] Sudan's support for the IPK was consistent with Khartoum's policy of promoting an Islamist agenda in the region and as a means of undermining Kenyan support for the rebel Sudanese People's Liberation Movement/Army.[8] The Sudanese government, however, at the time specifically denied allegations that it was training armed IPK insurgents in Sudan.[9] The radicalization of Muslim political discourse that occurred as a result of Sheikh Balala's influence has been partially attributed to the dispatch of Sudanese preachers to Coast Province apparently as part of the support given by Hassan al-Turabi's NIF to Sheikh Balala.[10]

The IPK's phenomenal popularity in the 1990s including its parliamentary seat victories proved threatening to the ruling KANU party politicians, who then reacted by vilifying the IPK and harassing its leadership. The KANU government and its supporters moved to drive a wedge between "Arab" and "African" Muslims as a way of diluting the IPK threat to KANU's hold on power. KANU politicians encouraged the establishment of an alternative "black African" Muslim party, the United Muslims of Africa (UMA), to rival the IPK. The IPK's opponents had launched a campaign of disinformation to characterize it as an expression of Kenyan "Arabs." This characterization was patently false, as much of the IPK's leadership, with the notable exception of Sheikh Balala whose father was from Yemen, could not be described as Arab Muslims.

The UMA has been described as little more than a political gang that included former members of Idi Amin's military regime in Uganda. The UMA used the race card and intimidating tactics in a bid to weaken IPK's popular support.[11] In an effort to undermine this support and that of other opposition parties, some KANU supporters also instigated election-related violence in 1997 that resulted in the massacre of hundreds of people in Likoni near Mombasa.

Sheikh Balala's firebrand role within the IPK was short lived. Although immensely popular on the streets of Mombasa, his frequently inflammatory rhetoric provoked a power struggle within the IPK that resulted in his expulsion from the party and a moderation of the party's hard-edged style. The Kenyan government later moved to repeal Sheikh Balala's citizenship while he was visiting Germany, with the consequence that he was unable to return to Kenya for several years. His removal from the party and the years spent in exile weighed heavily on Sheikh Balala's political ascendancy, and when he belatedly returned to electoral politics in an unsuccessful 2002 parliamentary race, he did so as a member of the Green Party. A 2003 political survey of Kenyans indicated that the IPK had maintained significant popularity.[12]

SOMALI MUSLIMS

With its largely Somali population, Kenya's North Eastern Province has been a focal point of jihadist organizing activities by both Al Qaeda and Al Itihaad. Al Qaeda-front and associated charities have a history of activism in the province and in the adjoining Gedo region of Somalia, and the province's porous border with unstable Somalia made it an easy entry point and a haven for Al Itihaad operatives and suspected international terrorists. Its geographical isolation from Kenya's center of power and its poor telecommunications infrastructure has often meant that the quality of information on the activities of extremist groups has been inconsistent. Nonetheless, since the late 1990s and as late as 2003, there were persistent reports of Al Itihaad activities among both Somali refugee populations and Kenyan Somali communities in this province. Al Itihaad has engaged in both military and ideological recruitment—seeking recruits for its militia and promoting its brand of Wahabism. The influence that Al Itihaad has wielded in the province may be explained in part by the fact that it once maintained a military stronghold in the Gedo region of Somalia that directly abuts North Eastern Province, that is, until Ethiopia forced the jihadist militia from Gedo in the late 1990s and effectively closed down the joint Al Itihaad-Al Qaeda camps located there. Social, economic, and political conditions in the province and its proximity to politically chaotic Somalia made it fertile ground for criminal activity operating from Somalia and the operation of extremist groups, such as Al Itihaad and Al Qaeda, and there has reportedly been a convergence of Al Itihaad, Al Qaeda, and criminal gang activity in the province.

Kenyan Somalis residing in North Eastern Province live in what is one of the most marginalized regions of the country. The province has been the least developed economically, and its recent history has been plagued by political and criminal violence. Incidences of banditry have been widespread; road travel has often required armed escort; and interclan fighting has been endemic. Lawlessness in the province worsened after the 1991 collapse of the government in Somalia, when hundreds of thousands of Somali refugees entered the province. The refugee camps became host to illegal trade in small arms, which heightened the insecurity in the province. Organized criminal groups used the province as a pass through for arms smuggling to Nairobi, where violent crimes increased, and on to other countries in the region. A 2003 UN report expressed alarm at Al Qaeda's involvement in the arms trade passing through the province from Somalia.[13]

Historically many in Kenya's Somali community have maintained a guarded if not hostile relationship to the central government. This political alienation is rooted in the *Shifta* separatist insurrections of the 1960s. After Kenyan independence in 1963, Somali rebels took up arms in a bid to force the integration of Somali-inhabited areas of Kenya into the Republic of Somalia, which had achieved independence earlier in 1960. The Somali government encouraged the rebels' separatist aspirations, but the Somali government failed to supply the Kenyan rebels with the weapons support that the rebels had expected. As a result, the newly independent Kenyan government managed to quickly suppress the rebellion, though sporadic insurrections continued to challenge the Kenyan authorities during the decade that followed. The repressive tactics of the government security forces since the insurrections nurtured resentment among many Kenyan Somalis against their government.[14] For instance, according to the Kenya Somali Community of North America, government forces committed at least four sizeable massacres of Kenyan Somalis since 1975 while KANU held power in the country.[15] It will be interesting to see to what extent the electoral transfer of power in 2002 from KANU to the National Rainbow Coalition government has begun to impact Kenyan Somali perceptions of their central government.

Throughout much of the 1990s until 2002, government policy requiring Kenyan Somalis to carry a second identification card in addition to their regular Kenyan identification card exacerbated antigovernment feelings within the Somali community. The government implemented this measure in an apparent attempt to deter illegal immigration from Somalia, but many Kenyan Somalis felt they were singled out because they were Muslim. In August 2002, then Kenyan President Daniel Arap Moi, ended the special identity card policy for Somalis, explaining that the government would henceforth rely instead on local elders and leaders to determine the citizenship of Somalis. However, Kenyan Somalis and other Kenyan Muslims have felt that their communities continued to be harassed by the government; and their leaders claimed that following Al Qaeda's 1998 bombing of the U.S. embassy in Nairobi and its November 2002 terrorist attacks near Mombasa, government discrimination, especially the demands for identity documents, against their communities worsened.

AL QAEDA AND AL ITIHAAD IN NORTH EASTERN PROVINCE

Both Al Qaeda and Al Itihaad have organized within Kenya's discontented Somali population and among the Somali refugee population. Bin Laden's organization used two charities, Mercy International Relief Agency and Help Africa Peoples, to carry out activities in North Eastern Province and in the Gedo region of Somalia, where the charities supported two joint Al Qaeda-Al Itihaad military camps in the mid-1990s.

Kenya: Jihadism in an Open Society

Militias of Al Itihaad and later the Al Itihaad-dominated Union of Islamic Courts have recruited among Somali youth in North Eastern Province. In 1997, police arrested five Kenyan youths who had been recruited by agents of the militia. The security sources in Garissa said that the recruiter belonged to a group of Kenyans who fled to Somalia at the height of the Shifta separatist rebellion in the early 1960s. In 1999, instances of Al Itihaad recruitment reportedly took place in and around the town of Garissa and among the Somali refugee communities at the nearby Dadaab refugee camps. Dadaab consists of three refugee camps with a combined population of around 130,000 individuals in 2002.[16] But again in November 2006, there were additional accounts of recruitment in the province by Somali militias. North Eastern Provincial Commissioner Kiritu Wamae said that the Kenyan government had compiled a list of youths allegedly recruited by "troops allied to the Union of Islamic Courts in Somalia."[17]

The growth of Islamic fundamentalism in the province, both among Kenyan Somalis and refugees from Somalia, has been noted by several sources, and has been attributed to Al Itihaad preaching. The now-banned Al Qaeda and Al Itihaad-allied Saudi-based charity Al Haramain actively promoted Wahabism in the province's mosques and schools. In 2001, Kenyan MP Fafi Barre Shill said that "thousands of residents in Hulugho division, including the town of Mandera" adjacent to the Somali border, had become affiliated with Al Itihaad, although others have disputed this account of Al Itihaad in Hululgho as an exaggeration.[18] In 2002, the Kenyan Constitutional Review Commission, however, did note an increased demand in North Eastern Province for the adoption of Islamic law. The members of the commission attributed the increased demand for the introduction of sharia to the call by Islamists made the previous year for the establishment of a caliphate in the province.[19] The creation of a caliphate to govern all Somalis has been the principal goal of Al Itihaad.

A researcher for the Washington-based Fund for Peace indicated in 2000 that "a more radical Islam was taking hold there [in the refugee camps] and was being imposed on those not interested."[20] After numerous interviews with refugees at Dadaab in 2003, the Lawyers Committee for Human Rights also reported that Al Itihaad members had infiltrated the camps, disguised as refugees, and that some of them were teaching "extremism" in local madrasas (Islamic schools) where tens of thousands of children and adults went daily for learning.[21] According to Monica Kathina Juma of the Center for Refugee Studies,

> Somali refugees have begun to conduct religious training that is akin to Taliban-styled madrasah classes in refugee camps, allegedly in preparation for defending Islam and Somali nationhood.

This religious training reportedly had an anti-American bent and played on refugee fears that the United States was out to punish Somalis for the 1993 armed opposition to U.S. forces that had been part of the UN humanitarian and national building intervention in Somalia.[22]

The Al Haramain Islamic Foundation, which supported Al Itihaad activities in Somalia, also supported Islamic schools, mosques, and social services in North Eastern Province and is known to have fostered a puritanical and fundamentalist brand of Islam.[23] When the Kenya branch of Al Haramain stopped operations after the ban on its operations due to its designation by the United Nations as a terrorist organization at the request of the United States and Saudi Arabia, the impact was readily felt in the province, where in Garissa District, for instance, children living in centers supported by Al Haramain reportedly were left homeless.[24] According to local Muslim leaders,

> The closure of Al-Haramain Islamic Foundation office in Nairobi has led to the closure of 20 centers and the loss of 200 jobs that cost the local economy K[enyan] Sh[illings] 13.2 millions [$200,000US] per annum which catered for the upkeep and education of more than 1,000 refugee and Kenyan orphans and destitute children at Dadaab, Ifo Dagahle and Hagardeera camps.[25]

However justified the banning of Al Haramain as part of a counterterrorism strategy, the action contributed to growing anti-Americanism in the Province.

Anti-Americanism in North Eastern Province became palpable. Local Muslims came to associate the United States with what they consider to be antiterrorism abuses by Kenyan security forces. In July 2003, Muslim leaders called for the closure of a newly established Kenyan antiterrorism police unit with offices in Garissa and in Mombasa. These leaders claimed that the unit had been created by the United States to intimidate and harass Muslims under the guise of fighting terrorism.[26]

Given the religious and political indoctrination by Al Itihaad, Al Qaeda charities, and Al Haramain and the fears of American reprisal in the province, it was not surprising that local residents reacted strongly in 2003 to the arrival in Garissa of a detachment of U.S. Marines on a goodwill mission. Hundreds of Muslims attempted to eject the marines from a Garissa hotel, and some forty people reportedly wound up injured during the incident. The marines, who had been stationed at Camp Lemonier in Djibouti as part of the counterterrorism Combined Joint Task Force—Horn of Africa, had arrived to provide medical and veterinarian assistance in the province.[27]

Some local Muslim leaders recognized the goodwill exercise as a misguided attempt to compensate for the loss of social services resulting from the cessation of Al Haramain charitable works in the region that followed the linkage that the United States and Saudi Arabia had made between the charity and Al Qaeda. The local population, which had ample knowledge of the counterterrorism objective of the Combined Joint Task Force based in Djibouti and awareness of warnings in the international media that the United States might intervened in Somalia to prevent it from becoming a haven for Al Qaeda, interpreted the goodwill gesture as a threat to its security. The local population was also aware that the 1992-93 U.S. military intervention in Somalia, which had also started as a humanitarian operation, had turned into armed conflict fueled by the arrival of foreign jihadist fighters. According to local Islamic leaders, the community feared that a U.S. military presence might attract Al Qaeda operatives intent on combating American forces, thus creating greater insecurity in the region.[28] To add fuel to the fire, local radical imams and sheikhs reportedly incited the faithful in mosques against the U.S. Marine-goodwill exercise, saying the medication that the soldiers were distributing were laced with toxic substances intended to wipe out the Muslim population from the world.[29] Although untrue, this message found a receptive audience among the already wary local population.

In an effort to calm down the alarmed population and dispel their fears about the presence of the Marines in their communities, the commissioner for North Eastern Province met with Muslim leaders. At their request, the marines switched the objectives of their mission from medical and veterinary assistance to infrastructural development, including sinking wells and making improvements to the physical plant of public institutions.[30]

CRIMINALITY IN NORTH EASTERN PROVINCE

North Eastern Province, with its porous border with Somalia, became an easy entry point for illegal immigration, the smuggling of arms and other illicit items, and the transit of suspected foreign terrorists. Somali criminal gangs reportedly mounted a transportation and communications infrastructure, of which both Al Qaeda and Al Itihaad have taken advantage. Kathi Austin of the Fund for Peace, who conducted extensive research in the Dadaab refugee camps in 2000, reported:

> I had specific information [about terrorist training in Dadaab] before Sept. 11 ... I was looking at arms networks going from Somalia into Kenya, and I ran into terrorists competing with criminal elements and clans to take advantage of those networks.

Political factions fighting inside Somalia carried out the violence and smuggling inside the camps.[31]

Austin reported that the camps had become a "nerve center for arms trafficking" throughout East Africa. The criminal gangs operating out of the Dadaab camps were responsible for "all sorts of illicit activity affecting downtown Nairobi," and she also reported that weapons traffickers "operate a sophisticated radio network linking Somalia, the camps, and Nairobi." Somali refugees have been able to communicate between Nairobi, the camps and Somalia using radio sets called *taars*. The Kenya government had been concerned that this informal communications network was being used by terrorists and other criminals to pass on information. Taars also interfered with official police and NGO frequencies, and the police carried out campaigns against their use.[32] With the introduction and widespread use of mobile phones in Kenya and Somalia in more recent years, the massive use of mobile phones for telecommunication between the two countries may have reduced the earlier reliance on taars for such communication.

In the Dadaab refugee camps, in late 2002, Kenyan authorities apprehended a group suspected of being operatives on a mission to launch a terrorist assignment, and had them deported on charges of having illegally entered the country. The group included eleven Iraqis and three Syrians who had illegally crossed into Kenya from Somalia using falsified travel documents. The group had reportedly made its way into the country on local bush trails known as *panyas*.[33] In 2005, at a Garissa checkpoint, Kenyan police also arrested a Sudanese national, Elbur Mohamed Ibrahim, who was holding documents suggesting that he had a role in the assassination of BBC correspondent Kate Peyton in Mogadishu. Kenyan authorities did not have enough evidence to hold him, and he was deported for immigration violations. The confiscated documents reportedly also included a list of *Al Islah* "operatives" from Somalia who had gone to Afghanistan for training. Al Islah is an Islamist organization in Somalia dedicated to providing social services, although many Al Islah members reportedly also belong to Al Itihaad; and there are reports that Al Islah has acted as a social welfare arm of Al Itihaad.[34]

AL QAEDA'S PRESENCE IN KENYA

After Osama bin Laden moved his Al Qaeda headquarters to Sudan in 1991, he set out to create an extensive operational command in East Africa that was centered in Nairobi and which carried out charitable works, business activities, military support, and arms trafficking activities in Kenya, in Somalia, in Tanzania, and reportedly in Uganda. As part of its campaign to undermine American military, diplomatic and intelligence capabilities in the region, Al Qaeda contemplated striking at American targets in Kenya prior to the 1998 bombing of the American embassy, but no action took place. Under the leadership of Al Qaeda's second in command and co-founder, Abu Ubaidah al-Banshiri, Nairobi served as "the nerve center of military operations in Somalia."[35] U.S. federal prosecutors have said that at least five group members crossed the border to Somalia to train and to supply logistic support to some of the fighters involved in the October 3, 1993 battle with U.S. Special Forces that left eighteen American military personnel and several hundred Somalis dead.[36] Evidence presented earlier in this book suggests that Al Qaeda support for operations in Somalia was far more extensive.

Between 1993 and 1997, Abu Ubadiah al-Banshiri and Wadih el Hage, the latter bin Laden's personal secretary, turned their attention to establishing a small business empire in East Africa. Bin Laden wanted Al Qaeda's East Africa operation to become financially self-sufficient after Sudan reneged on repayments of loans to him. With the loss of these funds, even someone as fabulously wealthy as bin Laden recognized that there were limits to his ability to finance his jihadist ambitions, and Al Qaeda cells would need to generate their own revenues. As a consequence, the two Al Qaeda leaders established diamond and gem mining and trading companies in Kenya and Tanzania. Ashif Mohamed Juma, a Tanzanian and brother-in-law of al-Banshiri, set up a company called Taheer Limited to mine diamonds and gold in Tanzania, and Al Qaeda and individuals connected with the organization bought property in Tanzania for the purpose of mining diamonds. Taheer Limited was most likely used to launder illicit diamonds from eastern Zaire (later the Democratic Republic of the Congo). After al-Banshiri's death in a ferry disaster on Lake Victoria in May 1996, el Hage found another partner, an unwitting Jordanian gemstone trader called Mohamed Ali Muraweh Saleh Odeh, who was based in Nairobi. In Kenya, el Hage found yet another unsuspecting partner in the then Kenyan assistant minister for agriculture, Dr. Joseph Misoi, and set about incorporating a company called Black Giant Mining. Although it never got off the ground, it appears that the company was going to be used for legitimate business purposes.[37]

El Hage also set up a company, Tanzanite King, in Nairobi and in Mombasa for trading tanzanite gemstones to Dubai and Hong Kong. The gems, unique to Tanzania, are mined at Mererani by small-scale miners. In 2002 testimony before the U.S. Senate Select Committee on Intelligence, the director of the Defense Intelligence Agency indicated that after the embassy bombings and the break up and flight of Al Qaeda operations in East Africa, that "there have been no further credible indications of al-Qaida involvement in gem trading."[38] Yet, reporting by the *Wall Street Journal* cast doubt on that assessment. The *Journal* reported in 2001 that a radical cleric, Sheikh Omar, at the Taqwa mosque in Mererani issued edicts that Muslim miners should sell their stones only to fellow Muslims. Radical Muslims had established a type of Mafia to dominate the trade. According to one informant, "Even if non-Muslims offer better prices for our stones, we are harassed by the fundamentalists not to sell to anyone but them. Many Muslim miners obey because they are scared of them." The mosque reportedly had been a hotbed of support for bin Laden in his struggle against the United States. According to this report, Tanzanian authorities were "100%" sure that Al Qaeda was behind this trafficking in Tanzanian gems to the markets in the Middle East.[39]

Other Al Qaeda operatives—the Egyptian national Abdullah Ahmed Abdullah, the Tanzanian, Ahmed Khalfan Ghailani, and the Comorian, Fazul Abdullah Mohammed—went on to use the knowledge that they gained from Al Qaeda's diamond-trading operations in East Africa to establish a diamond-buying laundering operation in Liberia and Sierra Leone in 2000—2001. Abdullah Ahmed Abdullah is believed to have been the mastermind of the bombing of the U.S. embassy in Nairobi. Ahmed Khalfan Ghailani and Fazul Abdullah Mohammed, an Al Qaeda computer expert, were involved in the Dar es Salaam bombing. Ghailani, Fazul Abdullah Mohammed, and Abdullah Ahmed Abdullah were familiar with the diamond and gemstone dealings of al-Banshiri and el Hage and had extensive diamond knowledge from diamond buying trips to Angola, to the Central African Republic and to Zaire.[40]

On the Kenyan coast near Mombasa, another Al Qaeda operative, the Yemeni-born Mohammed Sadek Odeh, used organization funds to set up a fishing business in 1994. The fishing business was a front for an arms smuggling operation, and profits from the fishing business was used to help support Al Qaeda operations in Kenya. Odeh was later convicted of murder in the United States for his role in the 1998 Nairobi embassy bombing.

After Al Qaeda's success in helping to drive out U.S. forces from Somalia, Odeh had moved from Somalia to the Mombasa area and used it as a central transit point in Al Qaeda's arms trade. Odeh used his fishing company as a cover to smuggle arms from both Somalia and Sudan as well as to export arms to the Taliban in Afghanistan. Odeh worked with the notorious Russian international arms dealer and former KGB agent Viktor But (Victor Bout) to smuggle arms to the Taliban. Al Qaeda reportedly smuggled Russian SA-7 missiles through Sudan to Kenya. But's air transport companies, Air Cess and Flying Dolphin, officially carried their cargoes from East Africa and the United Arab Emirates to Central Asia, but his Armenian pilots made landings in Kandahar, Afghanistan, where the Taliban unloaded the weapons cargo. In a fax captured by the Pakistani intelligence, sent by But's employees in Peshawar, the weapons deliveries were referred to with the code "fish from Tanzania" in reference to Odeh's fishing company."[41]

In Kenya, Al Qaeda also created or worked through existing Islamic charities. The potential offered by charities—as a source of finance, a network through which propaganda can be disseminated and a means of enhancing one's reputation among Muslims through humanitarian gestures—was not lost on Al Qaeda. The charities also functioned at times as a type of bridge between Wahabist-type evangelization and the call to jihadist action made by Al Qaeda members and sympathizers.

In Nairobi, prior to the embassy bombing, Al Qaeda worked through Mercy International Relief Agency and Help Africa People. Bin Laden and Mohammed Atef were both linked to the Mercy International Relief Agency, which gave bin Laden an identity card and helped give bin Laden cover. Mercy International was financed by "Saudi merchants." In its Pakistan operation the same charity also employed relatives of Ramzi Yousef, the mastermind of the 1993 New York World Trade Center bombing. One of the Nairobi bombers, Fazul Mohammed, traveled often to Somalia on behalf of Help Africa People. He used funds raised overtly in areas such as the Persian Gulf to implement an antimalaria project in Somalia on behalf of Al Qaeda's allied organization Al Itihaad and channeled support to two joint Al Qaeda-Al Itihaad militia camps in Somalia's Gedo region.[42] The Al Qaeda charities also carried out humanitarian activities among the Somali Muslim population in North Eastern Province, as did Al Haramain, that was subsequently linked to Al Qaeda and Al Itihaad.

Kenya: Jihadism in an Open Society

Al Qaeda justified its decision to attack American targets within Kenya by claiming that the government's orientation was overly pro-American. The embassy bombing aimed to hobble U.S. intelligence capacity in the region. The bombing killed 219 people including 12 Americans and injured around 5,000, mostly Kenyans. On the day after the 1998 attack, the Islamic Liberation Army of the People of Kenya, an Al Qaeda phantom organization, issued the following communiqué:

> The Americans humiliate our people; they occupy the Arabian peninsula; they extract our riches; they impose a blockade; and, besides, they support the Jews of Israel, our worse enemies, who occupy the Al-Aqsa mosque... .The attack was justified because the government of Kenya recognized that the Americans had used the country's territory to fight against its Moslem neighbors, in particular Somalia. Besides, Kenya cooperated with Israel. In this country one finds the most anti-Islamic Jewish centers in all East Africa. It is from Kenya that the Americans supported the separatist war in Southern Sudan, pursued by John Garang's fighters.[43]

Al Qaeda launched a second terrorist attack inside Kenya in November 2002, when it carried out a suicide bombing of the Israeli-owned Paradise Hotel in Kikambala near Mombasa and undertook a failed simultaneous missile attack to hit Israeli Arkia Air flight 582 departing from the Mombasa airport. These attacks were the first known Al Qaeda actions directly targeting Israelis. The suicide bombing killed ten Kenyans and three Israelis.

Bin Laden seems to have provided an explanation for this new tactic in an audiotape that he released a month prior to the Mombasa operations. In the tape he threatened the United States and its allies—Britain, France, Italy, Canada, Germany and Australia—and Israel. "You will be killed, just as you kill, and will be bombed, just as you bomb," he said. Another part of the tape included the sentence: "Our kinfolk in Palestine have been slain and severely tortured for nearly a century." The attacks are believed to have been bin Laden's "answer to those Arabs who ask why Al Qaeda is not attacking Israel."[44]

By the time of the 2002 attacks, Mogadishu had apparently replaced Nairobi as Al Qaeda's "nerve center" in East

Africa. After the 1998 bombings of the U.S. embassy, when the East Africa cell dispersed, a type of role reversal occurred, as Somalia began to function as a gateway for Al Qaeda terrorist activities in Kenya. From Somalia, Al Qaeda came to nest itself in Kenya's Coastal Muslim community, using coastal shipping routes out of Somalia; recruited Kenyans to participate in its activities; and plotted to bomb, once again, the U.S. embassy, in addition to launching terrorist attacks against these Israeli-associated targets. Weapons used in the Mombasa attacks were smuggled into Kenya by sea from Somalia, according to the United Nations, and since the attack, Kenyan authorities have apprehended a number of terror suspects who entered the country from Somalia or have been linked to Somalia.[45]

According to a UN report on the bombings, the Paradise Hotel bombers used converted fishing boats for transport on at least two occasions, including their escape back to Somalia from Lamu. Weapons shipped from Somalia originated in, or were routed through Djibouti, Eritrea, Ethiopia, United Arab Emirates, and Yemen. The missiles and launchers used in the attempted downing of the Israeli airliner came from either Yemen or Eritrea via Somalia. The two Strela-2 surface-to-air missiles were manufactured in the Soviet Union in 1978, and the two "gripstock" launchers were produced in Bulgaria in 1993. The smugglers had painted the launchers blue and white for camouflage.

The Comorian, Fazul Abdullah Mohammed, masterminded the attacks. He had ingratiated himself with the local Swahili community in Malindi and took a local woman as wife. Fazul Abdullah Mohammed was born in the Federal Islamic Republic of the Comoros, a Swahili-speaking archipelago off the coast of Mozambique and north of Madagascar, and as such he easily blended into Kenya's Swahili community in Coast Province. He attended a Wahabist school in the Comoros and at the age of sixteen received a scholarship to study at a Wahabist school in Pakistan. From there, he went to Afghanistan to join the Al Qaeda terrorist network. He traveled to the Sudan in 1994.[46] From this base in Malindi, Fazul recruited Kenyans and Somalis to Al Qaeda's cause. According to a UN report, several organizers of the Mombasa actions worked prior to the attacks as lobster fishermen along the coast.

Most of the Al Qaeda members who made it back to the Somali capital remained there for several months, living on cash allowances provided by a Sudanese financial controller, the UN panel reported. One member of the team, Suleiman Abdalla Salim Hemed, also known by the *noms de guerre* "Ngaka" and "Chuck Norris," was captured in a joint Kenyan-American operation in March 2003.[47] Reports have varied as to Abdalla's activities while in Mogadishu. One report said that he ran several businesses in Mogadishu and was protected by body guards; another report said that he worked as a driver for a major Mogadishu hotel. Kenyan authorities handed Suleiman Abdalla Salim Hemed over to U.S. authorities for trial for his earlier role in the embassy bombings.[48]

An uncorroborated 2002 claim by an Israel-based intelligence subscription newsletter reported that 150 Al Qaeda and Egyptian Islamic jihad fighters were stationed southwest of the Somali city of Xagar. According to this source, some members of the Al Qaeda team that carried out the 2002 attacks in Mombasa escaped from Kenya by flying to this camp. According to the newsletter, a coalition of Somali supporters of Osama bin Laden sheltered the Xagar fugitive community.[49]

COUNTER TERRORISM BACKLASH

Efforts of the Kenyan government to investigate and to prevent terrorist activities following the 1998 Al Qaeda embassy bombing and the 2002 attacks near Mombasa have added to the grievances described by Kenyan Muslims. The frequently-questionable quality of Kenyan journalism on terrorism issues, accompanied by a failure of the Kenyan government to adequately explain its counterterrorism activities to the public, appears to have contributed to the Muslim backlash against the government's counterterrorism policy.

The degree of Muslim concern over government handling of antiterrorism measures was born out by a 2004 survey analysis of Kenyan attitudes showing that Muslims and Christians differed significantly in their views of the matter. Among Christians, 74 percent of respondents gave the government positive ratings for its handling of the terrorism threat, 10 percent offered a negative rating, and 16 percent answered "don't know." On the other hand, among Muslims a much slimmer majority of 52 percent still gave support, but more than twice as many Muslims (24 percent) than Christians rated the government's counterterrorism efforts as "fairly bad" or "very bad," and 24 percent did not have an opinion.[50]

This author's review of Muslim reactions in the Kenya press after Al Qaeda's 1998 bombing of the U.S. embassy revealed a constant and vocal resentment on the part of many Muslim leaders of antiterrorism measures undertaken by the government. The first incident of Muslim backlash against government antterrorism actions occurred when the government sought to ban the activities of Islamic charities thought to be implicated in the embassy bombing: Help Africa People, the International Islamic Relief Organization; the Ibrahim bin Abdul Aziz al Ibrahim Foundation; Al Muntada Al Islami; and Mercy Relief International Agency. The banning of the charities became controversial because international Muslim charities have provided much-needed legitimate humanitarian assistance to Kenyan Muslims.

At the time of the announcement, the government spokesman sought to justify its actions: "These organizations are supposed to be working for the welfare of Kenyans, but are instead endangering Kenyan lives...."[51] The government explained, perhaps erroneously, that the ingredients for manufacturing the bomb used in the embassy attack had entered the country as part of a humanitarian shipment of food. It was only later the public learned some Muslim charities, such as Help Africa People and Mercy International Relief Agency, were Al Qaeda fronts.[52]

Alarmed at the effect of the banning on Muslim welfare activities in 1998, Muslim leaders challenged the decision to deregister the NGOs and called for a general strike to protest the closures of the charities. The leaders said the government's action sought to suppress Islamic activities in the country. "We are surprised when Muslim NGOs come to assist and improve the social and economic status of Muslims, the government de-registers them," said Abdulgafur Busaiddy, head of the Supreme Council of Kenyan Muslims. "This testifies that the marginalization of Muslims is not accidental, but deliberate," he added.[53] Kenya's high court ultimately reversed the government's deregistration of the charities, and Muslim leaders called off their plans for a nationwide protest strike. Muslim leaders were adamant in their claim that the Kenyan government had been pressured to carry out the ban by the U.S. government. "Otherwise why are they doing it after the embassy bombing? Are the two connected?" wondered one of the Muslim leaders, Ismail Aden Issak.[54]

The Kenyan government has investigated and imposed a ban on the activities of a number of NGOs funded from Arab countries out of a concern that some may have become financial conduits for terrorist activity and believed that it had ample reason to justify its actions. As previously noted, Al Qaeda operated through two charitable front organizations in Kenya, and the United States and Saudi Arabia linked the Kenya branch of the Al Haramain Islamic Foundation to both Al Qaeda and Al Itihaad, and Al Haramain has reportedly supported terrorist activity in a number of other countries, including in Somalia, where, according to independent researchers, its employees had been linked to the assassination of foreign aid workers. In addition, personnel of the World Muslim League, one of the largest charities created by the Saudi royal family, have reportedly worked for or with Al Qaeda in Kenya.[55]

In 2003, the government reportedly banned funding from Arab-funded NGOs, as part of its wider campaign against terrorism.[56] In the same year, the Africa Muslim Agency, an international NGO, threatened to pull out of Kenya because the Kenyan government deported two of its directors,[57] and in 2004 allegedly under pressure from the U.S. government, Kenyan government authorities deported the head of the Nairobi branch of the Islamic charity Al Muntada Al Islami for not having his work permit in order. Mhawiye Hussein Abu-Waid, a Sudanese, had been the subject of a police investigation that apparently failed to come up with substantial evidence linking him to terrorist activity. Al Muntada Al Islami is a charity based in the United Kingdom that reportedly receives substantial support from Saudi Arabia.[58] Al Muntada Al Islami, which was one of the charities temporarily closed down in 1998 after the Nairobi embassy bombing, maintained operations in North Eastern Province.[59]

The expulsion of Abu-Waid coincided with a crackdown against Al Muntada Al Islami in Nigeria, where authorities alleged that the head of the Nigerian branch of Al Muntada Al Islami, the Sudanese Wahabist cleric, Muhiddeen Abdullahi, had funded a short-lived uprising by Muslim youths in Yobe

State. The Muslim rebels called for the establishment of an Islamic state and fought security forces in a series of clashes that left two police and more than a dozen rebels dead.[60]

Some Muslim leaders in Kenya occupy positions on the local boards of these foreign-funded charities and often benefit personally from this relationship. These leaders appeared to have been unaware of the support that some of these charities have provided international jihadist terrorist groups. As U.S. officials privately conceded in the case of Al Haramain, only a small portion of the organization's total charitable giving found its way into Al Qaeda coffers.[61] Nonetheless, the relatively small amount of funding going to Al Qaeda and allied organizations has often proven to be of strategic value. In Kenya, Al Haramain support enabled Al Qaeda to establish its fishing business near Mombasa that acted as a front for an illicit international arms trade. This Al Qaeda business also provided critical support to the those carrying out the 1998 Nairobi embassy bombing. In Indonesia, Al Haramain support to an Indonesia terrorist group likely enabled the group to scale up its terrorist bombings in Bali.

Muslim leaders in Kenya asked the government to lift its ban on financial assistance from nongovernmental organizations based in Arab countries. Without the funds, development projects in Muslim areas, including health centers and Islamic schools, would suffer, they argued. Some Muslim leaders were openly critical of U.S. efforts to help compensate for the decline in Islamic assistance by providing resources to improve the quality of education in Islamic schools, saying that they wanted funds restored from Islamic sources.[62]

The police tactics in investigating terrorist activities, including the Al Qaeda actions of 1998 and 2002, have also provoked bitter protest from the Muslim community. Actions designed to weed out terrorists from Kenyan society resulted in what many Muslims regarded as intrusive discriminatory tactics against their communities, and so ironically these tactics may have helped create fertile ground for radical Islamist and jihadist recruiters.

The expression of Muslim concerns that the counterterrorism efforts unfairly discriminated against Muslims increased sharply after the Al Qaeda's 2002 Mombasa attacks. Government security forces had reportedly detained eighty Muslims on suspicion of terrorist links, giving rise to accusations that Muslims were being used as scapegoats, and that the cases were unduly influenced by foreign interference, pressure, and funding—a reference to the U.S. global war on terror.[63] After the large-scale investigations of the Mombasa terrorist acts, one young Mombasa resident, Ali Amin, complained, "Policemen, armed to the teeth have broken into our homes and arrested our mothers and sisters, put them through mental torture and released them without preferring any charges."[64]

Kenyan Muslim activists and human rights organization accused the Kenyan government of allowing foreign security agents to torture, interrogate, and violate the rights of Kenyans suspected of terrorism. They claimed that the government had permitted foreign security agents, in particular, the U.S. Federal Bureau of Investigation and Israeli security agents, to harass families and relatives of terror suspects. To illustrate their case, Kenyan human rights groups pointed to the prolonged and, so they argued, legally questionable detention of the brother of terrorist suspect Saleh Ali Saleh Nabhan as means to pressure him to reveal the whereabouts of his brother.[65]

The Kenyan government has acted to curb some of the excesses of its security forces involved in counterterrorism. For example, in response to protests by prominent Muslim leaders in Mombasa, then National Security Minister Chris Murungaru ordered, in December 2003, an end to unauthorized police swoops outside Mombasa mosques.[66]

Kenya's National Rainbow Coalition government showed considerable sensitivity to Muslim concerns in other areas. Perceiving that government security forces were overly zealous in combating Islamic terrorism, Muslim leaders opposed the 2003 proposal for "Suppression of Terrorism" legislation, which the government believed would give Kenya the legal framework needed to more effectively deal with terrorists. According to Amnesty International's 2004 Report,

> Suppression of Terrorism Bill...if enacted, would allow the police to arrest suspects and search property without the authority of the courts. It provided for the incommunicado detention of suspected "terrorists" for up to 36 hours, and the extradition of suspects without internationally agreed safeguards. The bill conferred on mem-

bers of the security forces immunity from prosecution for the use of "reasonable force" in the performance of their duties in fighting "terrorism."[67]

In response to Muslim outrage over the proposed legislation and concerns by human rights groups, the government postponed its enactment and initiated a review process that included Kenyan human rights groups to fine tune the draft law.[68]

KADHI COURTS

The effort to ban Islamic Courts in Kenya was another issue heightening resentment among Kenyan Muslims over their treatment. Muslim leaders became incensed over efforts by some Christian religious leaders to remove provisions for Islamic Courts, known in Kenya as Kadhi Courts, from a draft constitution. The Kadhi Courts, whose jurisdiction historically has been limited to personal law, i.e., marriage, divorce, and inheritance, have been enshrined in Kenya's constitution since independence. Then, when Kenya was engaged in a process of drafting a new constitution, elements of the Christian press appeared to have misled the public by distorting the scope and power of the Kadhi Court provisions in the draft constitution, saying that jurisdiction was to be expanded to commercial and civil disputes.[69]

Various prominent Muslim leaders reacted to the initiative to eliminate the Kadhi Courts by calling for actions that ranged from jihad to the establishment of a Muslim state if the Kadhi Courts were not continued. In April 2003, more than 2,000 Muslims demonstrated in Nairobi, and 8,000 protested in the predominately Somali town of Garissa in North Eastern Province.[70] The leaders, drawn from the Council of Imams and Preachers of Kenya and the Islamic Party of Kenya (IPK), said that Muslims deserved the courts, and that they would not relent in the struggle to have the courts enshrined in the new constitution. IPK chairman Sheikh Khalifa Mohammed charged that the plans to remove the Kadhi Courts were funded by foreign governments—a partial and apparently erroneous reference to the United States. He said, "We will stand firm and ensure that our rights are enshrined in the national constitution," and he charged that some Christian leaders were lying when they said that Muslims wished to turn Kenya into an Islamic state.[71]

Muslim leaders again reacted angrily to efforts by Christian church leaders to block the inclusion of the Kadhi Courts in the new constitution. In May 2004, forty Christian bishops threatened to have the draft constitution rejected at the referendum stage unless the Kadhi Courts were removed from it. Later in July, church leaders, drawn mainly from the Anglican Church of Kenya and Evangelical Churches of Kenya, filed a judicial petition seeking to have the country's judiciary declare that the inclusion of the Kadhi Courts in the new constitution is being done for the "sole purpose of acquiring political power, supremacy and control over Africa and Kenya by undemocratic means."[72]

Framers of the draft constitution ultimately tried to strike a compromise position on the contentious issue of the Kadhi Courts, but their solution left many Muslims and Christian leaders dissatisfied. Under the compromise solution, the proposed constitution would have established religious courts that would include Christian courts, Kadhi Courts, and Hindu courts. Jurisdiction of these courts was to be confined to "the determination of matters related to personal status as may be prescribed by an Act of Parliament." On the one hand, by providing courts for all faiths, the provision sought to placate the call from many Christian leaders to treat all religions equally. On the other hand, it managed to shrink the status of the Kadhi Courts to avoid favoring the Muslims alone. The provision seemed to have little popular support, and many Christian and Muslim leaders asked their respective faithful to vote against the proposed constitution in the referendum that took place in November 2005. The issue of the Kadhi Courts was one of several contentious issues in the draft constitution that was overwhelming voted down.[73]

IDEOLOGICAL IMPLICATIONS OF FOREIGN ISLAMIC FUNDING

According to David C. Sperling, a leading scholar of Kenyan Islam, international organizations and foreign Muslim communities have turned Kenya into the battleground of an ongoing religious "cold war." Saudi Arabia, Iran, and other Muslim countries offer scholarships for study overseas, sponsor social and cultural activities, and fund numerous projects and institutions, often in competition with one another. Local Muslim communities have often paid a price for these charitable acts, namely, the handing over of local community controls of Islamic affairs to foreign patrons.

> Generous propositions are made to build new mosques or madrasa, and to pay the salaries of the imam and religious teachers, but on condition that the local Muslim community benefiting from the grant hands over control (and sometimes the title deed of the land) of the mosque or madrasa, and allows the donor agency to appoint the imam and teachers. Viewed in this context, the objective of some of the donor agencies seems to be not so much to strengthen local Muslim communities, but rather to increase their own influence and control over those communities.[74]

As in many other countries, such foreign patrons have often promoted a Wahabist brand of Islam that often perceives the world in stark terms as opposed to the more tolerant form of Islam traditionally practiced by Kenyan Muslims. An incident that occurred in a mosque near Mombasa illustrates the type of conflict that has emerged between local Muslims and foreign patrons.

> A fight broke out during Friday prayers at the Aqsa Mosque in Kisauni between the local Muslim community and the officials of the Islamic Foundation after the local Kisauni community numbering more than 300 were forced to listen to a sermon given by a Muslim preacher who does not conform to their cultural values. A local Muslim preacher, Ustadh Bampini, who had been invited by the local Muslim community to lead prayers, was about to mount the stairs to the Minbar (pulpit) to deliver the Friday sermon when he was blocked by an official of the Islamic Foundation. The official told the congregation that Ustadh Bampini had no authority to deliver the sermon. He said that the person who had been delegated the duties of delivering the sermon was Ramadhan Alwa Juma. The congregation who had packed the mosque for Friday prayers then rose up and demanded the removal of the intruder to let Ustadh Bampini lead the prayers.[75]

The ideological orientation of mosque leadership assumes particular significance when considering that much of the debate within Islam in Kenya revolves around such religious practices as celebrating *Maulid* (Prophet Mohammed's birthday) and funeral prayers, which are usually carried out by the imam. These practices, considered heretical by the Wahabis of Saudi Arabia, have long been a part of Swahili Islam and the Islam practiced among various ethnic communities in the Kenyan interior. Most rural African Muslim communities in Kenya have had a tradition of celebrating Maulid, and many Kenya African Muslims first embraced Islam, attracted by the Maulid celebrations. Observing Maulid has thus come to symbolize the ideological conflict between "popular" Islam in Kenya and Wahabi Islam.[76]

INTERNATIONAL GRIEVANCES

The identification of Kenyan Muslim with the suffering of fellow Muslims internationally have reportedly contributed to a radicalization in the political outlook of Kenya's Muslim youth. Kenyan imams have preached in mosques about what they consider the injustices against fellow Muslims in Afghanistan during the U.S.-led intervention in Afghanistan and in U.S.-occupied Iraq, and Muslim youth can recite a litany of Israeli wrongs against Palestinians.[77] Both Mombasa and Nairobi have witnessed a number of protests against Israeli treatment of Palestinians and U.S. actions in Iraq, and Mombasa youth have rioted out of a sense of outrage of the perceived injustices meted out to Muslims.[78]

The international media, with its images of civilian casualties in Afghanistan, Lebanon, Iraq, and Palestine, have contributed to a growing anti-American and anti-Israeli sentiment among many Kenyans and most of all among Kenya's Muslim population. One middle class Muslim parent in Mombasa explained: "My children sit all day and watch TV, and they see Palestinian people being killed by Jews, Afghans killed by Americans, and they have no context. They don't understand it. They only see killing, and they become extreme."[79]

One of Kenya's most outspoken Islamic leaders, Sheikh Ali Shee, who is chairman of Kenya's Council of Imams and who preaches at one of Mombasa's more activist mosques, Sakina, has over the years spoken out against the injustice against Muslims internationally. Yet, he too has expressed concern that the political and social injustices are radicalizing the Muslim youth in Kenya. He has contended that his generation of Muslims have to face the challenge of seeing younger people drifting toward more extremist elements. "Al Qaeda is the hero for the young people…It's very difficult," he said, "…we have to solve the problem of injustice."[80]

NOTES

1. U.S. Department of State, Bureau of Human Rights, Democracy and Labor, *Interantional Religious Freedom Report 2003: Kenya*, http://www.state.gov/g/drl/rls/irf/2003/23714.htm.
2. David C. Sperling, *Islam and the Religious Dimension of Conflict in Kenya*, n.d., http: payson.tulane.edu/conflict/Cs%St/SPERLFIN5.html.
3. Kariuti Kanyinga, *Re-Distribution from Above: The Politics of Land Rights and Squatting in Coastal Kenya* (Uppsala: 2000), 94-96; Njuguna Muntonya, "Spectre of Violence Never Too Far Away," *Daily Nation: Monday Notebook*, September 30, 2002, http://www.nationaudio.com/News/DailyNation/Supplements/notebook/07102002/story4.htm.
4. L. Muthoni Wanyeki, "Kenya's Second Multi-party Election: Trends in Electoral Violence," *IPS*, n.d., http://www.ips.org/critical/watch/ken1.htm.
5. "New Move on Traditional Shrines Attracts Praise," *The Coast's Nation*, November 11, 1998, http://www.nationaudio.com/News/Daily Nation/1998/111198/Features/XX14.html.
6. Arye Oded, *Islam and Politics in Kenya* (Boulder: Lynne Rienner Publishers, 2000), 149.
7. Ibid., 152.
8. Gamal Nkrumah, "The Lure of Africa," *Al-Ahram Weekly On-line*, August 13-19, 1998, Issue no.390, http://weekly.ahram. org.eg/1998/390/in5.htm.
9. "Sudanese Envoy Denies SPLA Allegations of Support for Kenyan Opposition," *SWB*, March 25, 1995 [KTN TV, Nairobi, in English, March 23, 1995], http://www.sas.upenn.edu/African_ Studies/Newsletters/HAB395_SUD.html.
10. Phillipe Marchesine, *The Rise of Islamic Fundamentalism in East Africa*, 2003, http://www.african-geopolitics.org/show.aspx?ArticleId=3497.
11. *Human Rights Watch World Report 1995: Kenya*, http://www.hrw.org/reports/1995/WR95/AFRICA-04.htm#P184_66754.
12. Thomas P. Wolf, Carolyn P. Logan, and Jeremiah Owiti with Paul Kiage, *A New Dawn? Popular Optimism in Kenya after the Transition*, AfroBarometer Working Paper no. 33, March 2004, http://www.afrobarometer.org/AfropaperNo33.pdf+ Afrobarometer+Kenya+Muslims&hl=en.
13. Kevin J. Kelley, "How Al Qaeda Carried Out Paradise Hotel Bombing," *The East African*, November 11, 2003, http://allafrica.com/stories/200311111068.html.

Kenya: Jihadism in an Open Society

14. Walter O. Oyugi, Conflict in Kenya: A Periodic Phenomenon, 2002, http://216.239.39.104/search?q=cache:-DYQF0cNh5wJ: unpan1.un.org/intradoc/groups/public/documents/CAFRAD/UNPAN008267.pdf+squatters+Coast+kenya&hl=en; see Nene Mburu, *Bandits on the Border: The Last Frontier in the Search for Somali Unity* (Trenton: Red Sea Press, 2005).
15. *Stop the Massacre,* http://www.kenyasomalis.org/Gsa-massacre.html
16. In March 1999, the PanAfrican News Agency reported that Kenyan security agents had arrested an Al Itihaad member in Garissa who was recruiting young Kenya Somalis for its militia. "Regional: East Africa Refugees: EA Could Become a 'Terror Centre' Soon, *Africaonline*, November 25, 2002, http://www.ifj-pa.org/docs/mn020.htm; "Police Nab Militia Agent, *PanAfrican News Agency*, March 2, 1999 http://allafricacom/stories/printiable/199903020110.html.
17. Victor Obure, "I Have List of Hired Youth, Says Administrator," *The East African Standard*, November 6, 2006.
18. Stephen Muiruri, "Terror: Muslims Claim Mix-Up in Imam's Arrest," *The Nation*, December 11, 2001, http://allafrica.com/stories/200112100659.html.
19. "North Eastern Residents Press for Sharia," *The Nation*, June 11, 2002, http://allafrica.com/stories/200206100888.html.
20. Kevin J. Kelley, "Dadaab an 'Arms Centre,'" *The Nation,* November 18, 2000, http://allafrica.com/stories/printable/20011200098.html; Danna Harman, "In a Dire Kenyan Camp, Links to Al Qaeda," *The Christian Science Monitor*, December 18, 2002, http://www.csmonitor.com/2002/1218/p01s04-woaf.htm.
21. Alisha Ryu, "Somalia/Refugees/Terrorism," *VOANews*, January 24, 2003, http://www.globalsecurity.org/military/library/news/2003/01/mil-030127-2a181c54.htm.
22. Stephen Mgobo, "Lawyers Had Warned of Possible New Attacks in East Africa,"*CNSNews.com*, November 29, 2002, http://www.cnsnews.com/ForeignBureaus/archive/200211/FOR20021129c.html.
23. Office of Public Affairs, U.S. Department of the Treasury, *Treasury Announces Joint Action with Saudi Arabia against Four Branches of Al-Haramain in the Fight against Terrorist Financing*, Press Release JS-1108, January 22, 2004, http://www. ustreas.gov/press/releases/jus1108.htm.
24. Buthul Somali, *Our Madarasas are Now the Target! What Next!,* http://www.garissa.net/article7.htm.
25. Sheik Hussein Ibrahim Burale and Sheikh Muawiyah Mahmood, *Open Letter to Heads of All Diplomatic Corps in Kenya*, December 13, 2003, http://www.twf.org/News/Y2004/0229-Kenya.html.

26. "Demand for the Closure of Anti —Terrorism Units," *The Nation*, July 21, 2003, http://allafrica.com/stories/200307211227.html.
27. Darrin Mortenson, "Pendleton Marines Train in Kenya," *North County Times* (Oceanside, Calif.), January 19, 2004.
28. Burale and Mahmood, *Open Letter to Heads of all Diplomatic Corps in Kenya*, December 13, 2003, http://www.twf.org/News/Y2004/0229-Kenya.html.
29. Victore Obure, "40 Hurt in Anti-US Riot," *The East African Standard*, December 15, 2003; "Health Camp Rejected Over Terror Threat to US Men," *The Nation*, December 9, 2003.
30. Obure and Ongeri, "Marines Mission Shrouded in Mystery," *The East African Standard*, December 3, 2006, http://allafrica.com/stories/200612041176.html.
31. Kelley, "Dadaab an 'Arms Centre.'" Harman, "Dire Kenyan camp."
32. Cindy Horst, *Vital Links in Social Security: Somali Refugees in the Dadaab Camps, Kenya*, New Issues in Refugee Research Working paper no. 38, April 2001, http://www.jha.ac/articles/u038.pdf.
33. Stephen Muiruri, "Suspect Terrorists Sent Back to Kenya," *The Nation*, December 4, 2002, http://allafrica.com/stories/200212040045.html.
34. Cathy Majtenyi, "Terrorism Suspects in Kenya Said to Have Links to Journalist's Murder in Somalia," *VOANews*, February 22, 2005, http://www.voanews.com/english/archive/2005-02/2005-02-22-voa15.cfm; Victor Obure and Cyrus Ombati, "Ex-PS's Kin among Suspected Terrorists," *The East African Standard*, February 22, 2005; Dominic Wabala, "Four Terror Suspects Arrested," *The Nation*, February 22, 2005.
35. Kevin Kelley, "New Clues Emerge over Embassy Bombing," *The East African*, February 14, 2000, http://www.nationaudio.com/News/EastAfrican/14022000/Regional/Regional66.html.
36. Stephen Engelberg, "One Man and a Global Web of Violence," *The New York Times*, January 14, 2001, www.omaid.com/english_section/in_the_pres/binLadin_NYT_Jan14.htm#tap.
37. Global Witness, *For a Few Dollar$ More: How al Qaeda Moved into the Diamond Trade*, Report by Global Witness, April 2003, 28-40, http://www.globalwitness.org/reports/show.php/en.00041.html.
38. Vice Admiral Wilson, *Testimony to the Senate Select Committee on Intelligence*, March 21, 2002, http://www.fas.org/irp/congress/2002_hr/020602dia.html. According to *Washington Post* journalist, Douglas Farah, U.S. intelligence agencies have dismissed as unfounded press and other reports that Al Qaeda was involved in African gem trading in West Africa, and other sources have indicated that this dismissal may extend to Al Qaeda trading out of East and Central Africa. Douglas Farah,

Blood from Stones: The Secret Financial Network of Terror (New York: Broadway Books, 2004), 85-107.

39. Robert Block and Daniel Pearl, "Much-smuggled Gem Aids al-Qaida: Bought, Sold by Militants Near Mine, Tanzanite Ends Up at Mideast Souks," *The Wall Street Journal,* November 16, 2001, http://www.geocities.com/spyjaguar/161101.html.
40. Global Witness, *For a Few Dollar$ More*, 41.
41. Kevin Kelley, "New Clues Emerge over Embassy Bombing," *The East African*, February 14, 2000, http://www.nationaudio.com/News/EastAfrican/14022000/Regional/Regional66.html; Anssi Kullberg and Christian Jokinen, "Tracking the Merchants of Death," *The Eurasian Politician*, October 2003. Translation from the article published in *Kristityn Vastuu*, September 25,2003, http://www.cc.jyu.fi/~aphamala/pe/2003/mercdeat.htm.
42. Mark Huban, "Bankrolling Bin Laden," *Financial Times*, November 28, 2001, http://specials.ft.com/attackonterrorism/FT3FJ5RJMUC.html.
43. Islamic Liberation Army of the People of Kenya, August 11, 1998, text in Arabic published in London, http://www.african-geopolitics.org/show.aspx?ArticleId=3497#_edn3.
44. Paul Reynolds, "Al-Qaeda Suspected in Kenya Attack," *BBC*, November 28, 2002, http://news.bbc.co.uk/2/hi/africa/2523737.stm.
45. "Two Terror Suspects Deported," *The Standard*, May 20, 2004, http://allafrica.com/stories/200405200460.html; Stephen Muiruri, "Suspect Terrorists Sent Back to Kenya," *The Nation*, December 4, 2002, http://allafrica.com/stories/200212040045.html; "State Links Two to Al Qaeda Cell," *The East African Standard*, July 6, 2004, http://allafrica.com/stories/200407061166.html.
46. "The Journey of Haroun Fazul," *Frontline*, http://www.pbs.org/wgbh/pages/frontline/shows/saudi/fazul/.
47. Kevin J. Kelley, "How Al Qaeda Carried Out Paradise Hotel Bombing," *The East African*, http://allafrica.com/stories/200311111068.html; James Macharia, "Somalia Says Qaeda Suspect Handed to U.S. Agents, *Reuters,* March 19, 2003, http://www.intellnet.org/news/2003/03/19/18151-1.html.
48. Nation Team, "Terror Suspect Flown to US," *The Nation*, March 27, 2003, http://allafrica.com/stories/printable/200303270086.html.
49. "Mombasa Bomber Fazul's Secret Hideaway," *Debka-Net-Weekly*, December 13, 2002, 2, no. 18, http://archives.econ.utah.edu/archives/a-list/2002w51/msg00009.htm.
50. Thomas P. Wolf, Carolyn P. Logan, and Jeremiah Owiti with Paul Kiage, *A New Dawn? Popular Optimism in Kenya after the Transition*, AfroBarometer Working Paper no. 33, March 2004, http://

www.afrobarometer.org/AfropaperNo33.pdf+Afrobarometer+Kenya+Muslims&hl=en.
51. Judith Achieng, "Religion Bulletin-Kenya: Ruling on Muslim Charities Averts a Major Strike," *IPS*, September 18, 1998, http://www.oneworld.org/ips2/sept98/04_04_002.html.
52. Stephen Mbogo, "Kenyan Muslims Want Funding from Saudi Arabia, not US," *CNSnews.com*, March 16, 2004, http://www.cnsnews.com/ViewForeignBureaus.asp?Page=%5CForeignBureaus%5Carchive%5C200403%5CFOR20040316d.html.
53. Achieng, "Religion Bulletin-Kenya."
54. Frederick Nzwili, "Christian-Muslim Tensions Rising in Kenya," *All Africa News Agency*, October 5, 1998, http://allafrica.com/stories/199810050050.html.
55. Jonathan M. Winer, *Origins, Organization and Prevention of Terrorist Finance*, Testimony before U.S. Senate Committee on Governmental Affairs, July 31, 2003, http://www.iwar.org.uk/cyberterror/resources/terror-financing/073103winer.htm.
56. Mbogo, "Kenyan Muslims Want Funding."
57. "NGO Threat to Pull Out," *The East African Standard*, July 14, 2004, http://allafrica.com/stories/200407140133.html.
58. See Al Muntada Al Islami website: http://www.discoverislam.co.uk.
59. Otsieno Namwaya and Samwel Rambaya, "Why NGO Boss Was Thrown Out," *East African Standard*, March 6, 200, http://www.sudan.net/news/posted/7942.html.
60. "Kano Police Arrest Mastermind of Sudan-Saudi Inspired Bloody Revolt," *Mathaba.net*, February 25, 2004, http://www.mathaba.net/news/print.shtml?cmd[40]=i-42-8d08e484638feda19c15044c606aa68a; "Afrique: Montée des tensions inter-religieuses dans le nord du Nigeria," *AFP*, March 13, 2004, http://www.bethel-fr.com/voxdei2/afficher_info.php?id=8913.191.
61. Matthew Rosenberg, "Al-Qaida Continues to Siphon Charities," *Associated Press*, June 6, 2004, http://www.boston.com/news/world/africa/articles/2004/06/06/ap_al_qaida_continues_to_siphon_charities?pg=full.
62. Mbogo, "Kenyan Muslims Want Funding."
63. *Kenya: Muslims Tenions Rise and Churches Burn*, July 1, 2003, http://www.worldevangelical.org/persec_kenya_1jul03.html.
64. "Anti-terror Steps Irk Kenyans," *news24.com*, July 27, 2003, http://www.news24.com/News24/Africa/News/0,,2-11-1447_1393459,00.html.
65. Organizations critical of the practices of police and foreign security agents operating in Kenya include People against Torture, Release Political Prisoners, Independent Medico-Legal Unit, National Constitu-

tion Executive Council and Citizens for Justice, and the National Youth Movement. Jillo Kadida and Ngumbao Kithi, "Murungaru Bans Police Swoops at Mosques," *Daily Nation on the Web*, November 10, 2003, http://www.nationaudio.com/News/DailyNation/10112003/News/News1011200310.html.

66. Kadida and Kithi, ibid.
67. Amnesty International, *Annual Report 2004: Kenya*, http://www.amnestyusa.org/annualreport/index.html.
68. Patrick Mathangani, "Terrorism Bill to be Revised," *The East African Standard*, February 26, 2004, http://allafrica.com/stories/200402260080.html.
69. *Kenya: Jihad Threatened if Muslims Demands Are Not Met*, April 30, 2003, http://www.domini.org/openbook/kenya 20030430.htm.
70. Eliude Chisika and Victor Obure, "Muslims Protest over Kadhi Court," *The Nation*, April 26, 2003, http://allafrica.com/stories/200304280039.html.
71. Abdulsamad Ali, "Muslims Angered by Bishops' Stand on Review," *The East African Standard*, May 2, 2004, http://allafrica.com/stories/200405030233.html.
72. Nyakundi Nyamboga, "Clerics Sue Over Kadhis' Courts," *The East African Sandard*, July 15, 2004, http://allafrica.com/stories/200407150687.html.
73. Wangui Kanina, "Kenya: Kenya Referendum Campaign Gets Dirty," *New Vision* (Kampala), November 2, 2005, http://allafrica.com/stories/200511020402.html; Ali Abdi, "Muslims Want Bill Amended," *The East African Standard*, September 12, 2005, http://allafrica.com/stories/200509121009.html; Abdulkadir Hashim, "Muslim-State Relations in Kenya after the Referendum on the Constitution," *African Association for the Study of Religion*, 24 (November 2005), 21-27.
74. David C. Sperling, *Islam and the Religious Dimension of Conflict in Kenya*, http://payson.tulane.edu/conflict/Cs%20St/SPERLFIN5.html.
75. Ibid.
76. Ibid.
77. Dana Harman, "Why Radicals Find Fertile Ground in Moderate Kenya," *Christian Science Monitor*, December 6, 2002, http://www.csmonitor.com/2002/1206/p07s02-woaf.html.
78. "Muslims Take to the Streets over Military Actions," *The Daily Nation*, October 14, 2001, http://www.khilafah.com/home/Iographics/category.php?DocumentID=2423&TagID=2; Wawera Mugo and Ismail Wadham, "Muslim Youths Stage Protest against Israel," *Saturday Nation on the web*, September 8, 2001, http://www.nationaudio.com/News/DailyNation/08092001/News/News28.html.gz.

79. "Kenya's Muslims Debate Bin Laden's Role," *Associated Press*, December 3, 2002, http://www.foxnews.com/story/0,2933,71970,00.html.
80. Ibid.

Chapter Six

RADICAL ISLAMIC EXPRESSION IN TANZANIA
DOMAIN OF A GROWING MINORITY

In July 2004, Pakistani security forces, supported by U.S. agents, took into custody the Tanzanian national Ahmed Khalfan Ghailani in the city of Gurjarat after a fourteen-hour gun battle. The thirty-year-old Ghailani was a top Al Qaeda operative, known by aliases such as "Foopie" and "Ahmed the Tanzanian," who had been placed on the FBI's most wanted terrorist list for his alleged role in the 1998 bombing of the American embassy in Dar es Salaam.

According to Pakistani security officials, Ghailani was handed over to U.S. officials and flown out of Pakistan. Although he had been indicted in a U.S. Federal Court for the August 7, 1998 bombing of the U.S. embassy in Dar es Salaam and for conspiring to kill American nationals outside of the United States, U.S. authorities flew him out to an undisclosed location. Then over two years later, in September 2006, U.S. authorities transferred him and thirteen other prisoners to the detention center at the U.S. military base at Guantanamo Bay on the island of Cuba from secret overseas CIA prisons, where they had been held.[1]

After Ghailani's capture in Pakistan, his family and friends on the main Zanzibar island of Unguja were at a loss to explain how a quiet and religious youth made the transition to international terrorist.[2] In certain respects, the story lines of Ahmed Khalfan Ghailani's life—from pious Muslim youth in his native Zanzibar to hunted international terrorist—intersected with ideological crosscurrents and political trends that have characterized and influenced radical Islamic expression in Tanzania since 1990.

Ghailani's radicalization occurred during an era when groups of Tanzanian Muslim activists sought to gain adherents to their causes by exploiting growing suspicions between the Christian and Muslim communities, Muslim resentment of their real or perceived second class status, and frustration with the multiparty system's unfulfilled promise to deliver an alternating disposition of power in the country.

Ghailani hailed from the semiautonomous province of Zanzibar, which has come to earn a reputation as a hotbed of Islamic nationalist discourse that centered on the restoration of an Islamic government to Zanzibar and became intertwined with global jihadist grievances. Ghailani also served as a preacher in the fundamentalist *Tabligh Jamaat*—a normally apolitical missionary movement with roots in South Asia, but which in Zanzibar and other parts of East Africa has given rise to militant Islamist preaching and in the case of Uganda an armed insurrection. Sometime during his youth, Ghailani came across those espousing a jihadist ideology, possibly mujahidin veterans who had fought in Afghanistan against Soviet occupation, and under their influence he traveled abroad after secondary school, presumably to Pakistan and Afghanistan, for training in religion and ultimately in the use of explosives. Mujahidin returning home to Tanzania have reportedly played a role in radical Muslim politics in the streets of Dar es Salaam and in other cities, where some of them took part in the forced takeover of certain mosques.

Ghailani returned to Tanzania from his training abroad as an Al Qaeda operative, and in addition to the expertise that he provided in the embassy bombing, he reportedly learned the ropes of international gem trading. To help finance its operations in East Africa, Al Qaeda had set up companies to trade in diamonds harvested from Angola and Zaire and in tanzanite gems mined in Tanzania, where organized groups of radical Muslims sought to corner the tanzanite trade. After the 1998 embassy bombing, Ghailani fled to Pakistan and later made his way to West Africa, where he used his knowledge of gem trading to become a key figure in Al Qaeda's effort to profit from the illicit "blood diamond" trade from war-torn Sierra Leone through Liberia.[3]

The appeal of militant Islam has remained weak in Tanzania, and only a very small group of individuals like Ghailani have made the transition from Islamism to jihadist terrorism. When Islamist-inspired violence by Tanzanians has occurred, it appears to have been linked to foreign jihadist organizations and agencies which possessed the wherewithal to finance operations that supported their internationalist agenda. In 1993, for instance, NIF Sudan reportedly supported the short-lived jihadist efforts of *Baraza la Uendelazaji Koran Tanzania* (BALUKTA), known in English as the Tanzania Koranic Council. BALUKTA reportedly began training a jihadist militia and sponsored interreligious street violence in Dar es Salaam. As previously noted, Al Qaeda was behind the 1998 bombing of the U.S. embassy in Dar es Salaam, and officials of the Al Qaeda-linked, Saudi-based charity Al Haramain reportedly plotted to carry out terrorist attacks in Zanzibar and may have helped promote a spate of jihadist terrorist actions that hit Zanzibar in March-April 2004.

THE POLITICO RELIGIOUS BACKDROP TO RADICAL ISLAM

Political rhetoric that sought to drive a wedge between Tanzanian Christians and Muslims increased after the 1992 advent of multiparty rule, as political parties and radical Islamic preachers vied for popular support. Although no one knows for sure the religious composition of Tanzania's population, estimates of the percentage of Christian and Muslims in the country range from between one-third and one-half for each group.[4] Zanzibar is estimated to be about 95 percent Muslim. Many Muslim activists contend that Christian-dominated governments in both the colonial and postcolonial states have been guilty of discrimination against Muslims especially in education, which has disadvantaged them in the economy and in government service.

Despite the reinstitution of a multiparty system in Tanzania, no party other than the ruling *Chama Cha Mapinduzi* (CCM) has ever held power, either in the national government or in Zanzibar's regional government. As a result, the security apparatus of the state had continued, for all practical purposes, to function as an arm of the CCM. At times, these security forces have violently suppressed the opposition, including Islamist groups. This has been especially true in the Unguja and Pemba.

Islamist political agitation, which at times has taken the form of bombings and other terrorist acts, increased in Zanzibar, especially after government security forces brutally suppressed a 2001 opposition Civic United Front (CUF) protest of alleged electoral fraud by the CCM. Islamist anger was also aimed at the Western tourism industry in Zanzibar, which has been seen as having a corrupting influence on Islamic and local values. The attacks targeting tourism were likely intended to weaken Zanzibar's economy and thus to provoke a greater challenge to or collapse of the Zanzibar state.

On the mainland, Tanzania's commercial capital, Dar es Salaam, has been the scene of volatile "street" politics often led by firebrand Islamic clerics. The public preaching by such clerics, which began in the 1990s with political liberalization, often critiqued tenets of the Christian faith and earned the ire of the leadership of some Christian denominations. The Christian leaders then pressured the government to take action against these preachers, and the government, in an effort to preserve public order, imposed restrictions on certain Muslim religious activities. These restrictions gave rise to further resentment among Muslim activists.

RETURN TO AN ISLAMIC STATE

Although the objectives of radical Muslim activists often do not appear to be well defined or uniform, it is clear that many are frustrated by what they consider to be the failures of the secular state to redress their grievances. As a remedy, some aspire to restore an Islamic state in Zanzibar and to enforce sharia. Prior to German and later British colonialism, the Sultan of Zanzibar wielded considerable influence in large sections of what is now mainland Tanzania and Kenya. Apparently this vision of a restoration of Islamic rule would also ideally include areas of Tanzania and Kenya that remain predominately Muslim.

Muslim opposition literature in Tanzania has been replete with resentment of the 1964 Zanzibari Revolution that led to the dismantling of the independent democratically elected Zanzibari government.[5] In December 1963, the British gave Zanzibar its independence as a constitutional sultanate. One month later, in January 1964, it was overthrown, and by April 1964, postrevolution Zanzibar merged with Tanganyika to form Tanzania. Zanzibar then became a semiautonomous province of Tanzania with its own regional government and parliament.

The radical Muslim interpretation of these events amounts to a type of historical revisionism. According to the Islamist perspective, the specter of an Islamic state in the region triggered Christian politicians in Tanganyika and other African countries to conspire to rid the island state of its Islamic government.[6] The reality of Zanzibar's revolution was, however, far more complex, as a dimension of the revolution included a popular uprising of largely Muslim descendents of the African slave population against the descendent of the Arab slave and land owning class. However, the Islamist perspective pits Christian against Muslim and ignores the historic class and ethnic tensions that have existed among Muslims in Zanzibar.[7]

A year after the Zanzibari Revolution, Tanzania instituted a system of one-party rule on the mainland and in Zanzibar. The Tanganyika African National Union became the only legal party on the mainland, and the Afro-Shirazi Party, which was an actor in the revolution, became the sole political party in Zanzibar. The mainland and Zanzibari parties merged in 1970 to form the ruling CCM. The emergence of one-party rule stifled political dissent within the country, including the discussion of Muslim grievances.

MUSLIM EXPRESSION UNDER ONE-PARTY RULE

Within the politically intolerant climate of one-party rule, the government abolished an influential vehicle of Muslim expression, the East African Muslim Welfare Society (EAMWS), and created a quasigovernmental organization to represent Muslim interests in the country. EAMWS was founded in Mombasa in 1945 by the then Aga Khan, the leader of the Islamic Ismaili sect, with the aim of promoting Islam and raising the standard of living for East African Muslims. Asian Shiites, especially Ismaili, dominated and financed the organization, but the Aga Khan urged all Muslims in East Africa, the vast majority of whom are Sunni Muslims, to regard EAMWS as their organization. The EAMWS leader in Tanzania, Abdallah Fundikira, was one of the principal political rivals to President Julius Nyerere in the 1960s. EAMWS promoted a procapitalist or free market vision for Tanzania, at a time when President Nyerere was implementing his socialist agenda for the country. Because of its pan-Islamic and probusiness orientation, the prosocialist Muslims in Nyerere's party opposed EAMWS, and the Tanzanian government banned EAMWS in 1968.

President Nyerere attempted to control Muslim expression by promoting the formation of a national Islamic organization, *Muslims Baraza Kuu la Waislam wa Tanzania* (Tanzana Muslim Council) or BAKWATA, which after its formation maintained close ties with the ruling party. BAKWATA selected the country's Islamic legal authority, the *Mufti* (an Islamic legal scholar who interprets sharia) who served as a government employee.[8] Many Muslims felt that in the formation of BAKWATA, President Nyerere had discriminated against their religion, as the ruling party did not sponsor a parallel quasistatal organization for Christian denominations. This quasiofficial Muslim organization, then, became a thorn in the side of Muslims with political aspirations independent of the ruling CCM, and opposition to BAKWATA, then, became a focal point of resistance and resentment for dissenting Muslims during Tanzania's era of one-party rule and even later.

MUSLIM COMPLAINTS OF SOCIAL AND ECONOMIC INEQUALITIES

Muslim opposition intellectuals have contended that favoritism of Christians in the civil service and in the education system led to social and political inequalities in Tanzania. They have argued that the failure of the British colonial state to subsidize Muslim education (as it had done with Christian missionary schools) contributed to the development of substandard education for Muslims. According to University of Dar es Salaam Professor Hamza Mustafa Njozi:

> As far as access to education and employment are concerned, Tanzania today is divided into two major classes; the privileged and the underprivileged. ...the vast majority of Tanzanians who happen to be Christians are in the former category while the majority of citizens who are Muslims belong to the latter class. There is probably no serious researcher who can deny that Christians constitute a disproportionate majority of the best-trained minds in Tanzania. And since the majority of the finest medical doctors, lawyers, professors, engineers and professionals in other fields are Christians, naturally Christians also predominate in almost all key positions in government administration.[9]

Such inequalities, Muslim critics have argued, led to the growing political marginalization of Muslims. Muslim critics of the ruling CCM have pointed out that CCM has a history of favoring what they term as the "Christian lobby," and that the CCM has remained insensitive to Muslim grievances. They believe that the discrimination against Muslims has been a political betrayal of the many Muslims who were in the forefront of the Tanzanian independence movement. According to these critics, Muslim politicians were consistently marginalized in the CCM and its predecessor, Tanganyika African National Union, despite the fact that Tanzania's second president, Ali Hassan Mwinyi, who served from 1985 to 1995, was a Muslim born on Zanzibar.

THE EMERGENCE OF ISLAMIC POLITICAL RADICALISM IN TANZANIA

The origins of radical contemporary Islamic political thought in Tanzania may be traced to the 1975 formation of the "Muslim Writers Workshop," or *Warsha ya Waandishi wa Kiislam* in Swahili. The founders of Warsha were students of a Pakistani teacher, Muhammed Hussein Malik, whom the government brought to Tanzania to teach mathematics. Eventually BAKWATA employed Professor Malik to teach Islamic Studies in secondary schools in and around Dar es Salaam. Within ten years of his arrival, Professor Malik was able "to mold a strong following of disciplined and committed young men who began to see the injustices committed to Muslims in the Tanzanian society...."

> They harbored the desire to initiate a political movement in Mainland Tanzania graced by Muslim sentiments to free Muslims from the bondage of Christian dominance. It was in their view that a movement similar to the independence struggle initiated by Muslim patriots in 1950s which ousted the British from Tanzania should be organized. But this time the struggle had to be different. This movement, instead of pursuing the nationalist-secularist ideology articulated by Muslim founders of the independence movement, should strive to adopt in the new movement Islam as the ideology of genuine freedom. The decision for this change of strategy was because secularism had failed Muslims in the political system of Tanzania.[10]

Iran's Islamic Revolution in 1979 also influenced the Warsha group by reinforcing the idea that Islam could be wielded as a potent political ideology capable of mobilizing mass support.

Warsha managed in 1981 to help bring a more militant leadership, including Warsha members, into BAKWATA, whose leadership had been formerly handpicked by then President Nyerere. Warsha members began to use their position to reinforce Koranic and Islamic Studies in a number of secondary schools under BAKWATA supervision. In addition, Warsha began using the print media and radio to get its political message across to the larger Muslim community.

The CCM responded by restoring a more compliant leadership to BAKWATA. The government then acted quickly to remove Muslim schools from Warsha oversight. The government banned Warsha and declared its mentor, Professor Malik, a prohibited immigrant. He traveled to Nairobi and took up a position with a Saudi-based Islamic foundation, presumably Al Haramain.[11]

Warsha later established its own educational institution, Masjid Quba and Islamic Centre, but the government refused to register the "Muslim fundamentalist" school. Only later, in 1987, did the government allow the school to be registered, when a Muslim came to head the Ministry of Education.

CCM maintained firm control of BAKWATA, leaving Warsha and other Muslim organizations little recourse other than to demand the restoration of multiparty rule as a way to break CCM's political dominance of the Muslim community. For many years, Warsha's publication and another Islamic magazine, *Mizani*, were in the forefront of the campaign for the restoration of a multiparty system to Tanzania.

Growing Islamic Militancy: Government Violence and the Partisan Exploitation of Religion

The decade of the 1990s witnessed a growing expression of militancy among sectors of the Muslim population that followed the country's adoption of multiparty rule in 1992 and the playing of the religion card by some of those vying for political power. At times, members of the ruling CCM sought to discredit the opposition, especially the CUF, with charges that it harbored an Islamist agenda, and the CCM government acted to curb what it considered to be the growing Islamic militancy in the country by imposing restrictions on Muslim preaching practices.

For their part, some Muslim leaders began championing the growing grievances of the Muslim population in a bid to gain popular support for their position. Some Muslim activists began demonizing the CCM as the "Catholic Crusade Mission,"[12] a reference to the prominent role that Catholics have played in the CCM. This political dynamic of exploiting religion for political ends contributed to heightened tensions between Christian and Muslim communities with a government little able or unwilling to seek a resolution to the growing tensions.[13]

In spite of the heightened tensions between Muslims and Christians, a 2001 survey of Tanzanian attitudes showed that Tanzanians, both Muslim and Christian, on the mainland and in Zanzibar, have retained a much stronger identity as Tanzanians than as a member of a religious group.[14] This finding suggests that Islamists may have made little inroad in winning over mass converts to their cause. Rather, it would appear that radicalism remains the property of a small portion of the Muslim population, with the majority of Muslims aspiring for redress of their grievances through accommodations by the secular state.

A growing movement of Islamic fundamentalist preachers, who openly criticize Christianity during their public sermons and debates, has been one of the most visible expressions of Islamic radicalization in Tanzania.[15] The preaching of these clerics has contributed to the tension between Christian and Muslim groups. These preachers and their organizations have played a prominent role in the "street" politics of Dar es Salaam and Zanzibar. They have marshaled their supporters in vigilantism, civil protest, the takeover of mosques, and, in some cases, terrorist acts. Such preachers have reportedly also been active in Tanga, Tabora, and Kigoma.[16] In part, the radical clerics have been part and parcel of the international upsurge in Islamic militancy and fundamentalism inspired by the Iranian Islamic revolution and the international mujahidin of the anti-Soviet war in Afghanistan and supported by foreign, especially Saudi, Islamic charities promoting a Wahabist brand of Islam. NIF Sudan also tried to play a role in promoting an Islamist agenda through its support for BALUKTA.

In reaction to the street preachers, the leaders of some Christian denominations have turned to the government to take action against what they considered "blasphemous" propaganda. For instance, in early 1993, the country's Roman Catholic bishops issued a public statement against these preachers entitled *Tamko Rasmi la Baraza la Maaskofu Katoliki Tanzania Mintarafu Kashf za Akidini* (A Statement of the Tanzania Episcopal Conference on Religious Blasphemies). The bishops' statement and an accompanying denunciation of the offending clerics that was broadcast on Catholic radio reportedly inflamed Muslim fundamentalist passion and resulted in urban religious violence.[17]

TABLIGH JAMAAT

Some of Tanzania's radical Muslim preachers have also been linked to one of the largest Islamic international missionary societies, *Tabligh Jamaat* (Proselytizing Group). Its headquarters are located in Nizamuddin, New Delhi, India. The roots of Tabligh's religious ideology are found in the same school of Islamic thought associated with the madrasa in Deoband, India, said to have also influenced the Taliban in Afghanistan. Deobandi thought is an Islamic revivalist movement that developed as a response to British colonialism in India. Its approach has often been likened to the fundamentalist Salafist and Wahabist traditions within Islam, but the Deobandi movement is different in many respects from the other fundamentalist traditions, especially in terms of spirituality. For instance, Wahabist intellectuals have been known to look down upon the practices of Tabligh Jamaat as an impure form of Islam because of its Sufi roots. However, in East Africa, at a popular level there appears to be a blending of the Wahabist fundamentalism and Tabligh Jamaat's reformist tradition.

An important Tabligh international center is located in Raiwind, outside Lahore, Pakistan. Raiwind has regularly hosted an annual three-day gathering estimated at over one million Tabligh fundamentalist believers. This may be the largest assembly of Muslims after the annual *hajj* in Mecca.

Al Qaeda operatives have on occasion used membership in Tabligh Jamaat as a cover for their travels. The U.S. government, for instance, alleged that Al Qaeda cell members of Yemeni origin in Lackawanna, New York, used the annual gathering of Tablighis in Raiwind as an opportunity to join the Taliban and Al Qaeda in Afghanistan. According to leaders of the missionary society, Tablighis are supposed to refrain from political activity. Yet, many Tablighis appear sympathetic to international jihadist agenda. Indeed, at the annual gathering of the movement in Raiwind in November 2001, a *Los Angeles Times* staff reporter found evidence of support for Osama bin Laden among some of the Tablighis.[18] In Uganda, a faction of the Tabligh sect joined the armed rebellion of Allied Democratic Forces (ADF), which operated against Uganda out of eastern Zaire/Congo. The ADF was also reportedly responsible for numerous terrorist bombings in Kampala and in other Ugandan towns in the 1990s. The ADF sought to establish an Islamic state in Uganda, and some of its supporters have been trained in Al Qaeda camps in Sudan and later in Afghanistan.[19] The Ugandan ADF had also unsuccessfully sought support for its jihad from the Iraqi government.[20]

Zahor Issa Omar has been identified as one of the militant Tablighis in Zanzibar's Pemba Island. He reportedly traveled to mainland Tanzania, Kenya, and Uganda each year to preach. The preacher told the *Associated Press* that "There is an army of Muslims and they are fighting an army of non-Muslims — who are trying to destroy Islam." Such preachers in Pemba are supported by Saudi Wahabist charities and receive stipends that are considered generous salaries by Zanzibari standards. The Saudi charities direct the local preachers to such a degree that the charities fax to the local preachers suggested texts for sermons. Some Tablighis in Pemba have reportedly preached support for Osama bin Laden and Al Qaeda and opposition to the U.S. occupation of Iraq. An indication of the influence of these preachers in winning converts may be found in the fact that some of the several hundred foreign fighters captured by November 2003 in Iraq came from East Africa, according to U.S. Marine Brigadier General Mastin Robeson, commander of the Joint Counter Terrorism Task Force based in Djibouti.[21]

Two Zanzibari Tablighis were involved in the 1998 Al Qaeda car bombing of the U.S. embassies in Kenya and Tanzania. A U.S. court convicted Khalfan Khamis Mohammed in 2001 for the murder of eleven people in the bombing U.S. embassy in Dar es Salaam. Mohammed had received weapons and explosives training in Afghanistan at Camp Manakando, which was run by a group called *Har Qatar*. He claimed never to have been an Al Qaeda member. The other Tabligh missionary/terrorist is Ahmed Khalfan Ghailani, who was captured in Gurjat, Pakistan in late July 2004 during a joint Pakistani-U.S. raid.[22]

Traditionalist Mulsim leaders in Zanzibar have felt both threatened by and at odds with the Tablighis. Maalim Mohammed Idriss, a traditionalist imam and Islamic historian in Zanzibar, said the Tablighis and the Wahabis, who have sponsored them, have perverted the Islamic missionary tradition, which goes back centuries, and represent a threat to the region's Sufi traditions. According to Idriss, "the Wahabis are dangerous…the old men have become very disturbed, those following the old traditions have become very disturbed."[23]

UWAMDI

One of the first Islamist preaching groups that came to public notice in Tanzania in the 1990s was *Umoja wa Wahubiri wa Mlingano wa Dini* (Union of Preachers for Propagation of Religion) better known as UWAMDI, whose secretary general was Sheikh Swaleh Uthman Ngoy. Founded in 1987, UWAMDI criticized the government's use of the quasiofficial BAKWATA to manage Muslim religious and educational affairs.[24] Its publication, *Mizani* (The Balance), advocated the establishment of a multiparty system in Tanzania. The editor of *Mizani*, Khamis Muhammed, who was influenced by and wrote about Wahabism, described the Iranian Islamic Revolution as a source of inspiration, and in a 1990 interview, he advocated that the Islamic Revolution in Iran should be followed by all Muslims in the world.[25]

BALUKTA AND SUDANESE SUPPORT

BALUKTA, known in English as the Tanzania Koranic Council, sought to promote the reading of the Koran and the spread of Islam through financial and material support to Islamic schools. It was active in Dar es Salaam and Zanzibar. In April 1993, some BALUKTA members, under the leadership of its president, Sheikh Yahya Hussein, were involved in attacks against butcheries selling pork in Dar es Salaam. Three slaughterhouses were destroyed, and authorities arrested some thirty people. BALUKTA and its supporters had taken offense at the rearing and slaughtering of pigs that had become common in religiously mixed neighborhoods.[26]

Tanzanian Deputy Prime Minister Augustine Mrema charged that BALUKTA had recruited 500 young men to set up an Islamic Army.[27] Various sources have claimed that BALUKTA received financial support from Sudan, and another source suggested that it was backed by Iran.[28] In 1993, the Tanzanian government investigated reports that youths received military training at an Iranian-funded rice project at Ikwiriri, approximately 100 kilometers (62 miles) south of Dar es Salaam. Sudan was accused of being involved in giving military training to Tanzanians to topple the government, and the government responded by expelling Sudanese nationals.[29] BALUKTA members were also suspected and accused of plotting through mosques to topple the government by force,[30] of inciting against it, of trying to stir up riots between Christians and Muslims by disseminating inflammatory cassettes, and of intending to destroy churches. The government ultimately responded by banning the organization.

However, some Muslim activists have contended that the allegations that BALUKTA was preparing to launch jihad have been unfounded and have been symptomatic of journalistic sensationalism in Tanzania that has contributed to the stereotyping of Muslims and has fomented hostilities between Christians and Muslims. Other sources indicate that BALUKTA had, indeed, gone beyond its original intent to promote the reading of the Koran in Arabic and had advocated the establishment of an Islamic state if the CCM government failed to meet its demand; the sources on this incident do not provide, however, details of these demands.

1998: CRACKDOWN ON RADICAL CLERICS

Heavy-handedness of Tanzanian security forces in cracking down on radical Islamic preachers and on the democratic opposition appears to have contributed to the radicalization of Muslims, especially among the youth both in Zanzibar and on mainland Tanzania. Islamic polemicists have pointed to the March 1998 killings at the Mwembechai mosque in Dar es Salaam and the 2001 killings of opposition demonstrators on the islands of Unguja and Pemba as critical events in stirring up Muslim resentment.

In early 1998, Tanzanian authorities vowed to get tough on what they considered to be extremist Islamic preachers. Tanzanian President Benjamin Mkapa said his government would not tolerate "people who go about distributing cassettes, booklets and convening meetings where they insulted and ridiculed other religions."[31] The government then issued a "juristic ruling" restricting Muslim Eid prayers to the day that would be announced by the leader of the Supreme Muslim Council, Mufti Hemed. Many Muslims were reportedly incensed by the government's willingness to interfere in the practice of their faith.

After the ruling was issued, a Catholic priest, Father Camillius Lwambano, told audiences on Catholic *Radio Tumaini* in Dar es Salaam that he had heard Muslim preachers ridiculing the Lord Jesus Christ. The priest challenged the authorities to live up to their commitment to stop blasphemy.[32] In the crackdown that ensued, police rounded up a number of Muslim preachers. In the aftermath, Muslim demonstrators clashed with police, and on February, 13 police opened fire on a crowd gathered outside Mwembechai Mosque, leaving three or four Muslims dead and many wounded.[33]

The Mwembechai killing may have been a turning point in the growing militancy of radical Muslims. The killings occurred in February 1998, and in August 1998, Al Qaeda bombed the U.S. embassy in Dar es Salaam.

AL QAEDA'S FINANCIAL LINK IN TANZANIA: GEMS AND CHARITY

Until the August 1998 bombing of the U.S. embassy in Dar es Salaam, Al Qaeda's involvement in Tanzania appears to have been restricted to business. As noted in the previous chapter, from early 1993 onwards, the year when al Qaeda ran into financial difficulty because the Sudanese government had failed to honor contracts to bin Laden, a coordinated attempt was made by two senior Al Qaeda members, Abu Ubadiah al-Banshiri, and Wadih el Hage, to trade in diamonds, tanzanite and rubies with the aim of making the organization's operations in East Africa financially self-sufficient.

The two Al Qaeda operatives registered companies for the ostensive purpose of mining diamond, gold and tanzanite in Tanzania, and reportedly had land purchased in Tanzania for diamond mining. Their mining companies were probably largely used as a conduit for illicit diamonds harvested in eastern Zaire and Angola; and through a trading firm, Tanzanite King — a company operating out of Nairobi and Mombasa — Al Qaeda bought and sold tanzanite, a gem only found in Tanzania. After Al Qaeda pulled out of the Tanzanian gem business, following the 1998 embassy bombings, Muslim radicals sympathetic to the Al Qaeda cause were involved in the tanzanite gem trade and sought to corner the tanzanite market.

The Saudi-based Al Haramain Islamic Foundation allegedly provided support for Al Qaeda and plotted terrorist action in Tanzania, according to U.S. and Saudi governments. Al Haramain maintained considerable financial and business ties to Al Qaeda in a number of other countries. The orgnization also came to own a large number of mosques in Tanzania that promoted the Wahabist doctrine. Al Haramain owned 136 mosques and a boarding school in Tanzania.[34]

In January 2004, the United States and Saudi Arabia asked the United Nations to add the Tanzanian branch of Al Haramain to the list of terrorist organizations tied to Al Qaeda. Both governments charged that individuals associated with Al Haramain helped plan a foiled effort in 2003 to attack several hotels in Zanzibar frequented by Westerners.[35] The Tanzanian government deported officials of the charity, the Tunisian Abu Hubheyifa and the Yemeni Mohammed Ally Saleh al-Saad, aka Mohed, on violation of immigration laws.[36]

Al Haramain's interest in encouraging terrorist acts against tourism catering to Westerners appears not to have been limited to Zanzibar. The Saudi charity also helped finance the operation of the Indonesian terrorist organization, Jeemah Islamiah (Islamic Community); in October 2002, in the resort town of Kuta on the Indonesian island of Bali, it killed 202 people and injured another 209.[37] Linkages between Al Haramain and terrorism against Western-oriented tourism in as diverse locations as Zanzibar and Bali suggest a coordinated international strategy. In addition to discouraging Westerner, who were perceived as corrupting influences, from visiting Muslim-majority countries, the objective of these terrorist strategies appears to have been to damage the soft economic underbelly and ultimately the stability of the governments.

THE PEMBA MASSACRES

Tanzanian security forces committed gross human rights abuses, killing at least 35 people and wounding more than 600 others, when they suppressed opposition demonstrations in the islands of Pemba and Unguja in January 2001. This violence followed the hotly contested regional and national elections in Zanzibar in the year 2000, which many Zanzibaris believed was rigged in favor of the ruling CCM.

Tanzanian army and police opened fire without due cause on January 27, 2001, attacking thousands of supporters of the opposition CUF who were protesting against alleged electoral fraud. In the ensuing days, security forces, aided by ruling party officials and militias, went on a house-to-house rampage, indiscriminately arresting, beating, and sexually abusing island residents. Some two thousand Zanzibaris fled to nearby Kenya, though most returned following an agreement between the government and the CUF.[38] A government commission investigating the massacres admitted that the violations committed by the security forces could have been avoided with better training and equipment for crowd control, and called upon the government to compensate those who had sustained serious injuries.[39] According to Human Rights Watch, no one responsible for the 2001 abuses, including shootings of demonstrators, beatings, and sexual abuse, was ever held accountable.[40]

The politically-motivated violence on Unguja and Pemba took a decidedly religious tone, as some CCM members have tried to discredit the CUF by portraying it as Islamist. In the 2000 disputed elections on Zanzibar, the CCM supporters stigmatized the CUF as "Muslim radicals," bent on introducing sharia to secular Tanzania. According to these allegations and rumors, the CUF is funded by "Arabs" and has the aim of returning the sultanate to Zanzibar. Part of the effort to demonize the CUF has been to take advantage of the fact that CUF secretary general and two-time candidate for the presidency of Zanzibar, Seif Shariff Hamad, had been a member of the Muslim Writers Workshop and an associate of the Pakistaini Islamist, Muhammad Hussein Malik, who introduced the notion among some Muslim youth in Tanzania that Islam could be a political organizing tool.[41] Seif Shariff Hamad, however, had also served as chief minister of Zanzibar from 1984 to 1988 under CCM auspices.

While it has a significant Muslim membership, including strong support in predominately Muslim Zanzibar, the CUF is not an Islamist party. It was formed on the Tanzanian mainland by lawyers, activists, and politicians from various communities, including Zanzibar and mainland Tanzania.[42]

INCREASING MILITANCY OF MUSLIM RADICALS

Following the Mwembechai killings, the embassy bombing, and especially the Pemba massacres, there has been evidence of a growing militancy and recourse to violent actions by small groups of radical Muslims on the Tanzanian mainland and also in Zanzibar. They apparently justified the use of violence against Western *kaffurs* (nonbelievers), apostate Muslims, and supporters of what are considered the illegitimate, repressive and Christian-dominated government.

In August 2001, unknown assailants bombed two CCM offices in Dar es Salaam. The media implicated "Muslim zealots," reporting that the bombings followed a demonstration by about 170 Muslims who demanded the release of a radical cleric, Khamis Rajan Dibagula, arrested for defaming Jesus Christ.[43] Another radical cleric, which one source identified as "one of the main theological instigators for contemporary militant activism is East Africa," was Sheikh Ponda Issa Ponda. Sheikh Ponda has been a popular firebrand whose followers have taken to the streets to protest discrimination against Muslims and to champion an Islamist agenda. Sheika Issa Ponda is one of the leaders of the Committee for the Defense of Moslem Rights, and in this capacity, he exhorted fellow Muslims not to vote for the ruling CCM. On various occasions Tanzanian authorities have arrested Sheikh Ponda on sedition and murder charges, only to release him later.[44]

Issa Ponda's followers have reportedly been involved in the forceful takeover of disputed mosques in Dar es Salaam. He has been credited as being influential with members of *Simba wa Mungu* (God's Lions), a group alleged to be involved in mosque takeovers and in inciting attacks against foreigners and the "morally corrupt." One account attributes a bombing of a Zanzibari tourist bar to Simba wa Mungu. In 1999, police arrested the sheikh for inciting his followers against other religions. A week later, police canceled a Muslim demonstration that was organized to protest his arrest. The sheikh later was charged with seditious intent and released on bail; however, in February 2002, he was rearrested and charged with murder as one of the nine Muslim leaders held responsible for the Mwembechai mosque riots of 2002. Violence at the mosque began after police intervened and fired tear gas at a Muslim prayer meeting to commemorate the 1998 Mwembechai mosque riots; two persons, including a police officer, were killed in the 2002 riots. The charges against the sheikh were later dropped.[45]

Radical confrontation was also directed against more moderate Muslims. The return of Tanzanian *mujahidin* from Afghanistan have reportedly played a role in this. By 2003, it was reported that Islamists, known as *Wanaharakita* (the Swahili word for "activists"), had taken over some 30 of Dar es Salaam's 487 mosques, and Tanzanian jihadists driven out of Afghanisan in 2001-2002, after the U.S.-led intervention there, had moved into these mosques.[46] Somalia and Mombasa in Kenya were known to have been a recruiting ground for fighters against the Soviet Union in Afghanistan. Research by the author of this study has not been able to establish the extent to which Tanzanians joined the ranks of the mujahidin in Afghanistan. Nonetheless, the interplay between the Tablighis, the returning mujahidin, Al Qaeda and groups like Al Haramain appears critical to understanding the formation of the core of some radical Muslim groups in Tanzania.

Tanzanian authorities also broke up a plot to bomb BAKWATA headquarters in February 2002. During a search of the home of Sheikh Omar Bashir, imam of one of the largest mosques in Dar es Salaam, the police said that they found detonators and ten kilograms (22 pounds) of dynamite, as well as a passport showing that he had traveled to Saudi Arabia and other countries of the Middle East. The authorities alleged that the explosives were meant for an attack against the headquarters of BAKWATA, accused of a lack of enthusiasm in the "war against the infidels." Sheikh Omar Bashir, whose followers call themselves *jahidinis* (jihadist in Kiswahili) has preached opposition to the United States and support for the former Taliban regime in Afghanistan. He reportedly has condoned suicide attacks as a legitimate weapon in the cause of defending Islam.[47]

TERRORISM AND POLITICAL VIOLENCE IN ZANZIBAR

In March and April 2004, a wave of political violence threatened to take the island of Unguja down the road to open civil strife. A series of small-scale terrorist attacks on the island was most likely the handiwork of Islamist extremists whose identity remains unknown. Also unknown is the extent of international jihadist involvement, if any, in these attacks. It may be worthwhile nonetheless to bear in mind Al Qaeda's past involvement with Zanzibar. Al Qaeda had recruited the Zanzibari Tablighis who carried out the U.S. embassy bombing in Dar es Salaam, and as previously noted, there have been several reports about the effectiveness of the Tabligh preachers on Pemba and Unguja in promoting sympathy for the Al Qaeda cause. In addition, members of the Tanzanian branch of the Al Haramain Islamic Foundation, a group supporting Al Qaeda activities in several countries, were foiled in their alleged plot to bomb several hotels in Zanzibar in 2003.[48]

The terrorist attacks that rocked Unguja coincided with the fortieth anniversary of the union of Zanzibar and Tanganyika in April 2004. The anniversary is much despised by Zanzibari Islamists because it had followed the overthrow of the sultanate. Events heated up in March with the government's banning of a demonstration in Zanzibar town by *Jumuia ya Uamsho na Mihadhara* (the Revival and Propagation Organization), commonly referred to as Uamsho. Uamsho, a leading radical Islamist organization in Zanzibar, had called the demonstration in part to protest the government's appointment of a Mufti for Zanzibar. Uamsho argued that the Mufti should be elected by Muslims and not appointed by the government. Uamsho had also expressed its resentment of the Tanzanian government's alleged favoritism of Christians over Muslims; and Uamsho had also been decrying the growing Western influence in Zanzibar resulting from the growth in tourism.

The police said they banned the demonstration because some of Uamsho's leaders advocated the killing of Zanzibari leaders who were opposing the imposition of Islamic law in Zanzibar. Uamsho leaders admitted that at earlier rallies and in some of their literature and videos, certain preachers said that secular leaders should be killed, but they insisted that those were individual views and not Uamsho policy. Uamsho proceeded with the demonstration despite the ban; demonstrators reportedly pelted the police with stones, and the police fired back with tear gas.

In the weeks after the confrontation between Uamsho followers and the police, a series of terrorist acts took place. A Catholic church was set ablaze; a Catholic school bus was torched; explosive bombs were placed at the home of the newly appointed Mufti; a grenade was lobbed into the home of a Zanzibari government minister; a grenade was also tossed into a restaurant filled with foreigners, including a British diplomat, but failed to discharge; a bomb was found in another restaurant frequented by Westerners; and some electric transformers were destroyed.[49]

The small-scale character of the bombs deployed, incompetence in the use of explosives, and the recourse to low-tech methods such as arson suggest that the Zanzibar terrorist attacks lacked the planning and sophistication normally associated with operations financed by Al Qaeda and the Al Haramain charity. These factors indicate that the attacks were likely the result of local operatives without the benefit of outside help. The break up of Al Haramain's Tanzanian branch, which plotted attacks against tourist hotels on Zanzibar, may have translated into the relatively ineffective assault upon targets in Zanzibar.

The burning of Catholic buildings and the foiled bombing of the Mufti are also suggestive of an attempt to foment sectarian discord in Zanzibar. The attempted bombing of the Zanzibari ministers suggested a challenge to the state; and the targeting of tourist facilities an attempt to harm the economy.

The targeting of the tourists also highlights the tension that has existed between the tourism industry and those Islamists in Zanzibar who say that they are upholding traditional and Islamic values against what they consider to be the corrupting influence of the West. Islamist disgust with the impact of Western tourism is echoed in the opinion of Professor Seithy Chachage of the University of Dar es Salaam.

> They are up to no good these tourists. All over the Island whorehouses are popping up to cater for them. The so-called hotels coming by dozens on the beachfront are no more than dens of inequities. Tourists lure our girls here with wild promises of foreign travel. They then get them into the cocaine habit. The next thing you know, they get hooked. We want investment but not the sort that turns our sisters and daughters into whores and junkies.

Zanzibari youth have protested against tourism, claiming to be doing so in the name of the Islamic faith. Islamic religious leaders in many parts of Tanzania have joined in the criticism of tourism and its effects on the local culture and inhabitants. One preacher, Sheikh Kurwa Shauri, was imprisoned in Zanzibar after demanding the government abolish tourism, and, on dubious legal grounds, Zanzibari authorities deported him to his home base in Tabora on the mainland.[50]

Government officials and opposition leaders accused one another of responsibility for the terrorism. CUF leaders said the government had staged the attacks of March-April 2004 as part of an effort to discredit the opposition. Authorities said the violence was the work of jobless youth recruited by the CUF and local Islamists to foment unrest.[51] CUF leaders have denied any link to radical Islamic terrorism on Zanzibar. It is difficult to know to what extent Zanzibari officials are blaming the CUF for the radical Islamic violence merely as a way of discrediting the opposition party, or whether there may be indeed some truth to the allegation that at some level the

CUF may be leveraging radical Islamists groups as a way of fomenting popular discontent that can then be channeled into electoral support for the CUF.

What seems certain is that the CCM supporters engaged in some violence against the CUF during this period of strife. According to a *Voice of America* report, in addition to the terrorism attacks described above, opposition leaders had been the target of a wave of political violence, some of it attributable to CCM supporters. In one instance, a hotel owned by Naila Jiddawi, a former CUF parliamentary representative, was firebombed by a crowd led by local officials of the ruling CCM.[52]

Authorities responded to the terrorism by detaining at least two of the top leaders of Uamsho, Sheikh Farid Ali and Sheikh Kalid Azan. The former was released after a two-week detention. A Uamsho spokesman said he had been tortured by police and had to be treated for his injuries in a Dar es Salaam hospital.[53]

The government also restricted the activities of the CUF's paramilitary organization, banning in April the training exercises of its Blue and White Guards. The CUF, whose members felt vulnerable after the 2001 massacre of its supporters on Pemba, protested, saying that the guards had been organized merely to provide security for its members.[54] In response to growing political unrest in Zanzibar, in June, the Tanzanian government ordered a large movement of troops from the mainland to Pemba out of concern that political violence might spread there from Unguja; fearing another crackdown on its supporters, the CUF leadership once again protested.[55]

Concerns that Zanzibar might descend into even more violence led Zanzibar president Amani Abeid Karume to anger, declaring in July 2004 that his government would no longer tolerate politicians making "inflammatory" statements aimed at disrupting the peace in the isles. "I want to tell them that we are tired! We are tired! We are tired!" President Karume went on to warn CUF Secretary General Seif Shariff Hamad against implementing his reported threat to "set the country ablaze" if he was "robbed" of victory in the upcoming 2005 presidential election. "Which country is he referring to? Is he crazy? If he thinks that he can cause chaos in Zanzibar let him be assured that he is dreaming."[56] Yet, President Karume's supporters and government security forces apparently were behind most of the limited violence that was to occur in the context of the 2005 elections.

ZANZIBAR'S DEMOCRATIC MIRAGE

There is little doubt that Tanzania's failure to introduce free and fair elections in Zanzibar as part of the country's 1992 adoption of a multiparty system has encouraged the growth of Islamic militancy. Both the widespread fraud in Zanzibar's 2000 elections and the massive state repression that ensued pushed some Zanzibaris, especially youth disillusioned with the status quo, into the welcoming arms of radical Islamist preachers. Both moderate and radical Muslim leaders in Zanzibar have acknowledged that this political radicalization has taken place, and the flawed elections of 2005 may have done little to counter this trend.

In late 2005, the CUF once again lost the elections, and alleged that they had once again been stolen as a result of government fraud. International observers agreed that the election process was flawed, but they observed that the electoral performance was more transparent and better managed than in the past. The government was faulted both for the excessive deployment of security forces and for the excessive use of force.[57]

Opposition officials accused the CCM of deploying an irregular militia to intimate them through acts of violence. Zanzibaris gave this local irregular militia the popular name "*Janjaweed*" to draw an analogy with the notorious Janajaweed militias used by the Sudanese government to wreck genocide-like violence on the African populations of Sudan's Darfur region.

Nonetheless, political violence by government security forces in 2005 did not reach anywhere near the levels of the 2000 elections, in part, because both the CCM and CUF had reached a "Peace Accord" in 2001 that sought to moderate the political practices of the two parties and enhance the neutrality of the government in the electoral process.[58] In addition, at the height of the October 2005 Zanzibar electoral season, government, opposition, and Muslim leaders had made public calls for nonviolence during the elections, although five protestors and four police were reportedly killed in postelection violence in Pemba.[59]

Uamsho and other Islamist organizations have been prevented from establishing their own political parties, and some of these groupings opted informally to throw their support behind the secular CUF in the 2005 election. The Islamist leaders have contended, however, that election fraud and government unresponsiveness to people's needs have created an opening for them and their plans to create an Islamic state. Cofounder of Uamsho, Khalid Azan, reportedly said, "Democracy in Zanzibar has failed. Muslims are desperate. They are suffering. The only way for our society to move forward is through an Islamic state."[60]

How effective Uamsho and other fundamentalist groups will be in using religion as a political organizing tool to achieve the goal of an Islamic state is yet to be seen. It appears to be preparing the ground by preaching and recruiting youth to its cause. Radicalized by years of perceived marginalization, some young Muslims have returned from scholarships in Saudi Arabia and Pakistan with the view that religion may be the only force capable of rescuing Zanzibar from what they see as moral decay. In sermons by Zanzibar imams, local grievances have also become intertwined with rhetoric about international issues—what they consider to be the injustices of the U.S. military occupation of Iraq and what they see as U.S. support of Israeli policies toward Palestinians; and, in this way, local grievances are becoming part of a global Islamist narrative. Prohibited from having their own religious parties that might stand in elections, it is yet to be seen what measures Uamsho and other radical organizations may use to realize their vision of an Islamic state in Zanzibar.

Notes

1. "Prisoners: Ghost: Ahmed Khalfan Ghailani," http://www.cageprisoners.com/prisoners.php?id=1307; "Pakistan Hands over Ahmed Khalfan to US," *The News* (Pakistan), January 26, 2005, http://www.jang.com.pk/thenews/jan2005-daily/26-01-2005/main/main7.htm; Robert Burns, "Terrorist Suspects Arrive at Guantanamo," *Associated Press*, September 7, 2006, http://www.washingtonpost.com/wp-dyn/content/article/2006/09/07/AR2006090700719.html?referrer=delicious; and *Fourteen Senior Prisoners to Guantanamo*, http://universalprox.com/index.php?q=aHR0cDovL3d3dy5nbG9iYWxzZWN1cml0eS5vcmcvc2VjdXJpdHkvcHJvZmlsZXMvZm91cn

RlZW5fc2VuaW9y X3Bya XNvbmVyc190b19ndWFudGFuYW1v
LmhObQ%3D%3D.
2. Mwaka Nakasula, "A Journey into the Home of Ahmed Khalfan Ghailani," *Mirror*, August 17, 2004, http://www.ipp.co.tz/ipp/mirror/2004/08/17/18635.html, and Ali Sultan, "Kin Says Bombings Suspect Was Secretive,"*Associated Press*, July 31, 2004, http://www.phillyburbs.com/pb-dyn/news/91-07302004-340297.html.
3. See Douglas Farah, *Blood from Stones: The Secret Financial Network of Terror* (New York: Broadway Books, 2004).
4. U.S. Department of State, Bureau of Democracy Human Rights and Labor, *International Religious Freedom Report 2002*, http://www.state.gov/g/drl/rls/irf/2002/13859.htm; "East African Muslims and the 9-11th September Crisis," *Mambo!: The Newsletter of the French Institute for Research in Africa*, 3, no. 1 (2002).
5. An example of this literature is Nafeez Mosaddeq Ahmed, *Suppressing Dissent: The Crackdown on Muslims in Zanzibar* (London: Islamic Human Rights Commission, 2001).
6. Khatib M. Rajab al-Zinjibari, *Nyerere against Islam in Zanzibar and Tanzania*, http://victorian.fortunecity.com/portfolio/543/nyerere-and-islam.html.
7. See Michael F. Lofchie, *Zanzibar: Background to Revolution* (Princeton: Princeton University Press, 1965).
8. Rajab al-Zinjibari, *Nyerere against Islam*.
9. Hamza Mustafa Njozi, *Mwembechai Killings and the Political Future of Tanzania, Globalink Communications*, Ottawa, Canada, 2000, http://www.islamtz.org/mwembechai/.
10. Mohamed Said, *Intricacies and Intrigues in Tanzania: The Question of Muslim Stagnation in Education*, http://islamtz.org/nyaraka/Elimu2.html.
11. "Administration Steps up Patriot Act Defense," *Camera Wire Services*, January 30, 2004, http://www.dailycamera.com/bdc/nation_world_news/article/0,1713,BDC_2420_2616164,00.html.
12. "Latest Clashes Reveal Underlying Religious Tensions," *IRIN*, September 4, 2001, http://allafrica.com/stories/printable/200109040159.html.
13. U.S. Department of State, Bureau of Democracy, Human Rights and Labor, *Tanzania: International Religious Freedom Report 2001*, http://www.state.gov/g/drl/rls/irf/2001/5714pf.htm.
14. Amon Chaligha, Robert Mattes, Michael Bratton, and Yul Derek Davids, *Uncritical Citizens or Patient Trustees? Tanzanians' Views of Political and Economic Reform*, Afrobarometer Paper no. 18, http://www.afrobarometer.org/papers/Afropaper No18.pdf.

15. See Lawrence E.Y. Mbogoni, *The Cross vs. the Crescent: Religion and Politics in Tanzania from the 1890s to the 1990s* (Dar es Salaam: Mkuki na Nyota Publishers, 2005).
16. *The Dialogue is Encouraged: The Christian-Muslim Relationship in Tanzania*, http://www.vemission.org/english/news/artegn01-05-03.html.
17. Father Method M.P. Kilaini, *The Tanzania Catholic Church*, http://www.rc.net/tanzania/tec/tzchurch.htm.
18. Suleman Din, "U.S. Tablighis Fear Crackdown," *REDIFF.COM*, http://www.rediff.com/us/2002/sep/21us.htm; Rone Tempest, "A Quiet Throng Hope to Show 'Correct' Islam," *Los Angeles Times*, November 3, 2001, http://www.latimes.com/news/nationworld/world/la-110301meet.story.
19. Human Rights Watch, "Sudanese Government Military Support for Armed Opposition Forces," *Annual Report*, 1998, http://hrw.org/reports98/sudan/Sudarm988-06.htm.
20. "Papers Point to African Terror Link," *Sydney Morning Herald*, April 18, 2003, http://www.smh.com.au/articles/2003/04/17/1050172711464.html.
21. Chris Tomlinson, "Enterprise: Islamic Extremists Use Missionary Tradition to Recruit Fighters, Spread Anti-U.S. Message in East Africa," *Associated Press*, February 22, 2004.
22. United States of America v. Bin Laden, *et alia* (Defendants), United States District Court, Southern District of New York, March 19, 2001, http://news.findlaw.com/hdocs/docs/binladen/binladen31901tt.pdf; Judy Aita, "Court Hears of Confession by Tanzanian Charged in Embassy Bombing," *The Washington File*, March 20, 2001, http://usinfo.state.gov/topical/pol/terror/01032054.htm.
23. Tomlinson, "Enterprise: Islamic Extremists."
24. Rajab al-Zinjibari, *Nyerere against Islam*.
25. Abdulazis Y. Lodhi and David Westerlund, *Islam in Africa*, March 1997
26. Ibid.
27. "BALUKTA Calls for Shedding of Blood as 500 Youths Register for 'Jihad,'" *The Daily Mirror*, July 1993, http://www.tu-chemnitz.de/phil/english/chairs/linguist/independent/kursmaterialien/africa/texts/rep-splash-t.rtf.
28. Anneli Botha and Hussein Solomon, *Terrorism in Africa*, http://www.up.ac.za/academic/cips/Publications/TERRORISM%20IN%20AFRICA.doc.
29. Anneli Botha, *Political Dissent and Terrorism in Southern Africa*, Institute for Security Studies Occasional Paper, no. 95, August 2004, http://www.iss.org.za/pubs/papers/90/Paper90.htm.
30. A. Lusekelo, "Tanzania Outlaws Muslim Fundamentalist Group,' *Reuters*, April 29, 1993.

31. *Daily News*, January 5, 1998.
32. Njozi, *Mwembechai Killings*.
33. Amnesty International, *AI Report 1999: Tanzania*, http://www.amnesty.org/ailib/aireport/ar99/afr56.htm.
34. Fautine Rwambali, "Dar es Salaam Charity Leaves Behind $1.45m in Properties," *The East African*, February 23, 2004, http://allafrica.com/stories/printable/200402250069.html.
35. Office of Public Affairs, U.S. Department of Treasury, "Treasury Announce Joint Action with Saudi Arabia against Four Branches of Al-Haramain in the Fight Against Terrorist Financing, JS-1108, January 22, 2004, http://www.ustreas.gov/press/releases/js1108.htm.
36. Faustine Rwambali, "Tanzanian Charity Officials Expelled," *The East African*, February 16, 2004, http://allafrica.com/stories/printable/200402170849.html.
37. Mark Forbes, "Saudi Princes Linked to Terror Funds," *The Age* (Australia), March 5, 2003, http://www.theage.com.au/articles/2003/03/04/1046540187386.html; Zachary Abuza, "Beyond Bali: A New Trend for Terrorism in Southeast Asia?," *Terrorism Monitor*, 3, Issue 19 (2005), http://jamestown.org/terrorism/news/article.php?articleid=2369798.
38. Human Rights Watch, *Tanzania: Zanzibar Election Massacre Documented*, April 10, 2002, http://www.hrw.org/press/2002/04/tanzania041002.htm.
39. Amnesty International, *Tanzania*, http://homepage3.nifty.com/aigroup1/case/eafran/ar03/tananzaniaE.htm.
40. Human Rights Watch, *Tanzania: Zanzibar Election Massacre Documented*, April 10, 2002, http://www.hrw.org/press/2002/04/tanzania041002.htm.
41. Rajab al-Zinjibari, *Nyerere against Islam*.
42. Nathalie Arnold, *Religion in Zanzibar*, http://www.africa.upenn.edu/Urgent_Action/apic-020801.html; "Latest Clashes Reveal Underlying Religious Tensions," *IRIN*, September 4, 2001, http://allafrica.com/stories/printable/200109040159.html.
43. Giviniwa Paul, "Bomb Rocks CCM Offices as Over 170 Muslims Detained," *TOMRIC News Agency*, August 27, 2001, http://allafrica.com/stories/printable/200108270216.html.
44. The Jamestown Foundation, "Tanzania: Al Qaeda's East African Beachhead," *Terrorism Monitor*, 1, no. 5, (2003), http://www.jamestown.org/publications_details.php?volume_id= 391&&issue_id+2872; *The Express on Line*, http://www.theexpress.com/express155/opinion/opinion2.html; "Wanaharakati and Kuffar," *Africa Confidential*, 43, no. 8, (April 2002).
45. U.S. Department of State, *International Religious Freedom Report 2002*.

46. John Ngahyoma, "Tanzania Demo over Graves," *BBC*, August 8, 2003, http://newsvote.bbc.co.uk/mpapps/pagetools/print/news.bbc.co.uk/2/hi/africa/3136139.stm; "Muslims Plan Demo as Chief Mufti Dies," *TOMRIC New Agency*, April 10, 2002, http://allafrica.com/stories/printable/200204100382.html; "Police Ready for Probe over Mwembechai Deaths," *I'Afrika News Network*, March 25, 1998, http://allafrica.com/stories/printable/199803250048.html; Gorill Husby, "Tanzania: Islamist Ascendancy Threatens Peace," *IPS*, May 23, 2003, http://dehai.org/archives/dehai_news_archive/apr-may03/0946.html.

47. Phillipe Marchesine, *The Rise of Islamic Fundamentalism in East Africa*, 2003, http://www.african-geopolitics.org/show.aspx?ArticleId=3497; Paul Redfern "Al Qaeda 'Link' Threat to Tanzanite Business," *The East African*, December 3, 2001; Gorill Husby, "Tanzania: Islamic Ascendancy."

48. Kevin J. Kelley, "Saudi Charity Plotted to Bomb Zanzibar Hotels, US Charges," *The East African*, January 26, 2004, http://allafrica.com/stories/printable/200401270645.html.

49. "Zanzibar Leaders Attacked," *news24.com*, http://www.news24.com/News24/Africa/News/0,,2-11-1447-1501485,00.html; Elizabeth Kendal, "Zanzibar: Church Attacked as Islamist Zeal and Anger Rises," *ASSIST News Service*, http://www.assistnews.net/Stories/s04030093.htm; "Zanzibar Suffers Attacks," *news24.com*, http://www.news24.com/News24/Africa/News/0,6119,2-11-1447_1505129,00.html; Sukhdew Chatbar, *The East African*, March 29, 2004, http:allafrica.com/stories/printable/200403300839.html.

50. "Zanzibar: Tourism Industry Linked to Drug Trafficking," *Tanzania News Online*, March 25, 1998, http://www.africa.upenn.edu/Newsletters/tno16.html.

51. Cathy Majtenyi, "Political Tensions Rising in Zanzibar Ahead of Next Year's Elections," *VOANews*, May 19, 2004, http://quickstart.clari.net/voa/art/fy/3661C472-6703-4FC9-A4A77E9652727DAC.html.

52. Ibid.

53. "Militant Islamic leader held for questioning," *Associated Press*, April 12, 2004; Ally Salleh, "Zanzibar Group Leader on Sedition Charges," *Reuters*, April 13, 2004, http://www.alertnet.org/thenews/newsdesk/L13435971.htm.

54. Judica Tarimo, "Govt Bans CUF 'Military' Training," *IPPmedia*, April 2, 2004, http://www.ippmedia.com/ipp/guardian/2004/04/02/8141.htm.

55. "Rep Alarmed by 'Massive Troop Movement," *IPPmedia*, June 17, 2004, http://www.ippmedia.com/ipp/guardian/2004/06/17/13515.html.

56. Peter Nyanje, *Angry Karume Rolls Up His Sleeves*, July 11, 2004, http://home.globalfrontiers.com/Zanzibar/zanzibar_ news.htm.
57. National Democratic Institute, *International Observation Mission: 2005 Zanzibar Elections, October 30, 2005, Final Report* (Dar es Salaam, December 11, 2005).
58. Ibid.
59. "Nine Killed Following President's Win in Zanzibar," *Associated Press*, November 1, 2005.
60. Edmund Sander, "Discontent Brews in Zanzibar: Islamist Sentiment in the Tanzanian Archipelago Raises Tensions as Islands Hold Elections Today," *Los Angeles Times*, October 30, 2005; "Zanzibaris Adopting Stricter Form of Islam," *Associated Press*, July 5, 2005.

CONCLUDING REMARKS
THE CHANGING DYNAMICS OF JIHADISM IN THE GREATER HORN OF AFRICA (NOVEMBER 2006)

The success of the Union of Islamic Courts militias in extending UIC control over much of southern and central Somalia in 2006 marked a turning point in the recent history of militant Islam in the Greater Horn of Africa region. The jihadist epicenter in the region had effectively shifted from Sudan to southern Somalia. Under the National Islamic Front government, Sudan had emerged in the early 1990s as the principal sponsor of jihadism in the region and a state sponsor of international terrorism. The NIF Sudan and Al Qaeda then based in Sudan had provided inspiration, strategic guidance, logistical support, arsenal, personnel and funds to many jihadist groups in the region, including their Somali ally, Al Itihaad. Iran also provided both arsenal and training at critical times. With Al Itihaad leaders at the heart of the militarily triumphant UIC, it now appeared as though the hardliners within the UIC had grasped the mantle of jihadist ambitions in the Horn of Africa region.

However unacceptable and in need of urgent solution is Sudan's genocidal violence against its "African" populations in the Darfur region, the retreat of Khartoum from its jihadist policies and its political accommodations with the rebel Sudanese People Liberation Movement/Army and the National Democratic Alliance had brought the promise of important peace dividends to the region. The gradual moderation of the Sudanese regime meant regional *détente* and an end to Sudan's policy of waging proxy wars against its neighbors, Eritrea, Ethiopia, and Uganda. Armed groups that Sudan supported such as the Eritrean Islamic Front-Eritrean Islamic Salvation Front, the Islamic Front for the Liberation of Oromia (Ethiopia), the Allied Democratic Front (Uganda), and the Lord's Resistance Army (Uganda) appeared to atrophy as viable fighting forces once Sudanese and Al Qaeda forms of foreign support dried up or until these insurgencies found other supporters to help bankroll their armed struggles, such as with IFLO and Al Itihaad. However, as Sudan's growing moderation, which was reflected in its internal policies of reconciliation and political accommodation and in its increasing cooperation in the international counterterrorism effort, seemed about to free the region once and for all from the threat of jihadist-inspired violence, UIC-dominated southern Somalia emerged as the potential successor to NIF Sudan as a source of jihadist expansionism in the region.

The prominence of historic Al Itihaad figures within the UIC raised concern about the threat that the UIC posed to regional stability. There were primarily two reasons for this. First, Al Itihaad has articulated a vision of establishing a pan-Somali caliphate that seeks to unite into a unified Greater Somalia all the Somali communities in the region, including those communities in Djibouti, Ethiopia, and Kenya. Al Itihaad has a long-standing record of military and terrorist actions against Ethiopia to fulfill its irredentist aims, and there have been a number of credible reports of Al Itihaad organizing among Somalis in Kenya in a bid to create a base of popular support in Kenya's North Eastern Province for its vision of an Islamist Greater Somalia. The November 2006 declaration of UIC leader Sheikh Hassan Dahir Aweys that "we will leave no stone unturned to integrate our Somali brothers in Kenya and Ethiopia and restore their freedom to live with their ancestors in Somalia seemed to leave little doubt about his intentions toward Ethiopia and Kenya."[1]

Second, for many years, Al Itihaad leaders have cultivated ties and cooperated with the greater international jihadist movement, especially with Al Qaeda. Al Qaeda has provided critical support to Al Itihaad's operations within Somalia, and Al Itihaad members have reportedly provided support to Al Qaeda both inside Somalia and in its terrorist operations aimed at U.S. and Israeli targets inside Kenya. Sheikh Hassan Dahir Aweys has not shied away from his expressions of admiration for Osama bin Laden and has compared bin Laden to the historic Somali-Islamic nationalist figure, Mohamed Abdullah Hassan, who, from 1899 to 1920, led a fierce resistance to British occupation, especially in the way that he believes bin Laden and Abdullah Hassan have both been demonized by Western powers. Sheikh Aweys is also closely associated with a Somali terrorist cell under the command of Hasan Adan 'Ayro that has enjoyed intimate ties to Al Qaeda. For these reasons and many more, Al Itihaad leaders within the UIC must be regarded as an expression of the international jihadist movement in addition to being a manifestation of Somali politics.

The publicly visible UIC leader Shariff Sheikh Ahmed considered by many observers to be the moderate face of the UIC, repeatedly denied UIC links to international terrorism and declared as propaganda the notion that the UIC harbors an expansionist agenda in the region.[2] In August 2006, Shariff Sheikh Ahmed told a visiting Kenyan delegation that the UIC's ruling council had no expansionist ambitions to create a larger Somalia beyond its current territorial boundaries.

> Our aim was to secure the control of Mogadishu and throw the war lords out of the city. Our primary aim is to embark on a process of reconstructing the country and not to nurse ambitions to create a greater [state in] the Horn of Africa region as is being claimed.[3]

Shariff Sheikh Ahmed's statements of UIC intentions appeared at odds with Sheikh Aweys's international jihadist credentials and with his expansionist agenda toward Somali-inhabited regions of Kenya and Ethiopia. These irredentist views are also shared by some of his senior commanders including the Ogadeni Hassan Abdullah Hersi al-Turki.

Sheikh Aweys and his jihadist faction achieved an ascendant position in 2006—exercising command control of the

UIC's unified militias as the UIC extended its control over territory in southern and central Somalia. In this regard, an important distinction between the character of the National Islamic Front in Sudan and the Union of Islamic Courts in Somalia should be noted. In Sudan, the architect of the Islamist revolution and jihadist strategies of the NIF, Hassan al-Turabi, did not control the guns, and so when it became in the interest of military strongman, President al-Bashir, to sideline his jihadist ideologue al-Turabi to achieve more practical political and diplomatic aims, the wielder of military power, President al-Bashir easily won the day. Within the UIC, the champions of both an international jihadist and Somali irredentist agenda, that is, Sheikh Aweys and his Al Itihaad cohorts wielded military power. This appears to be the reality with which voices of suspected moderation within the UIC, such as that of Sharif Sheikh Ahmed, have to contend. It is also the reality that other moderates such as the businessmen, technocrats, and professionals in Islamist organizations such as Al Islah must confront as they consider the political options before them.

Adding to the volatility of the regional dynamics is Eritrea's support for Al Itihaad as well as for the Ethiopian rebel Oromo Liberation Front and Ogaden National Liberation Front operating out of Somalia. In providing significant support to the militias of these three groups, Eritrean intent to destabilize Ethiopia from Somali territory seemed clear. Indeed, in August 2006, the Ethiopian government reported killing thirteen members of the Ogaden National Libeation Front as they crossed into Ethiopia from Somalia, and Ethiopia renewed the already well-founded charge that Eritrea and the UIC were supporting the ONLF forces.[4]

The presence of foreign jihadist fighters, training and fighting alongside UIC forces, also suggests that Somalia has become an important front for the global jihadist movement, arguably in 2006 the third most important front after Iraq and Afghanistan. UN revelations that Hasan Adan 'Ayro organized more than 700 Somali fighters to travel to Lebanon to fight alongside Hezbollah in July 2006 in its war with Israel, if true, demonstrated how Somalia had become a training center for a broader jihadist movement. The UN reports of a Hezbollah-'Ayro linkage also gave credibility to reports that in 1993 Hezabollah supplied fighters to back up Al Ithaad and

Mohamed Farah Aidid in its fight against U.S. forces in Somalia.[5]

The hand that Eritrea is playing in Somalia may be part of a dangerous game, capable of opening a Pandora's box not only for Ethiopia but possibly for Eritrea itself. Al Itihaad leaders and their international allies appear wedded to pursuing the past jihadist regional strategy of seeking Islamist hegemony over the entire Horn of Africa region. In several password-protected chat forums, Al Qaeda supporters have reportedly made no secret of their intention to create a pan-Somali East African Islamic caliphate from which it can launch attacks on "infidel" states to the north of Somalia such as Yemen and Saudi Arabia. In the past, this vision of Islamist hegemony included the take over of Eritrea as a launching pad to operations in Yemen and in other parts of the Arabian Peninsula and Ethiopia.[6]

POSSIBLE CONSTRAINTS ON UIC EXPANSIONISM

As it extends its control over more territory, the UIC is likely to encounter a number of potential constraints, some of which arise from the strong clan identities of Somalis. As UIC militias expanded their reach into the southern port city of Kismayo, they became increasingly labeled as a force representative of the Hawiye clan, and at times more specifically as the Ayr lineage of the Hawiye's Habir Gedir subclan. Factional leaders from other clans such as the Marehan began to portray the UIC militias as "tribal" forces dressed in Islamic clothing.[7] The charge that the UIC was a vehicle of clan or "tribal" ambitions by opponents making a political appeal to both clan and subclan identities posed a challenge to the strategy of UIC, including its Al Itihaad leaders who seek to deploy Islam as a political ideology capable of unifying Somalis of different clan identities around a common religious political agenda—an agenda that offers the hope of peace and prosperity to people subjected to past indignities by colonial powers, by Siad Barre's repressive regime, and more recently by "warlords." Clan-based appeals to oppose UIC politicomilitary expansion may very well increase as UIC militias continue to move beyond areas where the Hawiye clan enjoys traditional dominance.

An expansionist UIC has also to contend with resistance from the self-declared Republic of Somaliland and the administratively autonomous region of Puntland. The presence of Al Itihaad figures within the UIC has posed fresh security concerns for both states. These two entities, which have achieved relative security in an otherwise insecure Somalia, have successfully resisted Al Itihaad attempts to gain politicomilitary footholds in their territories in the past.

In spite of the Somaliland government's intent to remain independent and not to reunite with the rest of Somalia, Somaliland leaders have expressed concern that the UIC may exploit irredentistlike support within the ranks of Somililand's own Islamist groupings. In an apparent allusion to the historic Somali-Islamic nationalist figure Mohamed Abdullah Hassan, Somaliland deputy justice minister Yusuf Ise Duale Tallaabo warned the Somaliland public against believing in "a new prophet" from Mogadishu.

> I tell the Union of Islamic Courts (UIC), who dream of capturing Burao and Hargeisa, that Somaliland is an independent republic that has restored its sovereignty in 1991. We have a government, national flag, internationally recognised borders and a constitution.... Somaliland is not Kismayo or Mogadishu.

Official Somaliland concerns about UIC territorial ambitions on Somaliland heightened after reports that one of Al Itihaad's founders and former military commander from Somaliland, Sheikh Ali Warsame, had traveled to Mogadishu to join Sheikh Aweys. Ali Warsame had led the 1992 Al Itihaad offensive to take northern Somalia, now comprising the region of Puntland and Somaliland, and to establish an emirate there. Since the defeat of his Al Itihaad forces in 1992, Sheikh Warsame emerged as a well-known religious leader in Burao, Somililand.[8] There have also reportedly been concerns within Somaliland's government that an Ethiopia intervention in Somalia would potentially spark a popular Somali nationalist backlash that could bolster support for the UIC among Somaliland's own population.[9]

Although there have been many reports of popular support for the UIC, especially within Mogadishu, because of its success in bringing a state of law and order to unruly Mogadishu through the defeat of the so-called warlords, there have also been reports of popular ambivalence and notable

Concluding Remarks

expressions of dissatisfaction with the austere cultural-religious code and authoritarianism being applied to the population by the emergent UIC government. UIC dictates that imposed conservative dress codes, restrictions on the press, the closure of independent radio stations, the banning of the consumption of the widely used mild narcotic *khat*, prohibitions against the viewing of films and televised football matches, imposition of taxation on businesses, forced observance of Friday prayers, and other revolutionary and totalitarian excesses have provoked popular protest in Mogadishu and in Kismayo. Popular resistance may also become a possible constraint on UIC political ambitions, though the UIC managed to suppress through arrest and violence such manifestations of popular resistance.

The Transitional Federal Government based in Baidoa has also been emerging as a focal point of regional and international resistance to UIC expansionism. The TFG was considered to be weak both militarily and administratively. Yet, having been formed with the support of InterGovermental Authority on Development countries, it has enjoyed substantial regional and broader international legitimacy. The IGAD countries of Ethiopia, Kenya, Somalia (TFG), Sudan and Uganda have committed the organization to dispatching peacekeeping troops to Somalia to bolster the TFG at a time when the TFG appeared increasingly vulnerable to being routed by UIC forces. The African Union had given its blessing to the IGAD peacekeeping project.

According to Kenyan Foreign Minister Rafael Tuju,

> The IGAD force is supposed to protect the Transitional Federal Government and Institutions, help train civilian protection force and establish a united civilian protection force for the whole of Somalia, including breakaway Somaliland and Puntland.[10]

Uganda became the first IGAD country to make a commitment of troops to the peacekeeping exercise; and in September 2006, Uganda reportedly sent an advance contingent of military personnel to the TFG capital of Baidoa, in spite of the fact the United Nations had not conceded to IGAD's request to end its arms embargo on Somalia.

The introduction of IGAD peacekeepers can easily be construed as a effort to counter the military power of the UIC, and the UIC has vehemently opposed the deployment of IGAD peacekeepers. At a rally organized in Mogadishu to protest IGAD's decision to send peacekeepers to Somalia, Sharif Sheikh Ahmed, for example, enjoined the crowd "to thwart any foreign military intervention in our territory from IGAD or anywhere."[11]

REGIONAL COUNTERTERRORISM

The rise of the Al Itihaad-led Islamic Courts has presented to counterterrorism strategists with the fulfillment of their worse fears: that Somalia might become a haven for international jihadists much like Afghanistan under Taliban rule or Sudan under the NIF government, both of which had hosted Osama bin Laden's Al Qaeda movement. Under the Al-Itihaad-led UIC, international jihadists appeared to have gained greater opportunity to expand their presence. UIC control of the international airport in Mogadishu and the key ports in southern Somalia has created the conditions for facilitated international travel and transport, and jihadists have achieved unprecedented, unfettered access to international sea lanes.

The vulnerability of ships in Somali waters to international terrorists is of concern to counterterrorism experts. The UIC has confirmed, however, that it stands against the rampant maritime piracy that plagued Somali waters in 2005 and 2006, and the UIC had claimed that it destroyed the pirate center of Haradhere in the Mudug region as UIC militias moved northward from Mogadishu.[12] Piracy in Somali waters appears to have been motivated largely by the demand of ransoms rather than as acts of terrorism, although it may be worth recalling that Al Itihaad units were involved in piracy in 1999, seizing the Tanzania-registered *MV Sea Johana,* en route from Mombasa to India near Kismayo and demanding ransom from the vessel owners.[13]

In the past, Al Qaeda has used the sea lanes both to support its terrorist operations inside Kenya and to deliver supplies and personnel to Al Itihaad in Somalia. Somali piracy has also affected ocean transport and tourist cruise ship traffic to Kenya's principal port, Mombasa. As a result, when the Kenya government put its military on high alert in September 2006 in response to what it described as the deteriorating security situation in Somalia, it ordered the Navy, the Kenya Ports Authority, and the marine police to monitor all shipping in Kenya's territorial waters. Only ships authorized to ply within the country's current 200 nautical miles limit would be allowed in Kenya's territorial waters. In addition, Kenya extended its territorial limit by 150 to 350 kilometers (by 93 to 217 miles).[14]

The United States have long been concerned that international terrorist organizations would seek to increase their presence in stateless Somalia, and after Al Qaeda's 9-11 attacks against the United States, the Pentagon received permission from Djibouti to establish a regional counterterrorism command center to deal with the international terrorist threats in the region. U.S. Special Forces set up a base at Camp Lemonier outside the city of Djibouti, and Central Intelligence Agency operatives are believed also to have been working out of Djibouti. The mission of Combined Joint Task Force-Horn of Africa, as the counterterrorism effort is known,

> is focused on detecting, disrupting, and ultimately defeating transnational terrorist groups operating in the region—denying safe havens, external support, and material assistance for terrorist activity. Additionally, CJTF-HOA will counter the re-emergence of transnational terrorism in the region through civil-military operations and support of non-governmental organization operations — enhancing the long-term stability of the region.[15]

The Djibouti-based group's area of responsibility includes the total airspace and land areas of Djibouti, Eritrea, Ethiopia, Kenya, Somalia, and Sudan in Africa, and Yemen on the Arabian Peninsula.

As discussed in Chapter 4, the attempt by the United States to find a military solution to the growing strength of the UIC failed to achieve its end. The United States had reportedly provided covert assistance to the Alliance for the Restoration of Peace and Counter-Terrorism (ARPCT), a grouping of clan-based factional leaders organized in Jowhar in February 2006. U.S. financial support was intended both to help organize the structure of a militia force created to counter the threat posed by the growing UIC movement and to see captured Al Qaeda operatives resident in Somalia who had taken part in the terrorist bombings of the U.S. embassies in Nairobi and in Dar es Salaam. However, the UIC forces routed the U.S.-backed ARPCT fighters and consolidated their authority over Mogadishu, shortly thereafter launching the UIC expansion to other areas of southern Somalia.[16]

The United States and Eritrea have been on opposite sides of the military fence in Somalia — the United States having supported the defeated ARPCT; Eritrea, backing with military arsenal the UIC which decisively defeated ARPCT forces. In its clandestine military support for the UIC, OLF and the ONLF, IGAD member country Eritrea stood not only in violation of the United Nations arms embargo for Somalia but at odds with its fellow IGAD countries intent on deploying a peacekeeping force in support of the TFG. Some diplomats have also suggested that U.S. financial support to the ARPCT group may have also been a violation of the UN arms embargo.[17]

U.S. State Department officials have considered Eritrea uncooperative in the global war on terror, and this has been one factor in the deteriorating relations between Washington and Asmara.[18] Matters between the two governments worsened after Eritrean President Isaias Afewerki publicly characterized the Bush administration as a negative force in the region and accused it of using terrorism as a pretext to destabilize Somalia. In a sign of further deterioration in relations, Asmara reportedly restricted the travel of U.S. diplomats in Eritrea to within a twenty-five mile radius of the American embassy in Asmara, and the State Department reciprocated in June 2006 with a similar restriction on the movement of Eritrean diplomats within the United States.[19]

REGIONAL POLARIZATION

The growing power of the UIC has led to a polarization of the conflict in Somalia and the wider region. Despite the UN arms embargo on Somalia, Ethiopia had sent troops into Somalia to help protect the TFG, and the United States had supported the Somali counterterrorism alliance that had battled the UIC. On the one side of politicomilitary regional fault line, there stood the TFG, Puntland, Ethiopia, Kenya, Uganda, increasingly Somaliland and the United States. On the other side of the fissure, there stood Eritrea, the UIC, OLF, and ONLF as well as the UIC's foreign jihadist supporters.

Concluding Remarks

Then in November 2006, a UN-sponsored panel of experts examining violations of the UN's arms embargo dropped a bombshell in a highly disputed report. It added Egypt, Libya, Saudi Arabia, Syria, Hezbollah, and Iran to the list of parties providing arsenal and training for the UIC, and it added Yemen to the list of those supporting the TFG in Baidoa and the authorities in Puntland. Most of the accused parties denied the allegations of breaking the arms embargo, but, if true, the widespread outside support provided a partial explanation of the UIC's recent military prowess and would be a startling, but perhaps not suprising, internationalization of the Somali conflict.[20]

This internationalization seemed capable of pulling the Horn of Africa region squarely into a larger struggle engulfing the Middle East region. In 2003, the U.S. overthrow of Iraqi dictator Saddam Hussein and its occupation of the land shifted the balance of power in the region, enhancing Iran's role as a regional power. In this shifting balance of power, Middle East countries and movements appeared to be vying to influence the course of events in Somalia.

Although most regional and international actors had called upon the TFG and the UIC to reach a negotiated settlement that would produce a power-sharing arrangement allowing Somalia to enjoy a broadly supported transitional government of national unity, such talks, which began in Khartoum in the summer of 2006 under the sponsorship of the Arab League, were likely to be arduous. The asymmetrical military equation between the strong UIC and the weak TFG and the vast ideological gulf that divides the two sides as well as the personal animosities such as that between UIC leader Sheikh Aweys and TFG President Abdullahi Yusuf meant that the way of negotiations would be strewn with many obstacles. In addition, the incorporation of the UIC into a new, internationally recognized Somali government will be a bitter, if not impossible, pill to swallow by the United States and other nations concerned about the global terrorist threat given the involvement of the international jihadist movement with a powerful faction within the UIC. The suicide car bombing attempt in Baidoa on the life of the TFG president in September 2006 suggested that the jihadist terrorist tactics used effectively in the Iraq and Afghan theaters had made their way to Somalia, and this has only added to concerns about the role of international jihadists within the UIC movement. The international jihadist movement has also little interest in seeing the success of power-sharing negotiations between the TFG and the UIC, as this would likely deprive the global movement of Somalia, which has proven to be an important base of operations since 1993.

Notes

1. "Islamic Leader Says Somalia is Greater," *Associated Press*, November 18, 2006.
2. 'We Deny That We Are Harboring Terrorists:" A Letter from Somalia's Islamic Leaders Aims to Allay Western Fears that the Country will Become a New Front in the War on Terror, Letter signed by Sheikh Sherif Sheikh Ahmed, Chairman, Islamic Courts Union, June 6, 2006.
3. "Council's High Command Says It Has No Expansionist Plans," *The Nation*, August 13, 2006.
4. Namrud Berhane, *The Reporter* (Addis Ababa), August 12, 2006.
5. Yossef Bodansky, *Bin Laden: The Man Who Declared War on America* (Roseville, Calif.: Prima Publishing, 2001), 80—90.
6. Jerry MacDonald, "Islamists in Somalia Spell Doom for All," *The East African Standard*, August 25, 2006.
7. Aweys Osman Yusuf, "Demonstrations against Islamists Happen in Bardhere as Islamists Confiscate Weapons in Kismayu," *Shabelle Media Network* (Mogadishu), September 27, 2006, http://allafrica.com/stories/200609270711.html.
8. Hassan Shiek Abdullah, "Somaliland Govt Fears Country May Fall to Islamists," *Shabelle Media Network*, September 29, 2006. http://allafrica.com/stories/200609290680.html.
9. Interview with Ethiopian diplomat, October 1, 2006.
10. Lucas Barasa, "Somalia to Get Peacekeepers," *The Nation*, September 6, 2006, http://allafrica.com/stories/200609060011.html.
11. "Huge Rally for Refusal of Foreign Peacekeepers Takes Place in Mogadishu," *Shabelle Media Network,* September 2, 2006, http://allafrica. com/stories/200609060006.html.
12. "Understanding Somalia," *Addis Fortune*, n.d., http://www.addisfortune.com/Understanding%20Somalia-6.htm.
13. Emily Wax, " Piracy Surges off Somalia's Coast," *The Washington Post*, April 4, 2006.
14. Mugo Njeru, "Troops Put on Alert as Tensions Rise in Somalia," *The Nation*, September 30, 2006, http://allafrica.com/stories/200609290948.html.

15. Combined Joint Task Force—Horn of Africa, http://www.hoa.centcom.mil.
16. "Somali Warlords Hold 'Secret Anti-Terrorism' Talks with US Agents: Witnesses," *AFP*, February 28, 2006; Emily Wax and Karen DeYoung, "U.S. Secretly Backing Warlords in Somalia," *Washington Post*, May 17, 2006.
17. Matthew Lee, "US Support for Somali Warlords May Violate UN Arms Embargo," *AFP*, May 11, 2006.
18. Interview with State Department Official, September 30, 2006.
19. "USA Restricts Movement of Eritrean Diplomats, Businessmen," *Gedab News*, June 22, 2006, http://www.awate.com/artman/publish/printer_4521.shtml; Interview with Ethiopian diplomat, September 30, 2006.
20. "Politics — Adding Fuel to Fire," *The Reporter* (Addis Ababa), November 18, 2006, http://allafrica.com/stories/200611200456.html; Samuel Siringi, "Governments Said to Be Propping up Rebellion," *The Nation*, November 20, 2006, http://allafrica.com/stories/200611200092.html.

POSTSCRIPT— FEBRUARY 24, 2007
THE BATTLE FOR THE HORN OF AFRICA AND ITS AFTERMATH

General Tambi of the Eritrean People's Defense Forces agreed to pay Evgueny Zakharov $1.5 million for an aging Soviet-era Ilyushin 76 transport aircraft. Zakharov was owner of Aerolift — an airline based in Johannesburg and registered in the British Virgin Islands; and he was pleased with the handsome price that General Tambi offered. It was $.5 million more than the market price for an Ilyushin 76 of its vintage and condition. Zakharov became suspicious, however, that the Eritrean military might use the plane to transport arms in violation of the United Nations arms embargo on Somalia, because the Eritrean official had asked that the July 21, 2006 contract between Aerolift and Eriko Enterprise of Asmara contain a secrecy clause. So, to protect himself from possible involvement in international criminal activity, Zakharov insisted the contract should specify that the new owners were not to use the aircraft to transport arms. According to Zakharov, the Eritreans concealed their plans and went ahead to use the aircraft to deliver three shipments of arms, a total of 140 tons, from the Eritrean port of

Masawa to Somalia in July and August. On the return flights, Zakharov said, "we transported lots of men in uniform — Arabian men in masks." When Zakharov's flight crews told him of the arms shipments from Eritrea to Somalia, Zakharov cancelled the contract with Eriko Enterprise.[1]

Zakharov's account of Eritrea's clandestine cooperation is a rare glimpse into the details of one of the supply operations in 2005 and 2006 that, according to UN reports, largely benefited the radical wing of the Union of Islamic Courts. As described previously in this book, support from elements of the international jihadist movement and from various regional actors including Eritrea helped the UIC both to consolidate its control over Mogadishu and other areas of central and southern Somalia and to prepare for the looming confrontation with Somali's Transitional Federal Government and its ally, Ethiopia. Zakharov's story also speaks to the extent that Eritrea was willing to collaborate with international jihadists with ambitions to create an Islamist state in Somalia with hostile intention to Eritrea's enemy, Ethiopia.[2]

As the UIC took control of a large swath of southern and central Somalia including the international airport in Mogadishu and the ports of Mogadishu, Marka and Kismayo in 2006, a significant number of international jihadists, including Al Qaeda members, converged on Somalia to set up bases of operation as part of a jihad against the TFG, Ethiopia and the United States. Some of the international jihadists expressed the dream of turning Somalia, Ethiopia and Egypt into Islamist states.[3] Their coming to Somalia may have partly been in response to Osama bin Laden's call to fight foreign forces on Somali soil, including proposed international peacekeepers. In a taped audio file placed on the Internet on July 1, 2006, the Al Qaeda leader proclaimed, "We will fight (foreign) soldiers on the land of Somalia ... and we reserve the right to punish them on their land and anywhere possible."[4] By the time of Bin Laden's call to arms, the Aweys-led faction within the Courts appeared to have been well advanced in the implementation of its plans to involve foreign fighters and trainers in taking control of Somalia and in achieving its broader territorial objectives in the region. The Sheikh Aweys faction had nurtured ties, not only vertically with Bin Laden but also horizontally with others in Al Qaeda and affiliated organizations.

Key to this horizontal cooperation was the Al Qaeda cell that had been active in Somalia since 1992, when Al Qaeda and Al Itihaad first worked together — at that time in opposition to the U.S.-led United Nations humanitarian intervention in Somalia.

Al Qaeda's Somalia cell included, among others, Abu Taha al-Sudani (aka Tariq Abdullah), and the Comorian, Fazul Abdul Mohammed. Al-Sudani is a suspected Al Qaeda member reported to be an explosives expert trained by Hezbollah who is close to Osama bin Laden. A Sudanese as his nickname suggests, al-Sudani married a Somali woman and had lived in Somalia since 1993. Al-Sudani was also believed to be the financier of the 1998 bombings of the U.S. embassies in Dar es Salaam and Nairobi. The Al Qaeda cell in Somalia appears to have acted as a liaison with both the larger Al Qaeda movement and other groups within the international jihadist movement, and it provided support, in the form of financing, strategic planning and troops, to the radical wing within the Courts led by Sheikh Aweys.[5]

With the convergence of internationalist jihadists in Somalia in 2006 and the establishment of numerous new training camps, the nightmare scenario of counterterrorism strategists seemed to be unfolding. Somalia had the makings of the third major front, following Iraq and Afghanistan, in the jihadist effort to dominate parts of the Muslim world and to undermine U.S.-led efforts to oppose international jihadism in Somalia, Iraq and Afghanistan.

The war in Afghanistan began on October 7, 2001, in response to the September 11, 2001 Al Qaeda attacks on the United States. This marked the beginning of the U.S. war on terrorism. The purpose of the invasion was to capture Osama bin Laden, destroy Al Qaeda, and remove the Taliban regime which had provided support and safe harbor to Al Qaeda. The forces of the North Atlantic Treaty Organization, of which the United States is a member, supported the U.S.-led intervention. The war successfully removed the Taliban from power, although by 2007 there had been a resurgence in Taliban forces. The war in Afghanistan had been less successful in achieving the goal of restricting Al Qaeda's movement.

In Iraq, Al Qaeda assembled contingents of international jihadists to oppose the U.S. occupation of Iraq that began in

2003 with the aim of deposing Iraqi strongman, Saddam Hussein. In its justification for its intervention in Iraq, high-ranking members of the U.S. administration implied that Saddam Hussein had played a role in the September 11 terrorist attacks, but this claim had subsequently been widely disputed. In its opposition to the U.S. military intervention in Iraq, Al Qaeda deployed terrorist tactics against both Iraqi civilians and supporters of the U.S.-backed Iraqi government, which had succeeded the Saddam Hussein dictatorship. Al Qaeda also waged war against U.S. military targets.

In Somalia, the jihadist newcomers who arrived in 2006 intensified the mujahidin training of young Somalis and foreign volunteers. In the camps, boys and young men underwent physical conditioning and training in the use of arms. Veteran Al Qaeda members instructed chosen Somali youths in the use of explosives — a rite of passage consistent with the jihadist fascination with bomb-making. The veteran jihadists also initiated Somali youth into the their cult of martyrdom that seemed to help the youths dispel the sense of victim hood, despair and low esteem that many of them seemed to share, and Somalia witnessed for the first time the use of suicide bombers both as a military tactic and as a form of political assassination.[6]

An incarcerated U.S. citizen awaiting trial in Texas in February 2007 for his collaboration with Al Qaeda in Somalia provided insight into some of these training camps. While in custody in Kenya following his flight from Somalia, Daniel Maldonaldo (aka Daniel Aljughaifa) had confessed to agents of U.S. Federal Bureau of Investigation details of his training in jihadist camps in the cities of Mogadishu, Kismayo and Jilip. In the words of the FBI agent taking Maldonaldo's confession,

> MALDONADO stated that while residing with the young mujahadin in Mogadishu, he became aware that al Qaeda members were residing and training in the same compound. A Yemeni who personally knew bin Laden, and MALDONADO, participated in nightly gatherings during which stories of bin Laden were told by the Yemeni. MALDONADO identified certain members at the camp as being al Qaeda, although he did not know for sure who all of the al Qaeda members were. MALDONA-

DO opined that al Qaeda fighters were given much more respect than members of the ICU [Union of Islamic Courts]. During discussions with the young mujahadin, they spoke about conquering Somalia, Ethiopia, and Egypt and making them Islamic states. MALDONADO learned about a major al Qaeda operative fighting in the southern part of Somalia whom he did not meet.[7]

A number of the jihadist training camps operated under the auspices of the *Shabbab*, or "Youth" in Arabic. Under Sheikh Hassan Dahir Aweys's protection and encouragement, the Somali terrorist cell, which had been established under the command of the Al Qaeda-trained Hasan Adan 'Ayro, experienced phenomenal growth. In August 2006, Sheikh Aweys and some of his Al Itihaad allies within the UIC formally transformed 'Ayro's organization into the Shabbab, which continued a close association with Al Qaeda. The former Al Itihaad commander and Al Qaeda-ally, Sheikh Hassan Abdullah Hersi al-Turki and 'Ayro emerged as top Shabbab military commanders. The Shabbab leaders reinforced the dominance of the Al Itihaad faction within the UIC military and decision making apparatus, thus contributing to the increasing radicalization of UIC policies and practice.

The formation of the Shabbab also represented a generational transition. The first generation of Somali jihadists — the old guard from Al Itihaad, which included veteran jihadists such as Aweys and al-Turki, — were cultivating a second generation of Somali jihadists under the more youthful and charismatic 'Ayro with his ability to attract boys and young men into the ranks of Islamist militancy.

The Shabbab increased to six the number of training camps under 'Ayro's supervision that were located in and around Mogadishu.[8] Hundreds, if not, thousands of poor, desperate boys and young men flocked to the Shabbab training camps. Other recruits were high school and university students. Still others were young men from the Somali diaspora, including some from Canada, the United Kingdom and Pakistan.[9] Estimates of the number of Somali youths that became Shabbab members ranged from 3,000 to 7,000. Before admission to this Somali mujahidin corps, Shabbab leaders conducted extensive and thorough background checks on candidates to assure that they were not spies. Shabbab members were set apart from other UIC-affiliated militia members by the use of distinctive red and white checkered head cloths, and they gained a reputation for their fierceness, so much so that civilians would flee in fear at the sight of the Shabbab red and white scarves.

'Ayro reportedly inspired many of Mogadishu's unemployed and desperately poor youth with a sense of hope. He encouraged them to defend their religion and their country against Ethiopia. One Shabbab member described 'Ayro as "a kind man, who fed Shabbab members, gave each of them a monthly salary of $70, and looked after the well-being of each member." Another said 'Ayro was inspirational and a father figure.

One young man, Abdi, who had performed well in the training camps, said that he and several hundred other standout students were flown to Eritrea. There, they received an additional two months of advance instruction in explosives and guerrilla war tactics from Somali and Eritrean trainers. "Abdi says he and the others were given lessons in making roadside bombs, car bombs, and suicide vests, using explosives material cannibalized from various weapon systems."[10]

Shabbab trainers encouraged the cult of martyrdom among their recruits, and Sheikh Aweys reportedly plotted to use suicide bombers both within Somalia and in the region to help achieve his ambitions. According to the *Somaliland Times*, in a letter dated September 28, 2006 from a body called the "Shura Council of the Preservation Alliance," Sheikh Aweys communicated the Shura's decision "to send 30 young martyrs to carry out explosions and killing of the Jewish and American collaborators in the northern region (Somaliland)." The letter named top leaders from the Somaliland government who were to be targeted for assassination. The Shura also planned to train as mujahidin 3,000 young men hailing from Somaliland who were currently living in towns and cities under UIC authority. They were to be used as part of the effort to topple the Somaliland government. And, as previously noted, the U.S. embassies in Kenya and Ethiopia warned in November 2006 that Sheikh Aweys had planned suicide bombings against prominent landmarks in the two countries. The UIC denied the U.S. charges.[11]

THE MILITARY CONFRONTATION

After the UIC gained undisputed control of Mogadishu and expanded its authority over other areas of Somalia in June-July 2006, the Ethiopian military sent forces into Somalia in a series of countermoves to protect its security interests from advancing UIC militias.[12] In July 2006, the Ethiopian National Defense Forces (ENDF) stationed troops, tanks and helicopters in and around Baidoa both to defend the TFG from advancing forces of the UIC and to train the TFG army, which was comprised of militias from diverse politicomilitary factions that had joined together to form the TFG. In August, Ethiopia reportedly also sent its troops across its border into the central Somali region of Hiraan to check UIC battle wagons from advancing beyond the city of Beledweyne toward the Ethiopian border. According to Addis, UIC forces had amassed in this area to launch a "final offensive" into Ethiopia.[13] In November, Ethiopian troops arrived at Galkayo in the Mudug region in support of forces of the autonomously administered region of Puntland, an Ethiopian ally, in a bid to check the northward advance of UIC militias.[14]

In response to the stationing of Ethiopian troops on Somali territory, UIC leaders, both hardliners from Sheikh Aweys's faction and moderates such as Sheikh Sharif Ahmed Sharif, used FM radio addresses and public rallies to demonize the Ethiopians as an invading Christian army and thus to incite the Mogadishu populace into rising up in jihad against the Christians and their Somali apostate allies. The demonization of Ethiopians as Christian crusaders was a stereotype contradicting the fact that Ethiopia has a large Muslim community, at times estimated at more than 50% of the country's population.

UIC leaders exhorted young men and medical personnel in Mogadishu and other parts of Somalia to join UIC forces on the front lines of the jihad against Ethiopia. The UIC conducted a food drive, a money drive and an AK-47 assault rifle drive in support of the impending war with Ethiopia.[15] One UIC leader reportedly fantasized on Mogadishu radio about UIC forces reaching Addis Ababa within six months.[16] The UIC's head of education, Fuad Mohammed Khalf announced that students would be required to participate in the jihad, and schools and universities would be closed down if a war between Ethiopa and the Islamists ignited.[17] In mid-December, Islamist leaders in Mogadishu distributed sermons written in Arabic to be read at all of the city's mosques. The sermon warned that "infidels want to put out the light of Allah by trying to force us to follow their way, democracy. . . Oh God give pride to Muslims and humiliate the enemies of your leaders."[18]

Some UIC leaders also declared jihad against the United States for its backing of the Ethiopian military and support given at the UN Security Council for the authorization of an African peacekeeping force for Somalia; this force was mandated to both protect the TFG and train its military. After the 9-11 terrorist attacks, the U. S. military, through its Combined Joint Task Force — Horn of Africa based in Djibouti, had begun training Ethiopian troops at camps inside Ethiopia near its border with Somalia; the Ethiopian trainees included the special forces unit called the Agazi Commandos.[19] In addition, it was an open secret that in 2004 the Ethiopian government had also counted on U.S. counterterrorism intelligence for limited covert operations inside Somalia against suspected Al Qaeda operatives,[20] and it was likely that Addis could rely on continued intelligence from the U.S. government in a war with the UIC.

In November and December 2006, events and rhetoric were escalating toward a major military confrontation over the future of Somalia and the entire Horn of Africa region. Jihadist ambitions to turn the region into an area of Islamist dominance were clear, and the backing of the UIC by outside regional actors such as Egypt, Iran, Saudi Arabia and Syria suggested that the governments of these countries wanted to counter the hegemony of a U.S.-backed Ethiopia in the region. American diplomatic strategists regarded Ethiopia as an "anchor state" in the region capable of acting as a bulwark against both jihadist terrorism and increasingly the "rogue state" behavior of Eritrea.[21]

In late November 2006, in response to the UIC's repeated declarations of jihad against Ethiopia, Prime Minister Meles Zenawi asked and received authorization from parliament to use force to protect the country, if peace talks between the TFG and the UIC failed. UIC leaders then responded to the Ethiopian parliament's authorization of the use of force by reinforcing its military positions around the seat of the TFG — Baidoa.[22] The UIC forces, which assembled near Baidoa, included Somali Islamist militias, jihadist internationalist fighters, Ethiopian dissidents and Eritrean units; the price they would pay in the approaching battle would be high.

With a growing number of Islamist forces in place, on December 12, UIC Defense Minister, Sheikh Yusuf Mohamed Siad Inda'ade, gave Ethiopia seven days to remove its troops from Somalia or face war. He claimed that there were already more than 30,000 Ethiopian troops on Somali soil to bolster the TFG administration of President Abdullahi Yusuf Ahmed.[23] Within days of the ultimatum, the TFG president, Abdullahi Yusuf closed the door on further peace talks with the UIC, saying that talks were no longer an option and warning that the UIC was allowing Al Qaeda to set up shop in the Horn of Africa. Abdullahi Yusuf's announcement that the peace talks had failed fulfilled the legal requirement set by the Ethiopian parliament for Prime Minister Meles Zenawi to take military actions against the UIC.

The Shabbab had sent significant numbers of young, largely inexperienced fighters to the Baidoa area to do battle. There is evidence suggesting that some of the more moderate Courts did not heed the call to wage war against Christian Ethiopia and its TFG "stooges," and kept their militias out of the ensuring battle. Moderates within the UIC reportedly believed that they had accomplished what they had set out to do by stabilizing the part of Somalia where the Hawiye clan was predominant, and that they had succeeded in achieving a political situation comparable to that of Somaliland and Puntland. According to this view, the UIC's military and political achievements had placed the UIC in an advantageous negotiating position with the TFG.[24]

Sheikh Shariff Sheikh Ahmed, Chairman of the UIC's Executive Committee, who was considered by many observers to be a moderate, seemed to echo this sentiment when he had earlier made public statements distancing the UIC from Bin Laden's call to oppose the interim government. "Bin Laden is expressing his personal views like any other person. We are not concerned about them. . . . His call to oppose the interim government represents only himself and not us," he said.[25]

The Aweys-led faction, including the Shabbab leadership, had reportedly been growing in power within the Courts movement, however: and, with this faction's Al Qaeda-connections, it was unlikely that negotiations between the UIC and the UN-recognized TFG had much chance of success. The Islamist hardliners would likely have found it very difficult to accept the establishment of a government of national unity in Somalia that would be capable of curbing the regional ambitions of Somali jihadists and their internationalist allies.

The rift between the moderates and the hardliners within the UIC was evident. In a revealing interview with the Voice of America's English-to-Africa Service, UIC's foreign minister, Ibrahim Hassan Addow, appeared to distance himself from the jihadist-Al Itihaad faction of the UIC led by Sheikh Aweys, Mr. Addow said Sheikh Sharif Ahmed was the UIC leader. When questioned about the UIC's intentions to incorporate portions of Ethiopia into a Greater Somalia, Mr. Addow stated that the program for a Greater Somalia was not an official position of the UIC — an apparent refutation of the public position of Sheikh Aweys to unite all Somalis into a single state.[26]

International mujahidin were interspersed among the Somali Islamist forces gathered at Baidoa. The foreign mujahidin reportedly hailed from Denmark, Egypt, Ethiopia, France, Jordan, Morocco, Saudi Arabia, Sudan, Sweden, Tanzania, Tunisia, United Arab Emirates, United Kingdom, United States, and Yemen, among other countries.[27] According to one Shabbab soldier, some of the Arab mujahidin camped near Baidoa spoke Somali reasonably well — an indication that they had lived in Somalia for some time. Others had arrived more recently, and there were reports of hundreds of militants having landed on the Somali coast.[28] The TFG Defense Minister, Salad Ali Jelle, said that the Al Qaeda operative, Abu Taha al-Sudani, was one of the commanders leading forces near Baidoa.[29]

A contingent of Oromo dissidents from Ethiopia were also preparing for battle against the TFG and Ethiopian forces. Some of Oromo youths had been encouraged by "religious men" in Ethiopia to go to Mogadishu. One of these Oromo rebels, who had been taken prisoner, said that he had undergone training in Eritrea; he said that he was "among 270

Oromos, training in Mogadishu. We were in a military camp in the capital."[30]

Eritrean forces, which had earlier provided training to Somali Islamist and Ethiopian dissident forces, provided support and field command for the battle that was to ensue. A TFG press release stated a unit of 500 Eritrean troops with artillery and other heavy weapons had reinforced Burhakaba near Baidoa.[31]

When the period for the UIC's seven-day ultimatum ended, its forces launched its operation to take Baidoa. The forces assembled on the side of the UIC proved no match to the TGF army backed by the ENDF, one of the largest military establishments in Africa. UIC's teenage fighters were pitted against the more experienced adult fighters of the Ethiopia and the TFG forces. Eyewitnesses described waves of young Islamist zealots being mowed down near Baidoa by superior Ethiopian fire power. Ethiopian warplanes entered the battle apparently unopposed by the surface-to-air missiles that Iran had reportedly furnished the UIC, and the Ethiopian air assault decimated the UIC battle wagons known as technicals.[32] Sheikh Aweys and other Al Itihaad leaders within the UIC knew all too well the fighting capability of the Ethiopian forces. The Ethiopians had routed Al Itihaad forces in 1996 and again in 1999, and yet Sheikh Aweys sent thousands of Somali boys and young men on what amounted to a collective suicide mission.

The ENDF was battle hardened. Its leadership had come out of the guerrilla army of the Ethiopia People Revolutionary Democratic Front that had fought to topple the Ethiopian former military dictator Mengistu Haile Mariam in 1991. The ENDF had also routed Al Itihaad in 1996 and 1999, fought to a stalemate in the 1998-2000 Ethiopia-Eritrean border war that was costly in terms of human life, and effectively countered the low-intensity insurgencies of the Oromo Liberation Front and the Ogaden National Liberation Front.

The Ethiopian forces also had the benefit of U.S. backing. As previously noted, after the terrorist attacks of 9-11, the Ethiopian army began to train in counterterrorism and counterinsurgency.[33] Element of the U.S. Combined Joint Task Force — Horn of Africa trained members of the ENDF at the Ethiopian Military Academy in Hurso, northwest of Dire Dawa, and in the build up to this war, there were more than 100 U.S. military soldiers in Ethiopia helping train Ethiopian troops. A U.S. official spokesman denied, however, that U.S. forces had entered Somalia. "Officially, we haven't put anybody in Somalia. The Americans don't go forward with the Ethiopians. They are training Ethiopians in Ethiopian." However, a U.S. defense consultant contradicted this official position by acknowledging that a handful of American advisors had entered Somalia with Ethiopian forces.[34]

Ethiopian, TFG, Puntland and other "secular" Somali factional forces struck back on three sets of fronts where the UIC and allied forces had massed—in the Bay region near Baidoa, along the upper Shabelle River valley in the Hiraan region near Beledweyne, and in Mudug near Galkayo. According to TFG government sources, the Ethiopian forces stationed in and around Baidoa deployed twenty T-55 tanks and four attack helicopters,[35] and a column including a large number of tanks moved through the Hiraan region, capturing the city of Beledweyne and driving on toward Mogadishu. The Ethiopian forces advancing from Beledweyne were accompanied by Somali factional leader, Mohamed Omar Habeb, aka Mohamed Dheere, who wished to reestablish his control over the city of Jowhar, which had earlier fallen to the UIC.[36] When the UIC forces battling at Baidoa perceived that the Ethiopian forces penetrating down from Hiraan region were about to outflank them, they beat a retreat south toward Kismayo.

In the Mudug region, Ethiopian and Puntland forces, along with a Somali militia representing the nascent semi-autonomous state of Galmudug under Abdi Qeybdid, attacked UIC forces defending the town of Bandiradley. The fighting pushed the Islamists out of Bandiradley and over the border south into Adado district in the Galgadud region of Ethiopia.[37]

The TFG and its allies had accomplished a complete rout of the UIC forces, and the Ethiopian air force played no small part in this, way laying UIC positions and retreating forces. The Ethiopian forces reportedly had the advantage of satellite photography intelligence furnished by the United States which allowed Ethiopians to pinpoint the enemy's whereabouts.[38] According to Meles Zenawi, Ethiopia's interest lay in destroying those forces that were a threat to his country, namely foreign mujahidin and Eritrean forces stationed in Somalia. "The rank and file of the Islamic Courts is not a threat to Ethiopia. It is not the enemy, and we are not pursuing them at all. As soon as they go to their clan bases, we just leave them be, because we have no problem with them," he said.[39]

With the retreat of UIC forces from the Baidoa region and the road to Mogadishu open to the TFG and Ethiopian forces, the UIC leadership abandoned Mogadishu, saying it had done so to spare further bloodshed in the city. Top UIC leaders, Sheikh Hassan Dahir Aweys, Sheikh Sharif Sheikh Ahmed and deputy chairman, Sheikh Abdirahman Janaqow, resigned and announced that the UIC was handing over the city's administration to the people of Mogadishu to avoid destruction and bloodshed in the city.[40] The Ethiopian Prime Minister offered a different view of the UIC retreat from Mogadishu; he said that its fall had been facilitated by negotiations with traditional leaders to avoid the Islamists from making a stand in the city as he had feared.[41] Combined TFG and Ethiopian forces occupied Mogadishu without opposition.

The TFG and Ethiopian forces pursued the fleeing UIC leadership and its fighters, many of whom were foreigners, to Kismayo and then beyond. Eventually the Islamist leadership fled to the most southern easterly corner of the country, many to the area of Ras Komboni once home to a joint Al Itihaad-Al Qaeda base and historic stronghold of Al Itihaad-Shabbab leader, Abdullah Hersi al-Turki.

At the request of the TFG president, the United States undertook on January 7, 2007 air strikes in southern Somalia from a small air base in eastern Ethiopia; that the United States launched its air attacks from Ethiopian soil was denied by Addis. The planes targeted UIC leaders in armed pick-up trucks moving across a remote stretch near the Kenya-Somalia border. The TFG said that more than 50 people had been killed, mostly Islamist leaders. Sheikh Abdirahman Janaqow was reportedly among the dead.[42] The United States also deployed support planes from Djibouti; and F-15 Es flew missions from Al Udeid air base in Qatar. Ethiopian forces captured the jihadist base at Ras Komboni,[43] and then on January 24, 2007 U.S. AC-130 gunships bombed suspected Islamist and Al Qaeda holdouts in the rain forests of Ras Kamboni and Kulbiyow.[44] Shabbab leader, Adan Hasan 'Ayro, was reportedly killed in the aerial assault.⁴⁵ A U.S. Navy flotilla searched for ships that might ferry Al Qaeda operatives fleeing from Somalia; and along the Kenya border, British, U.S. and Kenyan authorities cooperated to capture fleeing Al Qaeda members and other jihadist leaders and fighters.

THE NEXT PHASE IN THE AFRICAN JIHAD

The war in Somalia, which dealt a crushing defeat to Somali and international jihadist forces, may not have been the final chapter in the jihadist efforts to seek hegemony in Somalia and the Horn of Africa region. Elements of the defeated UIC reconstituted as the Popular Resistance Movement in the Land of the Two Migrations (PRM). In January 2007, the pro-UIC website, Qaadisiya.com, announced Sheikh Abdkadir as its commander in the Banadir region which includes Mogadishu. Soon after the Ethiopian-back TFG installed in the Somali capital, an urban insurgency began to target TFG officials and Ethiopian troops, and the city began to experience a near nightly barrage of mortars; and suicide bombings had taken place. The start-up of an urban insurgency in Somalia left the concern among commentators that an Islamist insurgency might be imitating the terrorist tactics employed by Al Qaeda and other factional forces in Iraq after the U.S.-led intervention toppled the government of Saddam Hussein. In tactics similar to those employed in Iraq, the insurgence targeted TFG police and officials in an apparent bid to discourage cooperation with the TFG.

The TFG was counting on the arrival of African peacekeepers to help stabilize Somalia and to replace Ethiopia troops who stayed in Somalia to provide TFG with protection as it set out to consolidate its authority. The African peacekeepers were an UN-Security-Council-sanctioned protection and training force under the auspices of IGAD and the African Union. Burundi, Nigeria and Uganda committed contributions of troops to the peacekeeping operation.

The PRM made it clear that it would resist the peacekeepers, and it placed a video on the Internet warning African Union peacekeepers to avoid coming to Somalia, claiming "Somalia is not a place where you will earn a salary - it is a place where you will die."⁴⁶ The PRM also threatened to carry out suicide attacks against the African peacekeepers.⁴⁷

The TFG refused to negotiate with moderates from within the UIC who had survived the war, including Sheikh Sharif Ahmed. With assistance from the U.S. government, he was given safe passage from Somalia, through Kenya, to Yemen. He eventually joined other UIC leaders in Eritrea. This refusal on the part of the TFG meant that Islamists, even moderates, might not find a home in the new political order that the TFG intended to create in Somalia, and this raised the prospect of a continued violent conflict between Somali Islamists and the TFG. It was also unclear how the rank and file of Islamists forces, including Shabbab members, might view the prospect of further armed struggle. Much would depend on the credibility that the surviving UIC leadership retained after leading untold numbers of youth to ready martyrdom in its confrontation with TFG and Ethiopian forces.

Gregory Alonso Pirio
February 24, 2007

Notes

1. Jon Swain and Brian Johnson-Thomas, "Arab States Trained Al-Qaeda Men to Fight in Somalia" *The Sunday Times* (London), February 18, 2007, http://www.timesonline.co.uk/tol/news/world/middle_east/article1400655.ece.
2. "Politics - Adding Fuel to Fire," *The Reporter* (Addis Ababa), November 18, 2006, http://allafrica.com/stories/200611200456.html.
3. United States vs. Daniel Joseph Maldonaldo, Criminal Complaint, Case No. H-07-125M, United States District Court, Southern District of Texas, February, 13, 2007, http://www.foxnews.com/projects/pdf/Maldonado_Complaint.pdf.
4. Inal Ersan, "Bin Laden Says US Plans Crusade in Somalia," *Reuters*, July 1, 2006, http://www.boston.com/news/world/africa/articles/2006/07/01/bin_laden_says_us_plans_crusade_in_somalia/?rss_id=Boston.com+%2F+News.
5. "Clashes Broaden between Somali Islamist and Government Troops" *AFP*, December 20, 2006, http://www.garoweonline.com/stories/publish/article_6576.shtml.
6. Aweys Osman Yusuf, "Car Bomb Explosion Causes Casualties in Baidoa," *Shabelle Media Network*, November 30, 2006, http://allafrica.com/stories/200611300742.html to the web November 30, 2006; Hassan Kalkata, "Suicide Car Bomb Kills Seven People near

Govt. Base, *Shabelle Media Network,* November 30, 2006, http://allafrica.com/stories/200611301111.html.
7. United States vs. Daniel Joseph Maldonaldo.
8. Al Sudani worked with Shabbab leader 'Ayro as well as with Gouled Hassan Dourad, an Al Itihaad member and one of the leaders of the Somali terrorist cell that gave rise to Shabbab. According to the U.S. Office of the Director of National Intelligence, Gouled Hassan Dourad and Al-Sudani had been involved with a plot to target the U.S. Combined Joint Task Force base in Djibouti. "Extremist" Splinter Group of Somali Islamic Courts Form," *Somiland Times,* Issue 238 (August 12, 2006), http://www.somalilandtimes.net/sl/2005/238/01.shtml.
9. Stewart Bell, "Somali-Canadians Join African 'Taliban' Some Return Home to Serve in Hardline Islamic Militia," *National Post* (Toronto), October 14, 2006, http://www.canada.com/nationalpost/news/story.html?id=8a4c3ee2-4ff7-4b4b-abb0-4f869abb6ca0&k=14788.
10. Alisha Ryu, "Eritrea behind Radical Shabbab Group in Somalia," *VOANews,* January 7, 2007, http://www.ethiomedia.com/addfile/shabbab_radicalism.html.
11. "Suicide Bombers Heading for Somaliland, *Somaliland Times,* Issue 248 (October 21, 2006), http://www.somalilandtimes.net/sl/2005/248/01.shtml; Matthew Lee, "Somali Islamists Threaten Suicide Attacks in Kenya, Ethiopia: US," *AFP,* November 2, 2006, http://news.yahoo.com/s/afp/20061102/wl_afp/somaliaunrestus_061102183544.
12. "Interview with Meles Zenawi," *Washingtonpost.com,* December 14, 2006, http:www.washingtonpost.com/wp-dyn/content/article/2006/12/14/AR2006121400820.html.
13. "Conflict in Somalia Turns toward Confrontation," *PINR Report,* August 2, 2006 in *Somaliland Times,* Issue 236, http://www.somalilandtimes.net/sl/2005/237/3.shtml; "Interview — Meles Speaks on Ethiopia's Mission in Somalia," *The Reporter* (Addis Ababa), January 6, 2007, http://www.ethiopianreporter.com/modules.php?name=News&file=article&sid=10964.
14. Aweys Osman Yusuf, "Islamists and Ethiopian Troops Exchange Mortar Shells in Galkayo," *Shabelle Media Network,* November 28, 2006, http://allafrica.com/storie/200611280247.html.
15. Jeffrey Gettleman and Mark Mazzetti, "Somalia's Islamists and Ethiopia Gird for a War," *New York Times,* December 9, 2006.
16. Interview by phone with Somali informant, February 6, 2007.
17. Aweys Osman Yusuf, "Islamists to Invite International Islamists in the Country," *Shabelle Media Network,* November 28, 2006, http://allafrica.com/stories/200611280248.html.

18. Anthony Mitchell, "Somali Leader: Peace Talks Not an Option, *Associated Press*, December 15, 2006, http://www.washingtonpost.com/wp-dyn/content/article/2006/12/15/AR2006121500434.html.
19. Michael R. Gordon and Mark Mazzetti, "U.S. Used Base in Ethiopia to Hunt Al Qaeda in Africa," *New York Times*, Febuary 23, 2007, http://www.nytimes.com/2007/02/23/world/africa/23somalia.html?pagewanted=2&_r=1&hp.
20. Interview with Ethiopian Diplomat, March 17, 2004.
21. Diverse Interviews with U.S. Officials.
22. "On the Brink of War: Government Seeks Parliamentary Action," *The Reporter* (Addis Ababa), November 25, 2006, http://www.ethiopianreporter.commodules.php?name=News&file=article&sid=10152>;voa29.cfm?CFID=112190857&CFTOKEN=98802003; Emmanuel Goujon, "Ethiopia Authorizes Action against Somali Islamists, *AFP*, November 30, 2006, http://www.wardheernews.com/News_06/November_06/30_Ethiopia_authorizes_force.html.
23. Andrew Cawthorne, "U.S. Condemns Somali Islamists' War Ultimatum," *Reuters*, December 14, 2006, http://nazret.com/blog/index.php?title=ethiopia_u_s_condemns_somali_islamists_w&more=1&c=1&tb=1&pb=1; Cathy Majtenyi, "Somali Islamists Threaten Ethiopian Troops," *VOANews*, December 12, 2006, http://voanews.com/english/archive/2006-12/2006-12-12-voa33.cfm?CFID=112189459&CFTOKEN=68813198.
24. "Somalia Radical Militant Youth Group Evolving Dominance: Analyst," *The Reporter* (Addis Ababa), October 9, 2006, http://www.ethiopianreporter.com/modules.php?name=News&file=print&sid=8975.
25. Abdul Rahman Yusuf, "Somali Islamic Courts Snubs Bin Laden," *Islam on Line*, July 2, 2006, http://www.islamonline.net/English/News/2006-07/02/06.shtml.
26. Monitoring of "Reporters Roundtable," *VOANews*, December 14, 2006.
27. The nationalities of mujahidin fighters were gleaned from many different sources, including "Government Reveals Foreign Islamist Fighters in its Custody," *Shabelle Media Network*, January 28, 2007, http://allafrica.com/stories/200701290935.html.
28. Salad Duhul, "Ethiopian Jets Bomb Airports in Somalia," *Associated Press*, December 25, 2006.
29. "Clashes Broaden between Somali Islamist and Government Troops" *AFP*, December 20, 2006, http://www.garoweonline.com/stories/publish/article_6576.shtml.
30. Aweys Osman Yusuf, "Arrested Foreign Fighters Admit They Helped Islamists," *Shabelle Media Network*, January 8, 2007, http://allafrica.com/stories/200701081035.html.

31. "Interview — Meles Speaks."
32. Jeffrey Gettleman, "Ethiopian Warplanes Attack Somalia," *New York Times,* December 24, 2006.
33. "Military of Ethiopia," http://en.wikipedia.org/wiki/Military_of_Ethiopia.
34. Jeffrey Gettleman, "Ethiopian Warplanes," and "Islamist Forces in Somalia Are on the Retreat," *New York Times,* December 26, 2006, http://www.nytimes.com/2006/12/26/world/africa/26cnd-somalia.html?ex=1324789200&en=0146fc553ed11707&ei=5090&partner=rssuserland&emc=rss; "Camp United," http://www.globalsecurity.org/military/facility/camp-united.htm.
35. Hassan Yare, "Ethiopian Tanks Roll in Somali Battle's Fourth Day," *Reuters,* December 22, 2006, http://www.alertnet.org/thenews/newsdesk/L22886890.htm.
36. "ICU Lost Key Towns,' *Somalinet,* December 25, 2006, http://somalinet.com/news/world/Somalia/6127.
37. "Battle of Bandiradley," http://en.wikipedia.org/wiki/Battle_of_Bandiradley.
38. Gordon and Mazzetti, "U.S. Used Base in Ethiopia."
39. "Interview — Meles Speaks."
40. "Somalia: ICU Leaders Resign as Ethiopian Army Nears the Capital," *Somalinet,* December 27, 2006, http://somalinet.com/news/world/Somalia/6223.
41. Barry Moody, "Interview-Hundreds of Jihadists Fought in Somalia-Meles," *Reuters,* January 28, 2007, http://today.reuters.com/News/CrisesArticle.aspx?sotryld=L2813410.
42. Jeffrey Gettleman, "More Than 50 Die in U.S. Strikes in Somalia," *New York Times,* January 9, 2007, http://www.nytimes.com/2007/01/09/world/africa/09cnd-somalia.html?hp&ex=1168405200&en=1c795b2adf6eaddb&ei=5094&partner=homepage.
43. Mohamed Olad Hassan, "Islamic Hideout in Somalia Said Captured," *Associated Press,* January 12, 2007.
44. Aweys Osman Yusuf, "U.S. Air Strikes on Southern Somalia Leave Casualties, *Shabelle Media Network,* January 24, 2007, http://allafrica.com/stories/200701240335.html.
45. Gordon and Mazzetti, "U.S. Used Base in Ethiopia."
46. *The Popular Resistance Movement in the Land of the Two Migrations,* http://en.wikipedia.org/wiki/Somali_People's_Resistance_Movement.
47. "Somali Insurgents Threaten Attacks," *Associated Press,* February 23, 2007, http://asia.news.yahoo.com/070222/ap/d8nf1hkg0.html.

INDEX

A

Abdhullahi, Muhiddeen 93
Abdullah, Abdullah Ahmed 56, 137
Abdullah Hassan, Mohamed 189, 192
Abdullah, Sheikh 21
Abdulmejid Hussein 65, 66
Abu Nidal Organization 20
Abu-Bakr, Ali Sheikh 51
Abu-Waid, Hussein 143
Addis Ababa, Ethiopia 23, 28, 58, 65, 80, 97, 207
Addow, Ibrahim Hassan 210
Aden Hotel, Yemen 55
Aden, Yemen 44, 92
Adow, Ahmad Jilow 89, 90
Aerolift 201
Afar 108
Afghan Arabs 22, 64
Afghanistan 2-4, 13, 20-2, 25, 29-30, 36, 45-6, 48, 55-6, 59, 66, 68, 78-9, 85-6, 92-3, 109, 112, 135, 138, 140, 149, 158, 166-7, 168, 174-5, 190, 194, 203
African Union (AU) 6, 32, 193, 214
Afro-Shirazi Party 161
Aga Khan 162
Ahlu Sunna wal Jamaa 96
Ahmad, Youseff 79
Ahmadiyya 96
Ahmed, Sheikh Sharif 95, 97-8, 207, 209, 210, 213, 215
Aidid, Hussein 50, 67, 69, 70, 85, 87
Aidid, Mohamed Farah 5, 52, 57-9, 67, 191
Ainte, Sheikh Hassan 86
Air Cess 138

Al Ansar Al Sunna (Defenders of the
    Tradition) 82
Al Azhar University 47
Al Barakat 84-5, 94
Al Haramain 27, 79, 94-5, 122, 131-
    3, 139, 143-4, 159, 164, 171-2,
    175-6
Al Islah 49-51, 93, 135, 190
Al Itihaad Al Islamiya (Al Itihaad) 2,
    43, 44, 46
Al Jamaa al Islamiya (The Islamic
    Group, Egypt) 20
Al Muntada Al Islami 142-3
Al Qaeda 1-5, 8-11, 13-4, 18, 20-9,
    31-2, 35, 38, 44, 46, 48-9, 54-64,
    66, 68, 78-9, 81, 84-5, 90-6, 98,
    105-6, 112, 115-6, 121-3, 128-
    31, 133-45, 150, 157-9, 167-8,
    171, 175-6, 187-9, 191, 194-5,
    202-5, 208-10, 213-4
Al Shifa pharmaceutical plant 29-30,
    85
Al Tabliq 93
Al Wahda 49
al-Banshiri, Abu Ubaidah 135-7, 171
al-Bashir, Omar Hasan Ahmad 13,
    15, 17, 22, 27-8, 30-1, 34-5, 190
al-Fadhli, Tariq Nasr 56
al-Fadl, Jamal 115
al-Mahdi, Sadiq 19
al-Saad, Mohammed Ally Saleh 172
al-Sanusi, Ibrahim 31
al-Sudani, Abu Taha 203, 210
al-Turabi, Hassan 4, 13, 16-20, 30-2,
    34-5, 57-8, 127, 190
al-Turki, Hassan Abdullah Hersi 62,
    189, 205, 213
al-Zawahiri, Ayman 18, 55, 106
Algeria 15, 21
Alliance for the Restoration of Peace
    and Counter-Terrorism
    (ARPCT) 96-7, 195-6
Allied Democratic Forces (ADF) 9,
    21, 24-5, 35-6, 167
Amer, Sheikh Mohamed 105, 110,
    116
Amin, Idi 24, 128
Anglican Church of Kenya 147
Aringa 24
Arkia Air 139
Arta, Djibouti 50, 88
Asmara, Eritrea 23, 35, 106, 111-2,
    114, 196, 201
Atef, Mohamed 2, 55, 59, 138
Attabani, Ghazi Salah al-Din 30
Atto, Osman Ali 69, 87-8
Aweys, Hassan Dahir 2-7, 9, 52, 56-
    7, 59, 66-7, 69, 78-84, 86-8, 90,
    93, 95-8, 188-9, 192, 197, 202-3,
    205-7, 210-1, 213
Awfi, Saleh 32
Ayr lineage 191
Azan, Sheikh Kalid 178, 180
Azhar, Maulana Masood 56

B

Baghdad, Iraq 36, 60
Baidoa, Somalia 6, 7, 9, 53, 96-7,
    193, 197, 207, 209-213
Bakonja 24
BAKWATA (Baraza Kuu la
    Waislam wa Tanzania or
    Tanzania Muslim Council)
    162-4, 168, 175
Balala, Sheikh Khalid 27, 126-8
Bashir, Sheikh Omar 137, 175
Bay region, Somali 6, 212
Beck, Fred 56
Beledweyne, Somalia 64, 207, 212
Berbera, Somalia 45
bin Laden, Osama 1-2, 4, 13-4, 18,
    20-2, 24-5, 28-9, 5-6, 59, 62-3,
    66, 68, 84-5, 90, 93, 95, 98, 105,
    112, 115-6, 121, 123, 135-9,
    141, 167-8, 171, 189, 194, 202-4

Index

bin Mahfouz, Khalid 28
Black Giant Mining 136
Black Hawk Down 5, 59
Bod, Hussein Johi 88
Bormama, Somalia 52
Botswana 53
Boutros-Ghali, Boutros 58-9
Brave, Somalia 86
Brigadier General Tekheste 113
British Broadcast Corporation (BBC) 7, 92, 135
Bula Hawa, Somalia 57, 63, 66, 68
Bulgaria 140
Bur Gabo, Somalia 62
Burao, Somalia 52, 79, 192
Busaiddy, Abdulgafur 142
But, Viktor (Victor Bout) 138

C

Cairo, Egypt 1, 18, 107
Caliphate 8
Camp Lemonier, Djibouti 133, 195
Canada 139, 205
Central Intelligence Agency (CIA) 31, 158, 195
Chad 15
Chama Cha Mapinduzi (CCM or Party of the Revolution) 68, 70, 82, 87, 93, 160
China 22
Civic United Front (CUF) 160, 165, 172-3, 177-80
Clinton, William 14, 59
CNN 59
Coast Province, Kenya 27, 122-27, 140
Cohen, Herman 53
Colombo, Salvatore 43
Combined Joint Task Force Horn of Africa 133, 195, 208, 211
Comoros 124, 140
Comprehensive Peace Agreement 16

Conference on National Reconciliation (Somalia) 58
Council of Imams and Preachers of Kenya 146
counterterrorism 3-4, 8-9, 30, 32-3, 91, 132-3, 141-2, 144-5, 188, 194-6, 203, 208, 211

D

Dadaab refugee camps, Kenya 131, 134-5
Dahlak Islands, Eritrea 116
Damazin, Sudan 21
Democratic Republic of Congo 24-5, 36, 136, 167
Deobandi movement 167
Derg 108-9
Dheere, Mohamed (Mohame Omar Habeb) 91, 212
Dheere, Sheikh Ali 82, 88
Dibagula, Khamis Rajan 173
Dire Dawa, Ethiopia 26, 65, 69, 211
Disuki, Ibrahim 50
Djibouti 5, 6, 9, 26, 50, 61, 88, 90, 93, 125, 133, 140, 168, 188, 195, 208, 213
Dubai 136

E

East African Muslim Welfare Society (EAMWS) 161
Eastern Province, Kenya 122-3, 125, 129
Egypt 15-6, 47, 50, 197, 202, 205, 208, 210
Egyptian Islamic Group 21
Eissa, Sheikh Mohamed 48
el Hage, Wadith 2, 136-7, 171
embassy bombings 29, 56, 68, 136, 141, 171
Equatoria Defense Force (EDF) 37
Eritrean Islamic Jihad (EIJ) 9, 21,

25, 35, 54, 56, 105-6, 108-17
Eritrean Islamic Jihad/Eritrean Islamic Salvation Front (EIJ/ EISF) 105-6, 109, 110-7
Eritrean Islamic Reform Movement 107
Eritrean Islamic Salvation Front (EISF) 105-6, 111-7, 188
Eritrean Liberation Front (ELF) 35, 107-9
Eritrean National Alliance (ENA) 35, 105-6, 111, 114, 117
Eritrean Peoples Liberation Front (EPLF) 109, 111
Ethiopian National Defense Forces (ENDF) 207, 211
Ethiopian Peoples Revolutionary Democratic Front (EPRDF) 64
Evangelical Churches of Kenya 147

F

Farid Ali, Sheikh 48, 51, 82-3, 149, 178, 192
Fatah al-Majles al-Thawry 20
Federal Bureau of Investigation (FBI) 31, 85, 145, 157, 204
Flying Dolphin 138

G

Garang, John 139
Gardez, Afghanistan 59
Garissa, Kenya 131-3, 135, 146
Garowe, Somalia 7, 53, 58, 92, 208
Gash Barka region, Eritrea 107, 109
Gedged, Eritrea 113
Gedi, Ali Mohamed 7, 98
Gedo region, Somalia 52, 57, 61, 63, 66, 68, 82, 128, 131, 138
Ghailani, Ahmed Khalfan 137, 157-9, 168
Ghion Hotel, Ethiopia 65
Golaha Fulinta Shareeada Islaamka (Sharia Implementation Council) 88
Golden Moor Hotel, Yemen 55
Gulf of Aden 44, 92

H

Habr Gedir subclan 59
Hamad, Seif Shariff 173, 178
Hamas (Harakat al-Muqawama al-Islamiyaa) 20, 33
Hamesh Koreb, Sudan 21, 115
Har Qatar 168
Haradhere, Somalia 194
Harakat Al Islah (Reform Movement) 51, 106
Harakat al-Jihad al-Islami al-Filastini (Palestinian Islamic Jihad) 20, 33
Harar, Ethiopia 26
Hargeisa, Somalia 44, 192
Harkat-ul-Mujahideen 22
Hawiye (clan) 46, 59, 81, 191, 209
Hayelom Araya, General 65
Help Africa People 63, 130, 138, 142
Hemed, Suleiman Abdalla Salim 91, 141, 170
Hezbollah (Party of God) 20, 79, 190, 197, 203
Hong Kong 136
Hubheyifa, Abu 172
Huroy Tadle Beyrow 114
Hussein, Abdi Ahmed 93
Hussein, Sheikh Yahya 169
Hutu 24

I

Ibrahim bin Abdul Aziz al Ibrahim Foundation 142
Ibrahim, Elbur Mohamed 135
Idriss, Maalim Mohammed 168
Ifka Halane Islamic Court 78-9, 81, 84, 96

Index

Intergovernmental Authority on Development (IGAD) 6, 70, 97, 193-4, 196, 214
International Islamic Relief Organization 142
Irad, Abdullahi 67
Iran (Iranian) 21, 22, 26-7, 44, 46, 52-3, 55, 57-8, 127, 147, 166, 169, 187, 197, 208, 211
Iraq (Iraqi) 21, 31, 36, 54, 60, 135, 149, 167-8, 180, 190, 197-8, 203, 214
Isaak, Ismail Aden 143
Isaaq clan 44, 46
Isaias Afwerki 105, 109
Islamic Front for the Liberation of Oromia (IFLO) 9, 21, 26, 65, 69, 188
Islamic Liberation Army of the People of Kenya 139
Islamic Party of Kenya (IPK) 10, 26, 122, 126-8, 146
Islamic Salvation Front 56
Ismail, Abdullahi Sheikh 70
Ismail, Mustafa Osman 30
Ismaile, Isse Haji 86
Ismaili Sect 162
Israel (Israeli) 36, 79, 90-1, 106, 116, 121, 139, 140-1, 145, 149, 180, 189-90
Italy (Italian) 43, 77, 79-80, 108, 139

J

Jaish-e-Mohammed (The Army of Mohamed) 56
Jalalabad, Afghanistan 13
Jama, Jama Ali 66, 91, 93
Janaqow, Sheikh Abdiraman 213
Janjaweed 179
Jeemah Islamiah (Islamic Community) 172
Jihad Oromo Ibrahim Bilisa 26
Jimale, Ahamad Ali 85
Juma, Ashif Mohamed 24, 83, 132, 136, 148
Jumuia ya Uamsho na Mihadhara (Uamsho or Revival and Propagation Organization) 176, 178, 180
Justice and Equality Movement 15, 34

K

Kadhi Courts 146-7
Kakwa 24
Kandahar, Afghanistan 138
Karume, Amani Abeid 178
Kate, Peyton 135
Kaya (Sacred Forests) 24, 126
Kaya region, Uganda 24
Kayihura, Kale 37
Kebessa Plateau, Eritrea 108
Kenya 2, 5-10, 14-5, 22-3, 26-7, 29, 49, 55-7, 61-3, 68, 70, 80, 90-2, 94-5, 115, 121-6, 128-30, 132, 134, 135-47, 149, 161, 167-8, 172, 174, 188-9, 193-6, 204, 206, 213, 215
Kenya African National Union (KANU) 123, 126-8, 130
Kenya Somali Community of North America 130
Khalf, Fuad Mohammed 207
Khamis Mohamed, Khalfan 55
Khartoum, Sudan 1, 2, 13-7, 19-23, 25-9, 31-3, 35-7, 53-4, 57-8, 65, 68, 85, 106, 112-4, 121, 127, 188, 197
khat 63, 193
Kigoma, Tanzania 166
Kismayo, Somalia 44, 52, 62, 70, 191-4, 202, 204, 212-3
Kony, Joseph 23, 37
Kunama 108

L

Lakwena, Alice 23
Lamu, Kenya 90, 140
Las Korah, Somalia 52
Lebanon 2, 20, 22, 78, 149, 190
Liberia 137, 159
Likoni, Kenya 128
Lords Resistance Army (LRA) 23-4, 35-8
Luuq, Somalia 57, 66
Lwambano, Father Camillius 170

M

Mad Mullah 47
Mahdi, Ali 59, 61, 82, 85
Majis al-Shura (Consultative Council) 3, 6
Malik, Muhammed Hussein 163-4, 173
Malindi, Kenya 140
Mandera, Kenya 131
Marehan clan 43
Marka, Somalia 52-3, 55-6, 70, 86-7, 202
Marxism-Leninism (Marxist-Leninist) 108
Masaleh, Umar Haji 69
Masawa, Eritrea 116, 201
Masjid Quba and Islamic Centre 164
Maulid (Prophet Mohammeds Birthday) 149
McCurry, Michael 58
Mecca, Saudi Arabia 127, 167
Medina University, Saudi Arabia 127
Meles Zenawi 208, 209, 212
Mercy International Relief Agency (MIRA) 63, 94, 130, 138, 142
Mererani, Tanzania 136
Mijikenda 124-6
Misoi, Joseph 136
Mizani 165, 169
Mkapa, Benjamin 170
Mogadishu University 51
Mohamed Abdi, Hasan Sheikh 82-3
Mohamed, Sheikh Khalifa 146
Mohammed, Fazul Abdullah 137, 140
Moi, Daniel Arap 130
Mombasa, Kenya 48, 53, 62, 90-1, 121, 126-8, 130, 133, 136-7, 139-41, 144-5, 148-9, 162, 171, 174, 194
Moro Liberation Front 21
Morocco 25, 112, 210
Mrema, Augustine 169
Mubarak, Hosni 28
Mudug region, Somalia 194, 207, 212
Muhammad, Sheikh Hasan 78, 89
Mukhabarat 31
Murungaru, Chris 91, 145
Museveni, Yoweri 27, 37
Muslim Brotherhood (Al-Ikhwan Al-Moslemoon) 16-7, 47, 51
Muwafaq 28
MV Sea Johana 62, 194
Mwinyi, Ali Hassan 163
Mwembechai mosque, Dar es Salaam 170

N

Nairobi 2, 5, 27, 29, 56, 62-3, 68, 80, 86, 90, 94, 96, 121, 129, 130, 132, 134-8, 140, 143-4, 146, 149, 164, 171, 196, 203
Nassir, Bekkah Abdul 36
National Army for the Liberation of Uganda 24
National Congress Party 16, 33, 35
National Democratic Alliance (NDA) 15-6, 23, 33, 35, 188
National Islamic Front (NIF) 4, 8, 10, 14-20, 33, 35, 57, 61, 105-6,

116, 122, 127, 159, 166, 187-8, 190, 194
National Rainbow Coalition 130, 145
Ngoy, Sheikh Swaleh Uthman 168
Nigeria 53, 143, 214
Nile West Bank Liberation Front 24
Nimeiri, General Jafaar 17
North Eastern Province, Kenya 10, 57, 61, 63, 94, 121-2, 124-5, 128-32, 134, 138, 143, 146, 188
Nugaal region, Somalia 7
Nur, Adan Abdullahi Gabyrow 70
Nur, Hassan Mohamed Shaatigaduud 70
Nyerere, Julius 162, 164

O

Odeh, Mohammed Sadek 137
Odeh, Muraweh Saleh 136
Ogaden 26, 45, 61, 64-5, 97, 190, 211
Ogaden National Liberation Front (ONLF) 64-5, 97-8, 190, 196-7, 211
Omar, Sheikh 137, 175
Operation Anaconda 59
Operation Desert Shield 54
Operation Restore Hope 2, 53, 56
Oris, Juma 24
Oromo Liberation Front (OLF) 25, 65, 68-9, 98, 190, 196-7, 211
Othman, Mohamed 57
Ottoman Empire 17

P

Pakistan 1, 22, 48, 53, 56, 80, 95, 124, 138, 140, 157-9, 167-8, 180, 205
Paradise Hotel, Kenya 90, 121, 139-40
Pearl, Daniel 56
Pemba, Zanzibar 124, 160, 167, 170, 172-3, 175, 178, 180
Persian Gulf 44-5, 115, 138
Peshawar, Pakistan 1, 2, 138
piracy 62, 194
Ponda, Sheikh Ponda Issa 174
Popular Arab and Islamic Conference (PAIC) 19, 31-2
Popular Resistance Movement in the Land of the Two Migrations (PRM) 214
Protestants 124
Puntland 7, 51-2, 66, 81, 88-9, 91-2, 192-3, 196-7, 207, 209, 212

Q

Qabri Dharhar, Ethiopia 65
Qatar 89, 115, 213
Qatar Charitable Society 115
Qaw, Somalia 52
Qeybdid, Abdi 212
Qoryooley, Somalia 69, 70

R

Radio Tumaini, Dar es Salaam 170
Rahanweyn Resistance Army 70
Raiwind, Pakistan 167
Ras Hotel, Ethiopia 65
Ras Komboni, Somalia 61, 213
Red Sea 32-3, 44, 109, 116
Red Terror, Ethiopia 108
Robeson, U.S. Marine Brigadier General Mastin 168
Robow, Sheikh Mukhtar 80
Roman Catholics 124
Rwanda 24

S

Salad Hassan, Abdiqasim 88
Salafism (Salafi, Salafist) 7, 166
Salihiyya 96
Salman, Amir Abu Bara Hassan 110-1, 113
Saudi Arabia 4, 20, 28, 32-3, 48, 50,

54, 68, 80, 89, 94-5, 109, 112, 115, 122, 127, 132-3, 143, 147, 149, 171, 175, 180, 191, 197, 208, 210
Seber, Eritrea 113
Security Council 59
Seyoum Mesfin 69, 97
Shabbab 205-6, 209, 210, 213, 215
Shabelle region, Somalia 86
Share, Barre Aden 90
Sheab, Eritrea 113
Shebah, Eritrea 113
Shee, Sheikh Ali 149
Shill, Fafi Barre 131
Shire Sheikh, Hasan 83
Shura Council of the Preservation Alliance 206
Siad Barre, Mohamed 4, 6, 43, 44-8, 58, 61, 91, 191
Sierra Leone 137, 159
Simba wa Mungu (Lions of God) 174
Soba, Sudan 22
Somali National Alliance 70
Somali National Movement 44, 46, 52
Somali Patriotic Movement 70
Somali Salvation Democratic Front (SSDF) 6, 52, 62
Somaliland 48, 52, 79, 81, 88-9, 191-3, 196, 206, 209
Soviet Union 45-6, 48, 59, 140, 174
State Department 19, 28, 32-3, 58, 196
Stinger missiles 2
Sudanese Liberation Army (SLA) 34
Sudanese Peoples Liberation Movement/Army (SPLM/A) 14-6, 22-3, 29, 33, 38, 127
Sufism (Sufi, Sufist) 7, 18-9, 51, 81, 96, 124, 167, 168
Sultan of Zanzibar (Sultanate of Zanzibar) 124, 160
Supreme Council of Kenyan Muslims 142
Supreme Somali Islamic League 50
Swahili 124-5, 140, 149, 163, 174

T

Tabligh Jamaat (Tablighis) 24, 158, 166-8, 175
Tabora, Tanzania 166, 177
Taha, Ali Osman Mohamed 31, 52, 203, 210
Taheer Limited 136
Taliban 3, 29, 78, 86, 93, 132, 138, 166-7, 175, 194, 203
Tallaabo, Yusuf Ise Duale 192
Tambi, General 201
Tanga, Tanzania 166
Tanganyika African National Union 161, 163
Tanzania 2-5, 8- 9, 10, 14-5, 22, 27, 29, 56, 63, 68, 95, 115, 122, 124, 135-6, 138, 157-71, 173, 175, 177, 179, 194, 210
tanzanite 136, 159, 171
Tanzanite King 136, 171
Tanzim al Jihad (Islamic Jihad Squad) 20
Tareq Bin Ziyad 64
The Group for Adherence to the Book and the Sunna 67
Tigray region, Ethiopia (Tigrinyan) 108
Tigre 108-9
Total Somali Liberation Tigers 92
Transitional Federal Government (TFG) 6-9, 52, 70, 78-80, 96-8, 193, 196-7, 202, 207-14
Tuju, Rafael 193

U

U.S. Marines 133
Uganda Peoples Defense Force 24

Umbarger, Deena 62
Umoja wa Wahubiri wa Mlingano wa Dini (UWAMDI or Union of Preachers for Propagation of Religion) 168
Unguja, Zanzibar 124, 158, 160, 170, 172-3, 175, 178
Union of Islamic Courts (UIC) 2-3, 6, 8-9, 38, 49, 78, 80, 95-8, 131, 187-97, 202, 204-14
United Arab Emirates 89-90, 94, 138, 140, 210
United Methodist Committee on Relief 62
United Muslims of Africa (UMA) 127-8
United Nations 2-3, 5-6, 9, 23, 28, 53, 58, 66, 78, 114, 140, 171, 193, 196, 201, 203
United Nations Mission in Ethiopia and Eritrea 114
United Nations Operation Somalia II (UNOSOM II) 58
United Somali Congress (USC) 4, 46, 52
University of Addis Ababa, Ethiopia 109
University of East Africa, Bosaso, Somalia 51

W

Wahabism (Wahabi, Wahabist) 7, 17, 51, 81, 105, 122, 129, 131, 138, 140, 144, 148-9, 166-9, 171

Wahdat Al Shabab Al Islam (The Unity of Islamic Youth) 48
Wamae, Kiritu 131
Warsame, Sheikh Ali 48, 51, 192
Washa ya Waandishi wa Kiislam (Warsha or Muslim Writers Workshop) 163-4, 173
World Muslim League 143

X

Xagar, Somalia 90, 141

Y

Yahya, Abdul Qadir 79
Yalahow, Musa Suli 88
Yassin, Mohamed Osman 32
Yemen 4, 15, 22, 25, 32, 55-6, 80, 90, 112, 115, 127-8, 140, 191, 195, 197, 210, 215
Yemeni Islamic Jihad 55
Yobe State, Nigeria 144
Yousef, Ramzi 138
Yusuf Ahmed, Abdhullahi 6, 52, 66, 209

Z

Zaire 24, 29, 136-7, 159, 167, 171
Zakharov, Evgueny 201-2